MOUNTAIN _

MOUNTAIN DANCE

When two worlds collide, what will survive of us?

Stewart Wellings

You Caxton Publications
Oxford & Shrewsbury

Acknowledgements

Thank You Liliana, Ali and Matty - for everything. I Love You.

Thank you Mum and Dad.

Charlie and Bob (aka Chink and Egger) and their families. xx.

Family stories and a memoir: *'Poor Man's Paradise'* written by my Uncle, Ron Wellings (and transcribed by his daughter, my cousin Jean) which inspired me to write this story. My wife Liliana's story has been handed down orally from her family.

Writing this book would not have been possible without the great help of Nick Passmore and Quentin Shaw whose editorial wisdoms energies and enthusiasms kept me on track. Nigel Emery has been a great support regarding computing and pictures. Steve Edwards, a great friend, has been professional and helpful with publishing.

Many wonderful people have helped me along the way – friends and family too numerous to mention here – they know who they are – thank you all.

And finally, Pontesford Hill (Earl's Hill) has been the gift that keeps on giving: always there, a haven for a tired soul, brain or body.

Contents

PROLOGUE

Dizzy Heights

As my fingers loosened the cam to allow it to seat in the crack, it happened. The rock was not attached to the mountain, it was only jammed in. I had not slapped it to test it; it had looked solid... it was about half a metre square and was heavy. It slid off onto my arm. The full weight of it was on my arm and my bent knee underneath on a foothold. My other arm was on a handhold; if I let go I would fall. What could I do?! The weight was too heavy for me to lift with my one arm. I tried to wriggle my knee to enable me to lift it up in the hope of combining a knee and arm 'shoogle' movement to try and inch it back into where it had come from; but the weight was crushing me further down by the second. The only thing I could do was release it; but it would fall towards Al and Gav directly below. It was going to go that way with me as well if I didn't do something quick anyway, so it was the lesser of two evils.

*****

Towards the end of a summer term at University Gavin Burke had come up to stay. He, Big Al and I had headed to Ben Nevis for some rock climbing, as the forecast looked good. We camped by the CIC hut under the great North Face. The hut is named after Charles Inglis Clark, built by his parents as a memorial for their son after he was killed in the First World War. It is owned and operated by the Scottish Mountaineering Club. Not being members of this august association, we were happy to camp nearby, taking our water directly from the Allt a' Mhuillin, the burn that rises there. The Ben's alpine ridges and faces were framed by our tent flap.

We had decided on an open face route on the side of the North East Buttress, Raeburn's Arête. The route is approximately 230 m (750ft) long and brings the climber out onto the 'first platform' of the North East

Buttress. The route is graded as 'severe', which, in the grand scheme of things is relatively straightforward to the experienced climber. Al and I had been climbing together for almost a year, through the winter too, with all that that entailed. Gav and I had met in Alaska a few years earlier.

It was my lead, and things were going well. I was approaching an obvious belay spot that fitted with the guidebook description. I unclipped a 'friend' from my harness[1]. This meant that should I fall, the device should hold me, as long as those below were holding my rope and paying attention. Gav and Al were competent, and this had boosted my confidence. I removed the device from my harness loop, seeing a crack that looked like it would be the right size to accommodate it.

*****

I shouted warnings, telling them what I was going to do; what I had to do. I was shaking; my voice was croaky; my mouth was dry; I was sweating.

"BELOOOOW!!!!!!"

The huge rock cannoned down the steep pitch below me. It hit a ledge and burst into pieces, but not before severing the sheath of the rope and cutting several strands. Shaking with emotion, I had to climb further to find a safe place to stop and belay.

Sometime later Al and Gav joined me at the stance; but as they came up I noticed there was a big lump in the rope where they had had to knot it. There were serious faces all round until we had finally got down safely.

Al had to leave us to go back to Glasgow to work: he was on shift 'on the door' of the Lime Club Nightclub off Sauchiehall Street where we both worked as bouncers.

The next day Gav and I climbed Observatory Ridge, finding more loose rock there as well. On the summit we could at last relax in the sunshine of a late May in Scotland.

Back at the tent, Gav and I struck camp and headed down the Glen in the Ford Escort I had bought off a mate, with some money that Dad

---

1   A 'friend' is a camming device that jams in a crack in the rock and, when clipped back into the trailing rope, should offer some security as a running belay.

had given me: he was very pleased I had managed to get to university. On Skye Gav was full of the joys. A good ol' Maldon Essex wide boy, he had moved up to London and sought his fortune working at his passion as a photographer. He was imminently to marry Nimmy March, actress and adopted daughter of The Duke and Duchess of Richmond, whom he had met when they were on a Buddhist retreat. Gav and I were rekindling our mutual love of the hills, and as yet I had not met Nimmy. The wedding was to be at the ancestral home, Goodwood House in Sussex, one of the stately homes of England. I was to represent Gav at the ceremony, reciting a poem to Nimmy 'Phenomenal Woman' by Maya Angelou the American poet.

'But Gav, are you sure about this, mate?! I feel very honoured, but, mate, I'm just a Salopian drunkard, knowworrimean?!'

Chapter 1

Beginnings

Their World and the end of the Age of Innocence

Around the time Queen Victoria died a baby was born. She would go on to become a Queen Consort then the Queen Mother. She lived to be over 100 years old and her royal life is well documented. She lived and loved in Castle Mey near Dunnet Head in the far north of Scotland. Nearby, at the same time, another young girl was born; Jean Melville Harper faced a life of toil, domestic service, emigration and struggle. She died at just over 50 years old. I never met her, but she was my grandmother.

A hard wind blows from the east and the north. Jean Melville Harper had been born and raised near Castletown in Caithness. Her parents lived in a croft in the open countryside. When a cousin died suddenly in an accident, no one could attend the funeral because the snowdrifts were so deep. Life was hard and the chances of employment very poor. Jean and her two sisters, Bessie and Jessie, grew into young women but despite being good scholars they had to travel to find jobs. Later in Edinburgh all three, near each other but far from home, would find employment in domestic service in the city.

The rolling hills and fields south of Shrewsbury have been farmed since ancient times. They form a divine tapestry of hedges, counterpane fields and country lanes threading through, stitched together to offer one of the best possible views: look south from Lyth Hill and you see a view framed by the Wrekin, Wenlock Edge, Caradoc, Lawley, the Longmynd and Pontesford Hill. Here families would work the land for the landowners, poaching and gamekeeping, gathering and reaping and sowing. Children played, worked, gleaned, hopped, skipped, laughed and cried through the long summer days of plenty and the bitter harsh scrimping pinching winters, having very little, but wanting for nothing. They walked everywhere, but in deference, knowing their place. A poor man's paradise.

Ned Wellings and his wife lived under Lyth Hill at Exfords Green in the parish of Condover. Ned was (by and large) a gamekeeper. They had one son and seven daughters. Charles William Wellings, 'Charlie', was the eldest of the tribe, born on 29th April 1898 in Ashby de la Zouch Derbyshire. No one knew why they went there, but they soon came back to Shropshire. Charlie was followed by Ede, Nancy, Lil, Sally and three other sisters. Charlie was my Grandfather.

Charlie Wellings' early schooling had been at the old chapel up the bank just through the wood near the windmill on Lyth Hill: a small white painted building facing south, looking out over the wood and towards the Long Mynd. This was an idyllic setting to grow up and learn in a time of innocence and bliss.

Shropshire lads continued to work the land as they always had done. Threshers and traction engines were being used alongside horsepower now. Charlie Wellings followed this way, the way of his fathers, and started working as soon as he had left school at 14. Children then were expected to do chores for the family working before and after school, as well as walking to and from school. The school was at Condover, a distance of a couple of miles along the cart tracks between the hedges from Exfords Green. He was well versed about what was expected of him and had the stamina to complete a full day of farm work in the employ of the Estate.

A few balmy summers followed as the young Charlie grew up working.

'At the age of 14 he started work for Mr Roach (later Youngs) at the baker's shop in Condover, as well as delivering bread and groceries in the village of Condover.'

The Kaiser was rattling sabres in Europe, and alliances were forged, sides taken. The fateful day Franz Ferdinand was assassinated changed the world forever, and Charlie was to leave and play his part in the war.

'You don't look old enough to me!' barked the recruiting sergeant. 'Come back tomorrow when you are old enough!'

And so he did, to join the Shropshire Yeomanry as an *ostler* (horseman). Country boys were good with horses, and the British Army needed them at the Front. In his brand new uniform Charlie bade farewell to his beloved family and walked out of the door with his kitbag over his shoulder, his ginger hair hidden under his shiny cap badge.

'He was posted to Ashington Barracks in Northumberland. He was so proud of his pony there called 'Gypsy'. In a letter to his parents from Ashington he complained about the wet weather and also requested his mother to send him 'a good rough towel as mine are more like teacloths.' Arriving home on leave at night having walked up from Shrewsbury station he slept on his kitbag in the porch as he did not want to wake his parents.'

(Extract from Poor Man's Paradise – Ronald George Wellings 2007)

During one spell of leave there was a joyous homecoming: a new addition to the family, his youngest sister Winifred ('Win') was born in 1915.

Charlie was sent from France to the Irish Easter uprising at Dublin in 1916. This was a week before he turned 18.

What horrors went on for the next few years can only be guessed at. The Shropshire Yeomanry was decimated on The Somme. Charlie was transferred to the Seaforth Highlanders, perhaps, as he said, because his ginger hair gave him a Scottish complexion.

Charlie didn't talk about his time in the trenches much. If pushed he would lift his shirt sleeve and show the indentation where the shrapnel hit him just below his shoulder. He was hit by shrapnel twice. He would make light of things when he could: he recalled how they had to urinate on handkerchiefs and hold them up to their faces to staunch the effects of mustard gas before standard issue gas masks became available. He remembered a German biplane, quite possibly *'The Bloody Red Baron of Germany'* Baron von Richthofen, buzzing his platoon whilst he was in the latrine: a bullet both sides of him, and another funny story to recount to alleviate the memories crowding his mind, finding solace in dark humour.

'One day in the trenches a sergeant ordered Dad to cut some of the soldier's hair and gave him a comb and a pair of scissors. He continued to cut hair for

the rest of his life. People often called at home to have their hair cut. He always did it for free. When we children complained of perhaps he had cut off a bit too much hair here and there, he would say 'There's only 2 weeks difference between a good and a bad haircut'

Now a fully established 'Seaforth Highlander' Charlie was stationed at Edinburgh Castle following the 1918 Armistice. The young soldiers in their kilts were very popular, and they soon became acquainted with girls in the city, amongst them Jean Melville Harper the domestic servant.

Charlie and Jean's courtship was brief and they were soon married at Leith near Edinburgh. After he was demobbed from The Seaforth Highlanders they moved 'Up North' to live with Jean's parents in Caithness in the dark and cold.

A dead straight road cuts south inland through the flow country a few rough miles south-east of Castletown. Here at a lonely raised crossroads a farmstead stands against the elements. By curious co-incidence the farmstead is called Lyth (but pronounced 'Lithe'), and it was here, into this blank relentless post-war land to Charlie and Jean was born Edward Benjamin Charles Wellings at Lyth on Friday 13th February 1921.

Charlie was now a war veteran, a husband, and a father by the age of 22. Like hundreds of thousands of young men returning from serving their country, he had returned to very little. As the war ended they would return to unfamiliar stations hundreds of miles from their families. Kitchener, it was claimed, had connived with politicians to send thousands to their deaths in the last months of conflict, knowing that Britain was winning the war, but fearing possible civil unrest as young men returned, restless and underemployed, to a country changed beyond measure by the huge cost of the victory. There was evidence of 'demobbed' troops being moved to battalions far from their homes. Of those that returned, many looked out to a world from behind eyes inured to suffering, minds devoid of feeling, empty of ambition, drained and hopeless. Where was the heroes' welcome? What had been won, and for whom?

You were meant to doff your cap, defer to the status quo and carry on as best you could. Charlie and Jean moved down to Shropshire with little

Eddie. These post war years were far from the age of innocence he had left behind.

'... They moved down to Lyth Hill and were able to rent for a short while a small wooden bungalow in the garden of Windmill Cottage on Lyth Hill. The rent was 8 shillings a week in the winter and 10 shillings in the summer because of the view.

Our sister Jean (Jean Melville Elizabeth Wellings) was born in the windmill in Sept 1923. Mum pronounced her name as they do in Caithness, and our Grandmother at the Keeper's Cottage, heard it as 'Sheenie'. She was the person who first called Jean "Sheila", a name she was called for the rest of her life, over 80 years. Mary Webb the author lived on Lyth Hill at the time, and she gave presents at Christmas to local children. In a letter from London to Mrs. Thorne, Mary Webb asks about Mrs. Wellings and asks if Sheila is Jean.

By June 1925 our little family had moved into the house called 'Coppice Gate', Lyth Hill, where our parents rented 'rooms' from Mr. and Mrs. Hodges. I was born there in June 1925 and later christened Ronald George at Annscroft Church. Mary Webb bought the bonnet I was christened in. [2]

Around this time another family, the Bays family, had emigrated to Canada from Peterborough, England. Their sea passage across the Atlantic was followed by a journey across the prairies to establish a homestead out west of the Great Lakes. Eventually there were thirteen children in this family, my grandmother Marjorie Bays being the youngest. Her favourite siblings included Norman, Reg, and two tiny 'tots', Flo and Cath. There were several comings and goings between Canada and England as the family expanded in search of work and business. Spinster Cath, who was 4 foot 9 inches tall, with thick rimmed dark blue tinted glasses settled in Church Stretton where she enjoyed sherry, kept a budgie and lived to be 100 years old. She told stories of the cold cold winters on the prairies: a man wearing seven hats stealing a cooling pie from the window sill; houses being moved by huge trucks over the ice, bitter winds blowing. She would recite little ditties such as 'brown shoes leather laces, walking up the market places', cackling away in her raspy little sherry voice.

---

2   Extracts from - Poor Man's Paradise – Ronald George Wellings 2007

Her sister Flo became a teacher at Snowhill in Birmingham working in the same classroom for 50 years. She used to send cakes in the post to the family in South Shropshire; you could in those days.

When she retired she moved over to Church Stretton where she and Cath lived on the Burway, tight in to the side of the Long Mynd. They were nicknamed Effie and Beakie by their doctor, on account of their initials.

*****

White spikes pierce an azure blue sky - Chopiqualqui, Rondoy, Taulliraju, Tocllaraju, Cayesh, Huandoy, Pisco and the jewel in the Crown: Alpamayo. This is the land of the Incas. Travel in the Andes is fraught with danger, always has been: roughly hewn roads cling to mountain sides above huge airy drops into steep canyons. Mudslide, flood avalanche and earthquakes leave their scars.

Peru has a volatile geological history. Its backbone, the Andes is the longest mountain chain in the world. Thrust skywards by the Pacific and Nazca tectonic plates, running north to south these mountains push up to 6768m (over 22,000ft); the summit of Huascaran, Peru's highest peak, dominating and brooding above the town of Yungay in the Cordilerra Blanca. But in 1908 it was Annie Smith Peck, a trailblazing American proto-feminist who became the first person to scale the ramparts of Huascaran.

Peru 'a poor man sitting in a golden chair', suffered invasion by the Conquistadors, struggled for independence, managed to throw off its chains and tried to hold on to its mineral wealth ancient treasures and cultural heritage. Victorian engineers from Britain brought the railway to Peru and helped this country into a modern nationhood.

By 1911 there were sufficient transport links in Peru for the archaeologist Hiram Bingham and his team to travel from sea level at Lima up to Cusco, ancient walled city state of the Inca Empire, 3,500m above sea level. In the July of that year they ventured out and found at the edge of the jungle, hidden in vines, the fabled fortress city of Machu Picchu. The beaten pathways of tourism would inevitably reach this wonder of the world. Almost as a by-product of this, aircraft flying south of Lima first saw the bizarre giant drawings of the Nazca lines, etched in to the desert by ancient civilisations, perhaps as a signal to alien life, but invisible from the ground. The mysteries of Peru were beginning to be uncovered.

The town of Pomabamba, hidden far to the north and east, remained untouched, unknown and unknowing. It lies tucked away on the hidden eastern side of Peru, where the watershed empties east into the Atlantic from the Amazon, below the mountains and above the jungle.

Pomabamba translates as 'Puma land': a folkloric town with a vast strung-out hinterland of farms and their arable strips. Windowless thatched adobe smoke-grimed shacks at best kept the elements out and at worst kept brutality, disease and deprivation within. Bitter night cold, midday suns that burns; katabatic winds that bake exposed skin. Toil is etched and ingrained in the feet and hands of the people tending cattle, tilling terraced crops of potatoes, always walking. Wrapped in ponchos, felt hat and *'yankee'* soled sandals, they roam quietly through the landscape, collecting brushwood, oftentimes alone.

Wrestling is sport in these parts. Men fight men and women fight women in rule-less bare knuckle contests. Itinerant workers travel from town to town and wrestle outside in the dirt within a ring of howling frenzy for money in bitterly fought contests. Spectators drink themselves into oblivion as they watch and gamble on the outcomes; side fights spill out into the raw starry nights where the cold air and the dusty dryness stick in the maw and the pounding *'sorroce'* headache of altitude buzzes under the temporal lobe. This is leisure for a community banded together through struggle: you had to be strong: work, fight, or die.

Julio Escudero Roca was a renowned wrestler around Pomabamba. He was also a ladies' man, strong and swarthy, of tall Latin stock, a descendant of the invaders, rather than the Inca stock that made up the majority of the population. At school Julio was intelligent but rebellious. He argued with his teachers and corporal punishment was the response. He fought because he was from a family with land and he was arrogant. No one could tell him anything, his parents included. Julio was very interested in the world and read whatever he could, but he wanted to do it entirely on his terms. Hence there was no schooling for Julio and there was only one person who mattered to Julio: himself.

Julio's fists got him into a lot of trouble but they also earned him a living. As a '*peleador*' he was an itinerant wrestler travelling wherever the fighting took him. He had a manager (who lost some teeth when he crossed Julio). The way out of this life was to walk. Over high mountain passes, dodging *banditos*, hoping for a safe house and the chance of some work to steal or fight, to hitch a lift on a passing truck or cart down and down, day after day to a hoped-for sanctuary soon revealed as the squalid shanty-towns of Lima. After his journey, he felt the warmer sun on his back but always kept an eye, always watching out for danger, aware of the chance of a knife at his throat. Arriving in Lima without a friend or family member has always been fraught with danger.

Julio roamed far and wide, even wrestling in the *Colliseo Cerrado del Puente del Ejercito* in Lima: the enclosed colliseum which still stands by the Rio Rimac – the talking river. Julio was used to having his own way but he had to fight for it, and that included fighting for his women. His eye had fallen on a pretty young woman, Maria: tiny, but strong and agile. Alas she was already married. Maria's two elder brothers warned her off this crazy wrestler, reminding her that she was married. Whilst her husband was away buying supplies in Huaraz Maria flirted with Julio and dismissed their concerns. She was falling under his spell, blind to his many faults.

Late one night Julio hatched a plan. It was simple and effective: he crept up on Agualita Maria in the darkness, scooped her up into a sack and ran away with her!

*****

Charlie and Jean Wellings were on the move again, but not very far this time with children Eddie Jean and Ron. Before Ron was one year old they had moved down into Lythwood in Bayston Hill, which was easier for journeys in to Shrewsbury and to find work. As tenants of the lodge included in the tenancy was the job of

'...opening the large cast iron gate to the drive leading up to Lythwod Hall, for the few cars used by people travelling to and from Lythwood Hall.

'...From the Lodge we moved across the road into 'Yew Tree Cottage'. The house was very damp and Mum suffered for the first time from asthma. A few years later we moved into the bungalow next door. The roof and sides were made of corrugated iron and when it rained or hailed the noise was terrific. Dad soon got the garden 'shipshape'. There was a large walnut tree in the corner of the garden. Mum pickled some of the walnuts which tasted nicely with cold meat.

'About 1932 our family was on the move again, this time to a bungalow called 'Little Towyn' about 100 yards down the road. It was a very small bungalow built of wood and asbestos with 2 bedrooms, a living room with a small pantry and a veranda open to the front and sides. There was a shed built on the back, and there was a boiler and we had a large box or bench with a bowl for personal washing in cold water. We also used it as a bathroom. There was a corner of the wash house partitioned off where the toilet was, that had to be emptied once a week in the garden. There was no drainage, inlaid water or electricity and only a stove for heating and cooking in the living room.

'As the youngest in the family I was often favoured. Dad visited our grandparents sometimes on a Sunday evening, and he would take me on the crossbar of his bike. They lived at Dorrington and he always went via Condover School, Young's shop and Condover Hall, and he would tell of his experiences there. In the winter he would have a carbide lamp on his bike to light the way and I warmed my hands from the heat of it.

'Dad (Charlie) often had long periods of unemployment; one period lasted 2 ½ years. He had to 'sign on' at the Labour Exchange in Shrewsbury every weekday and was paid 26 shillings a week in 'dole money'. From that amount 14 shillings a week was to pay the rent, leaving 12 shillings (60p) a week to pay for food, clothing, heating etc. for 2 adults and 3 children. They were very hard times for all poorer people.

'One advantage of living in a 'poor man's paradise' was the fact that by growing their own vegetables, families could sustain a somewhere near staple diet. There were many wild rabbits, and Dad and his father were experts at catching them in snares. Mum roasted a rabbit in the oven, with onions, sage *and thyme and perhaps thin slices of fat bacon… sometimes our own vegetables were supplemented with a swede from a farmer's field, or some water cress when in season. 'Dad was willing to take employment anywhere to earn some money; one place he worked at was the 'rag and bone shop' in Barker Street. Now and then a 'rag and bone' merchant would come walking round most districts with an old pram and would call out loudly: 'Rags and bones!' He would sell his load and also rabbit skins to the 'rag and bone shop'. They would send them in bags to companies who would treat them for use in industry. It was a poor job, but Dad was willing to earn money if he could. Now and then that job caused a number of 'hunting experiences', looking for a flea which had found a home in Dad's clothing.'*[3]

Houses were gradually being built along Lythwood Road as modern Bayston Hill started to take shape.

'Now and then Dad also worked as a labourer for some of the local builders. He also dug holes for electric light poles to supply electricity from the newly built Buildwas Power station. He said he had dug many of the holes for the electricity line to Bishops Castle. Often water would seep into the holes making the work very difficult. For some time he worked with Harry Titley from Hook-a-Gate, digging wells in many places. When Harry needed a haircut he would walk up the Hanley Lane on a Sunday morning and Dad would cut it for him. They could talk for hours. Dad worked later for Jones and Griffiths, the builders at Bayston Hill, and also for many other firms when they built the many houses erected at Upper Pulley and Lythwood.

'Dad's last employer was John Good, a master builder. He wrote to us: "Working with Charlie was certainly an education for me; everything had to be so neat and tidy. In those days all digging was done by hand and we did a lot of it together. I was always amazed by the way he stuck at it and made it look easy, with the result being a straight, plumb and very neat job. Nowadays when I dig a trench I like to think that Charlie would approve."

'When Dad was unemployed he always had plenty of jobs to do. He repaired his own bike made from spare parts, mended punctures, repaired all our boots

---

3   Poor Man's Paradise – Ron Wellings 2007

and shoes, as well as keeping his garden in shape, and spent many hours finding firewood.

'Somewhere about 1930 Mum and Mrs. Addis each bought a Singer sewing machine from a man called Mr. Fenn. He cycled around the district collecting the weekly payments of sixpence until the sewing machine was paid for. Times were very hard and perhaps they did not have the money. A few times they both hid in the washhouse giggling like schoolgirls until Mr. Fenn had gone.

'Even though we were hard up, when gipsies came to our door selling their homemade clothes pegs Mum would always buy a few pegs or give them perhaps a piece of bread and margarine to eat. As children we never realised we were poor, as most people were in similar circumstances. At bedtime Mum would light a candle and put us to bed. After we had said our evening prayer, she blew out the candle.

'Coal was delivered by horse and dray by Tom Sharpe who lived at Lythwood Hall. Another coalman was Roberts from Coleham. He had a lorry which never moved very fast so we children at times hung on the back of the lorry and got a 'lift'. It really was a dangerous practice. Once I fell off and hurt both my knees. Mum bandaged them with pieces of old sheets, and I had sore knees that afternoon when Mum took us children to see the opening of the new Shrewsbury By-pass (Oteley Road).

'...on the 11ᵗʰ November in 1934, Sheila and I were walking home with Ron Thomas, and just before we came to our house he suddenly said: "Your Mum is going to have a baby." Sheila and I both said he was daft to say that, but next day when we arrived home from school a neighbour, Mrs. Mabel Braddick, was in our house and said to us, "Come with me, I have a surprise for you." Mum was in bed and she had our little brother⁴ by her side. It was rather a shock for us, but we soon accepted him in the family and he got plenty of care and attention from all the family. The small space of 'Little Towyn' became even more cramped with a cot and a pram.

'My position of being the youngest in the family was changed by Robert's arrival. He was christened the next Spring, Robert Melville (a family name on Mum's side), at Grove Lane Methodist Chapel. I remember Eddie and I

---

4   The authors father

helping to lift the pushchair over the stiles on the way across the fields to Grove Lane.

'Of course with a baby in the family there was more washing to be done, with lots of napkins and baby clothes. As stated earlier, washing facilities were very primitive. Mum still had many serious attacks of asthma, and Sheila was often absent from school to look after Robert and Mum.

Robert spent a lot of time with Mum, he did not have many playmates as we others had to attend school. Robert invented a 'make believe' playmate that he called Michael Parton, and he spoke a lot about him, and they 'played' together in the garden at 'Little Towyn'.

'One very important milestone for 12 Bayston Hill families in October 1938 was being chosen for one of the 12 council houses which had been built on George Davies' field on Lansdowne Road, by the Atcham Rural District Council. They were named Rural Cottages.

Everyone had moved out of very poor houses which had been very overcrowded. Most tenants were pleased to get away from their private landlords, who often had made life quite difficult for them, and for most of them the rent then payable to the Atcham Rural District Council was less than they had paid before to private landlords. Our new rent and rates was 7 shillings and 1 penny a week. A rent collector came every week for the money.'[5]

Life was starting to improve for Charlie, Jean, Eddie, 'Sheila', Ron and Robert in Bayston Hill. Their council house had a garden and an outside privy and a butt for collecting rain water. Eddie had been working long hours, including Saturday nights delivering meat for Sunday dinners (there were no fridges in those days). Sheila increasingly had to help Jean whose asthma was worsening and Robert, now four years old had been diagnosed with a hole in the heart and he required extra help and attention.

*****

My maternal grandfather Alexander Stewart was born in Birmingham to a well-to-do middle class family. His father was a bank manager, a Scot

---

5   The above are excerpts from Ron's memoirs: Poor Man's Paradise (2007)

from Aberdeen. His father ended his life in a lunatic asylum. Alexander (Alec) and his two sisters lived comfortably well in Birmingham. They had a maid and ladies who 'did' for them – cleaning, washing and ironing. Mother kept the house, changing in to her best clothes to receive visitors in the afternoon. Dinner was taken in the evening when Father returned from work. The author P. G. Wodehouse was a relation.

Some of the Bays family had returned to Birmingham from Canada after the war. Marjorie was now a young teenager, her many siblings spread through England California and Manitoba, Canada.

Alec Stewart had met Marjorie Bays in the late 1920's in Llandudno when they were both on holiday. Alec worked at a bank and soon they were courting and then married. Ann was their firstborn, arriving in January 1935, Margaret[6] followed on December 4th 1938 and youngest Liz in 1943.

---

6   The author's mother

Chapter 2

A Just War, A Brighter Future

Fighting and Working For a Better Way

On September 3rd 1939 Prime Minister Chamberlain spoke to the nation, declaring Britain was at war with Germany.

Eddie(Ed), now eighteen, signed up, joining the Royal Air Force as a Radio Operator. After basic training he was posted to the Far East. Sheila joined the Women's Royal Naval Squadron, 'the Wrens', and was posted to Hayling Island in Hampshire, near Portsmouth. Ron was only fourteen when war was declared but within a year had started work on the railway as a freight guard. This work precluded him joining the forces as it was a 'reserved' job so Ron enlisted in the Home Guard.

Eddie (Ed) was away from Britain for the whole war. As a radio operator in Burma he was in the thick of the action. Working under pressure, never sure of what the Japanese would do next, he and his fellow airmen were living a life fraught with danger. Once he had to make another call in to a formation of over twenty aircraft as he had sent them 180 degrees the wrong way, spotting his error just in time. The squadron leader shook his hand when he returned from that sortie.

Getting mail was not always good news. One of his colleagues received a letter from a fiancée saying that it was all over between them as she had met an American G.I. He walked into the jungle and shot himself. Events like these were not only terrible for morale but also gave the position away to the enemy, upping the stakes in a deadly game.

Ed's squadron were wrong footed in the jungle by the Japanese who landed behind their lines at night. A hasty escape was under way as the Japanese launched a surprise attack. Ed and crew got out onto the runway and took off whilst under attack, just escaping by the skin of their teeth. The date was Friday 13th February 1942, Ed's 21st birthday.

Ed was never captured but did not return home for four years. Upon his return, on London's Paddington station in all the hubbub and bustle he bumped into Sheila and they travelled joyously back to Shrewsbury together on the train. Ed was placed in 'jankers' for two weeks as he was supposed to be posted up to Scotland[7] but he disobeyed orders so as to return home briefly to his beloved family in Shropshire.

Sheila had been given the nickname of 'Puss' whilst in the Wrens, and it stuck. She had been part of the support team for Operation Neptune, the massive D Day landings on the beaches of Normandy the biggest seaborne invasion in history.

Ron worked on the railways when freight movement was critical; most had to be done at night with minimal lighting for fear of German attack. Derailments were not uncommon, particularly with a long train of wagons. This happened on one occasion at Chirk Viaduct. There being no communication between driver at the front and guard at the back, Ron, realising his situation, carried on as trained: running back along the rails over the viaduct in the dark with a big drop on either side to place three detonators at intervals on the track before returning as quickly as possible to his train. The following train driver would hear these detonators under his wheels and recognise this as the signal to stop and avoid a collision with Ron's unlit derailed train ahead.

Charlie too played his part. At nearby Bomere Pool he helped string cable across the pool to sabotage the chance of boat-planes landing on the water. Luftwaffe returning from raids on Liverpool would jettison bombs over Shropshire waking people for miles around.

On one occasion an enemy bomb scored a direct hit on the railway sidings at Hook-a-Gate less than a mile away. Charlie came running down the stairs shouting: "The buggers am here! The buggers am here!"

Young Robert suffered ill health with his heart defect and was not allowed to play outside with his friends, which was a misery for him.

---

7   presumably because he was born there, although he left as an infant

However, he was becoming quite a scholar and was bright at most subjects. Pressure for social reform led to R.A. Butler's 1944 Education Act. This was among the first signs of the post war coalition - building a country fit for heroes to return to. Perhaps lessons had been learned from the return of demobilised soldiers in 1918?

The '11+' exam and free school meals appeared, school costs reduced and Robert was in the first cohort accepted to the Priory Grammar School under the new education act. How many came from rural working class backgrounds and how many were upper middle class boys from the town? It may not have been so easy to fit in there. But Robert had been lucky to be the youngest in some ways – to miss the war and the lean times of the Depression years. Despite poor health, he was able to follow an educational path that had been denied to Ed, Ron and Puss.

*****

In Peru there is a certain kudos being born in the capital city Lima, setting one apart from being a '*Chollo*' a 'Rustic'.

Julio the wrestler and his kidnapped wife Maria had their first child in Lima, probably on 9th January 1945. Christened Jorge Escudero Valverde, he grew up tall, strong and swarthy like his father, with slicked back jet black hair. He was followed by six sisters. It is probable that Julio fathered many other children too. Family sources have it that Julio did not provide for his family. He drank and his wife was now very submissive.

Crecencio Vasquez lived in Llamellin, dirt poor and on the same eastern side of the Andes as Pomabamba. He worked in agriculture but hated it. He had beautiful handwriting and was very academic; he was always reading, anything he could get his hands on. Through this he gained the respect of the community. His nickname was 'Gringo Kishi' on account of his looks, ginger hair and green eyes. His favourite phrase was '*ablando en oro*' – 'speak in gold' or 'tell the truth'. His wife Ignacia Acuña, a teacher, died when their daughter Herlinda was 6 years old. They lived in Coto near Llamellin. Herlinda would become the mother of Liliana Escudero de Wellings.

*****

After the war when Ed Wellings was 'demobbed' he moved down to Hereford, where Ron was working on the railway. Puss had found work with the Forestry Commission. Home life at Lansdowne Road Bayston Hill became quiet again for Robert. In 1948, aged 13, he and his mum Jean travelled by train to Castletown. This was the first time Jean had been 'home' for 26 years.

Charlie was a regular at The Fox pub. He would come home on occasion roaring drunk and fall asleep in the chair. Once Jean covered his (now bald) head in cochineal as he snored, producing tears of suppressed laughter from all, then, quickly wiping it off before he blurted awake. Usually though he would be outside on a Sunday morning digging and preparing veg for the Sunday dinner.

The trio of sisters Ann, Margaret and Liz Stewart were children still. Their mother despaired as roisterous girls Ann and Margaret would shout out of the window 'We've got scabies! We've got scabies!'

Rationing was making things scarce, even for the middle classes. Ann and Margaret were both allowed a bite of a banana, something of a luxury, as Liz, still a baby was only allowed *'a sniff!'* During this time they lived in Hereford and there was an air raid on the nearby munitions factory at Rotherwas. Travelling people and pedlars would call. A woman came with a child and he asked the family if he could 'have jam'. The woman turned on his impudence, how dare he speak without being spoken to? 'Jam I sez! You ain't 'avin' no jam!' This became a family saying for decades.

Ed met Mavis, a Liverpudlian of Irish descent who was a teacher. They were married in Hereford, and had two children Janet (b. 1950) and Andrew (b. 1953). Robert was studying for his A Levels at this time and was accepted at Cardiff University to study Medicine.

Queen Elizabeth II was crowned Queen in May 1953. A day prior to this news had reached London that Hillary and Tenzing had become the first people to summit Everest. Life was improving but rationing continued until 1954, nine years after the war had finished.

During the war, Ron had become politicised and would become the secretary of the Shrewsbury Labour Party. At a meeting in Bayston Hill Memorial Hall he asked the sitting Conservative MP, Sir John Holt, a couple of pertinent questions in front of an audience:

'Do people realise our MP has only asked two questions in the House? One: "How many hump back bridges are there between here and London? And, two: "What are the ingredients in the House of Commons puddings?"'

Ron was castigated for this by fellow audience members. Charlie, Daily Mirror reader though he was, may have had some sympathy for Ron but was from the age of deference and not 'rocking the boat'. Later Ron was harangued when canvassing for the party, Hilda Norris up at Castle Lane threatened to throw a bucket of water at him.

"Round here people would vote for a donkey if it had a blue rosette pinned on it!" he opined.

Through his socialist connections or the Railway, Ron attended a study tour to New York in 1954. He had met Else Deilendorf, a Danish girl working in England and were married that year. They bought a small mid terrace house on the Ellesmere Road in Shrewsbury near to the railway sidings.

Jean's asthma had become much worse. She made one final trip to her beloved Caithness before she died in March of 1954 and is buried in the cemetery on Roman Road in Shrewsbury. She was 54 years old.

Robert was having a difficult time at university as funding cuts were squeezing the education system. Exam results were posted on the noticeboard in descending order of success. A short way down was a red line. Everyone above the line was to stay at university and everyone below was out. Robert's name was the first one under the line. He had no option but to return to Bayston Hill. Puss, always pragmatic, helped him get a job working up with the Forestry Commission in North Wales based at Betws-y-Coed. It was here he learnt to drive, round the forestry roads in a type 1 Land Rover. He once rolled it over on the A5 scaring a young pregnant neighbour who witnessed it into going into early labour!

The Stewart family moved from Hereford to Church Stretton, the girls Ann Margaret and Liz now teenagers. A small cottage tucked tightly into the Long Mynd at the top of the steep Burway hill became their home. A short bridleway led down into Carding Mill valley, where Marjorie worked at the tea rooms. She adored her life there.

Margaret Stewart had finished secondary school at the Priory and worked at the Ministry of Agriculture in Shrewsbury as a typist before deciding to train as a nurse. Robert Wellings moved on and was now doing hospital orderly work. Whilst lighting his pipe, sitting among the sluices at the Infirmary behind St. Mary's Church in Shrewsbury, in came Margaret with some laundry. 'What are you doing tonight, nurse?' he asked.

They were soon 'going steady'.

Working hard, Marg and her fellow student nurses also had plenty of funny stories to tell: skeletons in beds, 'apple pie beds' collecting all the patients' false teeth in a bucket for cleaning, only then to realise no one knew whose was whose! A disabled man was rolled out of bed completely, his glass eye rolling away into a corner.

Robert and Margaret had parted but got back together again after she asked him out to the big event, The 1961 Red Rose Ball. They decided to get married that October. The previous year her sister Ann had married Alan Newman, a tall, dark policeman. They married at St. Lawrence's Church in Church Stretton. Robert (Bob, as he was now known), and Marg followed suit the next year. Charlie came down from Bayston Hill with Sheila. Ed and Mavis' daughter Janet was bridesmaid and son Andrew was pageboy. The reception was at Studio 54 in the town and the bride and groom honeymooned in North Wales, spending their first two nights of wedded bliss at the Bull Inn in Newtown. The smell of burning fish had accompanied them there: Marg's younger sister Liz's boyfriend Alan Wildblood was a local mechanic and had been trusted to service their car before they went away, strapping kippers to the exhaust manifold for good luck! Arriving in Newtown, the bride drank seven gin and tonics before being carried to bed, collapsing asleep in her clothes. It was only on the second night that she found that Marjorie had sewn her nightie up and it's only then that we can assume the fun started!

Ron and Else had migrated to Denmark the previous year with their two young daughters Jean and Marie and did not attend Rob and Marg's wedding. Liz married Alan at the same church two years later.

I was born in The Queen Elizabeth Hospital in Edgbaston, Birmingham, weighing in at a healthy 8 lbs on 25th August 1962. I was Stewart Melville Wellings: Stewart, mother's maiden name: Melville, dad's mother's maiden name.

Bob and Marg's first house was a maisonette in Hollybush Lane in Stourbridge. Above them lived a motorcyclist who kept a pet monkey. The Cold War was in its darkest depths, the Cuban Missile Crisis keeping everyone on tenterhooks and The Berlin Wall and The Iron Curtain was very new. My brother Charles Gavin Melville Wellings was born, also in Birmingham, on 4th November 1964. Auntie Liz nicknamed him 'Chink' for some reason and it stuck. Marjorie had breast cancer and died on 26th November just 22 days after her grandson Chink was born. A wooden seat in her memory sat just by the cattle grid where the Burway steepens and leads out up onto the Long Mynd proper.

Our youngest brother Robert Paul (Paul, after Paul McCartney) was born in Copthorne Hospital Shrewsbury. He arrived, weighing 5lb 9oz; things had not been easy with the birth and he had required a full blood transfusion. When he came home Chink and I, (Scoob as I was to become known) had to be very careful around him. He would be known as Robs, Bob and then for some reason 'Egg Boy' or 'Egger'. Ann and Alan had Cheryl, David and Peter, Liz and Alan had Helen and John. All of us cousins were born between 1962 and 1968.

Bob and Marg and their small family had come back to live in Bayston Hill. Bob's research at the University had been cut and Bob now worked for Hoechst UK, a German pharmaceutical company, as a medical representative. His area covered all of Shropshire, Mid and North Wales, including Anglesey.

Being a Medical Rep involves having a good working knowledge of how drugs work and of persuading doctors of the merits of these products. Although it wasn't what he had hoped for originally he was good at it and it was a good job with good terms and conditions, salary and pension. Bob had to stay away quite often to reach outlying areas in North Wales. He had to work long hours, including evening presentations, and occasionally a conference, but the job suited him. He stayed with the company for 28 years. He had an interest in maths and completed an Open University degree in the subject. He was a fine upstanding pillar of the community.

He had moved us to a fairly new family house in Overdale Road in Bayston Hill. Chink was just a baby then and Mum put him in the airing cupboard sometimes to keep him warm. It was only 'round the corner' to Puss and Charlie's house in Lansdowne Road. Charlie Wellings was 'Gramps' to us lads.

Around this time (1965) Marg's sister Ann and Alan and family emigrated to Canada, the prairies of Saskatchewan where Alan took up a post, transferring to the Royal Canadian Mounted Police.

Ed, Mavis, Jan and Andy had moved to Liverpool at the height of Beatle mania, to a big Victorian house up in Crosby, near the seaside at Blundellsands. Mavis was a teacher and Ed was an Education Welfare Officer – trying to keep Liverpool kids in school.

Our world remained very small. We played on the Overdale Road; there were a couple of houses opposite us, but otherwise just open fields. A weeping willow tree grew in the bottom of the garden and we could run down to it from the French windows. We also had a 'Sprite Musketeer' caravan parked in the drive.

Overdale Road had a couple of shops: Mr Davies the butcher and Mr Jones, grocer and general shop. Behind us lived my play mate Mark Fletcher. Behind his house was Longmeadow Junior School. Nick Preece, oldest of four children lived opposite the school. We would become best mates.

On Sundays we would go to church. The church, about a mile away abutted the old village common, (which had been the centre of 'old'

Bayston Hill before it expanded) opposite The Compasses pub. Everyone, to us it seemed, went to church. Revd John Fieldsend, a Jewish survivor of Hitler's concentration camps, was the vicar. At Sunday school we were told by Mrs. Maddison in no uncertain manner, stamping her heel on the wooden floor for emphasis: "2000 years ago, Jesus died on the cross for our sins!" I am surprised we could hear that over the din we all made before we were taken into our various groups for bible study.

This was the same building in which Ed, Puss and Ron had completed their schooling in before the war, and Dad, before he went to the Priory Boys' School. When Sunday school was over, we would all spill out and run around the corner to meet our parents and the rest of the congregation exiting the church through the graveyard, shaded by yew trees.

I knew that eventually if I wasn't careful Jesus would catch my heart and I would become one of them, a Christian! I really didn't want to be as even then, as a small boy, I recognised in these adults that their blind faith didn't answer my naïve simple questions with the same plausibility our school teachers did. But the thing was, most of my school mates went there, and we all had a great laugh shouting and singing!

After Sunday school we would pile back in the car and Dad would drive all of 50 metres and park up behind The Compasses and then go in for 2 or 3 pints. We would be placated with a bottle of Coke, a straw and a packet of crisps with a little blue salt sachet as we sat listening to 'Family Favourites' on the car radio before Dad drove home and Sunday lunch.

One afternoon Mum hosted a Tupperware party for some of her young mum friends, and they all sat around eating cakes and drinking from cups and saucers. It was a warm sunny day and I caused a commotion by bringing a frog in, cupped in my hand, and dropping it squarely into Mum's lap. She wasn't keen on frogs apparently.

The older kids nearby made a go-kart from an old pram, some sisal to steer it and a cardboard box to make it look like a tank. We thought it was great, easily pleased as we were. During a very cold winter we built a huge stand-in ice cave by hollowing out a snowball we had all rolled up. It was just outside the kitchen and Mum passed us out hot cheesy pastry twists to keep us warm as we played; our breath steaming, rosy cheeked, our red knitted mittens on strings patting the snow.

My 4th birthday was on 25th August 1966. Mum and Dad bought me a dog. This black and white mongrel came with a free tin of dog food and a lead, and went by the name of Hercules. The night before my birthday, unbeknownst to me, 'Hercy' escaped and went off round the village, leading Dad a merry chase as he went looking for him in the car, driving around in his dressing gown. That was the first of the many times 'Hercy' disappeared, always on the sniff-out for the nearest bitch.

Hercules accompanied Mum, Dad, Chink and me on our very first trip to Scotland. Dad had a company car, a Cortina, and had bought the smallest tent possible – a simple square of white canvas with a pole at both ends and guys to peg it out, no flysheet or sides or groundsheet. The first night we all slept in the tent on the bonny banks of Loch Lomond. There was no bridge at Ballachulish then, only a ferry. From there it is still a very long way to Caithness. We went up to stay with Dad's aunties in Castletown - his mother Jean's sisters Bessie and Jessie and the family up there. Bessie was very small and had a squint and an arm that was fixed at a right angle to her body. She was so happy that we had come to visit the Castletown branch of our family. She always remembered our birthdays, spidery written cards sent with love.

When we returned home I started at Junior School at Oaklands Bayston Hill, a brand new purpose built school. We didn't know it but we were Generation X, the youngest of the 'baby boomers'. We walked to and from school in our shiny shoes with our mothers, some pushing prams. We were a very different, more affluent band than the poorer ragamuffins of our parents' and grandparents' era. Fathers of my friends were employed in places such as Ironbridge Power Station, the Barracks at Copthorne, and also at the large corporate Post Office Telecommunications, usually career jobs.

Puss often looked after us at Lansdowne Road on a Saturday. She would get us involved in making or painting something or other, something made from toilet rolls and egg boxes. Perhaps unlike other young children, on occasion we would be drinking 'Cinzano' and lemonade with a slice of lemon while we did this. We would stay over, sleeping in the back bedroom, overlooking Longmeadow School. At bedtime we would play "Moles" - racing under the covers down to the bottom of the bed and back up, gasping for air, laughing. Then Puss told stories about boys, who (quite coincidentally) had the same names as us, and went exploring space in a rocket!

Gramps would be in the living room on a Saturday afternoon with the curtains drawn so he could see the television. He and his old friend Bob Trickett would sit in front of the black and white set and watch the wrestling. Bright and sunny outside, inside they sat in Stygian gloom shouting at the screen 'stamp on his head!' or 'hit him!' Bob Trickett's hearing aids squealed away, but they both sat glued to the set impervious to the din. Bob's badly deformed arthritic hands gripped the seat, his ladies' handbag, which he used as he could undo the clasp, though only with difficulty, dangling off the armrest. We had to be quiet as mice when the football results were read out at 5pm as Gramps assiduously checked his pools results to see if he had won a fortune. He never did though.

*****

The Beatles had reached Peru by the late 1960's and 'tocadisco' parties were becoming popular, although for Saint Day holidays 'banda de musica folklorica' – local folk music groups were favoured. It was at one such festival – Fiesta de San Juan Bautista, that Jorge Escudero Valverde met Herlinda Acuña. Herlinda escaped her aunties and she and Jorge were soon making a go of it in Lima. Jorge had a rich 'uncle' – a mysterious family friend or confidante who offered to go into partnership with him. Jorge had seen televisions being imported at the docks and decided this was where the future lay. His uncle helped him rent some premises and they started to sell television sets and other electrical goods.

Liliana Escudero Vasquez was born to Jorge and Herlinda on 18th November 1968 in Ancon on the north side of Lima by the coast. Maria (1971), Julio (1972), Jorge (Polaco) (1973), Maribel (who died in 1974 aged just 9 months) and Mabel (1977) followed. Everyone slept in one room, including Jorge and Herlinda, a simple room, concrete walls no decoration.

Huaraz is the main town of the Cordilerra Blanca, sitting around the 3000m contour (about 10,000 ft) under Laguna Churup, with the improbably sharp peak of Cayesh dominating, above steep snow ice guarding its ramparts. The hidden laguna is a day's hike from the town, with a dip in the icy grey waters, silted from glacial action, the reward after negotiating the final scramble. The views back show the town nestled below the much lower and rounded Cordilerra Negra. But look in a northerly direction and some of the biggest mountains in the whole of the Andes – Ranrapalca (6162m), Ishinca (5530m), Tocllaraju (6032m), Copa (6188m): a host of peaks around the 6000m/20,000ft mark. Dominating everything on the skyline are the twin peaks of Huascaran Norte (6664m) and Huascaran Sur (6768m). Himalayan in stature, the highest peak in Peru and the fifth highest in all the Americas, it scowls at you as if to say: "You may try, but will you succeed?"

Monterrey, Carhuaz and Yungay are the main towns as you head northwest away from Huaraz up the Rio Santa valley. These colourful small towns are well kept, each with its *plaza de armas* (central square) neatly planted with exquisite flowers: gentians, violets, *chinchircuma* – a shrub with red flowers, *taqllosh* and *quenual* trees. Shops selling iron hardware, ice cream, beer and Inka Cola face out from the shade. School girls in well-pressed pleated skirts, shiny shoes, bright smiles and sleek black plaited hair pass by in pairs, arms hugging books closely. Outside the town, away from the *canalettos* that terrace and allow water to run to feed the flowers and hydrate the population, all appear dusty and barren.

The old town of Yungay today lies buried, just the tops of the palm trees from the square, a twisted bus carcass, a reverential silence where a sweet daily humdrum should be…

31ˢᵗ May 1970 is a day etched in the psyche of the people of the Andes. One of the most devastating earthquakes the world has ever seen hit the area. Measuring 7.7 on the Richter scale, its force was so huge it dislodged a vast swathe of Huascaran Norte's peak, sending it crashing to the glacier thousands of feet below: perhaps a million tonnes of rock and ice avalanched into the Llanganuco valley by now travelling at 200mph, part of this tsunami of death flew over a 200m high ridge thought to protect the town. In a deathly instant Yungay town disappeared, buried under 10 metres of debris. An estimated 18,000 died that day, only 240 survived by running to the cemetery hill above the town. Throughout the region an estimated 100,000 people died and a million were left without homes. International aid was flown in to a hastily constructed airport.

Chapter 3

Children

Sunday July 20, 1969 was a warm day, and crowded around a black and white television set inside 20 Overdale Road many adults watched the first men to walk on the moon. We kids were not interested. It was something for the grown-ups. We hadn't got our heads around the idea of a man on the moon; what about the cheese? Anyway, I had just had my tonsils removed and did not want to be inside.

Our school was used as a polling station for the 1970 General Election. This was the first election where people above the age of 18 could vote. Dad was a Conservative councillor, and we stayed out late that night running errands as he was involved in helping the local MP, Sir John Langford Holt (MP from 1945 – 1983), that same MP that Ron Wellings had had a run in with after the war. The 1970 Election was a victory for Edward Heath's Conservative party with a 4.5% swing from Harold Wilson's Labour Party, who had been in power for most of the 1960s. None of this meant anything to us junior school children of course; we were in a club where the entry requirements meant picking a scab and eating it!

Shillings were replaced by shiny new five penny pieces which confused us as decimalisation superseded the pounds, shillings, tuppences, pennies and ha'pennies that we knew. Staying in Bayston Hill we moved house about half a mile to Broad Oak Crescent. Our new house was Number 17 and it was at the top of a *cul de sac*, round the bend and up the hill. Whilst unpacking as we moved in, Dad found a large cardboard box, scrawled on the side in my seven year olds handwriting the words 'I hope this is full of wollop'![8]

'Gramps' Charlie Wellings had carried the bricklayers their hods as they built these semi-detached three bedroom houses in 1961 (when he

---

8   'wollop' = alcohol.

was sixty three). Here we could play by the little stream that ran through the fields below our houses. This place we christened 'Cavern Camp' for the stream cut deeply under overhanging willow trees and was shady and cool in the summers.

Our new back garden was a safe place for Mum to bring up three young boys. The lean-to between the house and the garage was a playschool, which had been run by Flo Hewitt and had been sold as a going concern, and so every morning sixteen little darlings aged between three and five came to play. Mum and Brenda Fletcher would organise games, supervise the sandpit, the climbing frame, the swing. Milk drinking time was accompanied by watching 'Playschool' on TV, allowing Brenda and Mum a quick coffee break.

As an eight-year-old I was invested into the Cub Scouts. The Scout hut, a small wooden building, dark and dingy, on its last legs tucked away behind the Vicarage on the Common not far from Sharpstones Quarry, was part of the fabric of 'Old Bayston Hill'. On one memorable expedition Akela, Mrs Ann Ballard and her other helpers, 'Baloo' and 'Shere Khan', marched us down to The Compasses bus stop on the A49 where the whole pack – Nick Preece, Nigel Emery, Peter Thompson, Peter Fieldsend the vicar's son, Dave Lewis among them boarded a service bus. At Church Stretton we alighted near the traffic lights, ready for a mass ascent of Caer Caradoc. Up on the top among the ancient earthworks and heather we ran amok, laughing, carefree. I knew the Stretton Hills and The Stiperstones, as Auntie Liz and Uncle Alan lived in Church Stretton. At the tender age of six I had embarked upon a cycling trip to visit Grandpa Stewart who lived ten miles away at the top of the Burway on the Long Mynd. The roads were quieter then but big lorries bore down upon this unwary, unknowing and therefore fearless young cyclist.

Bill Braddick, steely eyed and straight of back, an old soldier of the Great War, corralled a gang of us into joining his Kazoo Marching Band, rehearsing on The Common so as to be ready for any Summer Fair, Fete or Garden Party that might have need of our services. We had cardboard hats held under our chins, with elastic and red piping down our white trousers and contrived tunics. I carried the big bass drum, not because of any sense of rhythm but because I could actually lift it! We marched up and we marched down, and 'The Red River Valley' was all we had in our dribbling spit repertoire.

Life in Broad Oak Crescent was always busy because of the playschool. We were all packed off to Longmeadow School so Mum could get ready for the daily influx of playschool children. We would walk ourselves to school. I would walk Hercy the dog up to the Glebelands and arrive a few minutes late to school as a result. Occasionally Hercy would escape from the nursery children. When he did he would make his way up to our school.

"Stewart Wellings! Take your dog back home – now!"

I would be handed a skipping rope by Mr. Butler or Mrs. Kinrade and drag Hercy out of the long jump sandpit, scuff the sand over where he had peed, and walk him back home. I didn't mind doing this, being with my lovely dog, and I never rushed back to school.

Headmaster Mr. Beddoes had taught my dad. The whole school would gather for assembly every morning, Mr. Beddoes at the front; we, cross-legged on the wooden tiled floor, beatifically smiling up at him. "I'm waiting!" he would bellow as a way to quieten us down. "Gunna wait a bit longer!" we would whisper to each other anarchically, trying not to snigger too loudly. Miss Simmonds would accompany us on the piano as we would sing a hymn. We had nicknames for most things and so it was with hymns. Our favourite was 'O Jesus I have Promised' - 'The Bubble Car Song' as we called it – something to do with its bouncy rhythm. There was a school choir too, though not for the likes of us 'nitwits'.

Being a chunky little fellow, I was often used by Miss Roberts as the 'rammer' to ram the waste paper in to the class bin when we were working on some project or other with vast amounts of toilet roll tubes, cardboard boxes, glue and paper. Nib pens dipped into ink, topped up by an ink monitor, was how we learnt handwriting. Roger Dean, long haired and artistic, was our milk monitor, bringing in a small crate with

1/3 pint bottles in it each day until milk for school children was stopped by Margaret Thatcher.

Our biggest adventure around this time was a school trip down to Berkeley Castle in Gloucestershire. Despite throwing a snowball which smashed Gramp Charlie's front window, on New Year's Day – Gramps took his belt off to me, such was the severity of the crime – I was allowed to attend the trip. The Chelsea v Leeds United forthcoming FA Cup final was the hot topic and we sang a lot: 'Blue is the colour, football is the game...' There was also a trip to Ludlow Castle. For some children these trips were as far as they had ever been.

One evening Mum and Dad left me in charge of the house as they had to visit Grandpa Alec Stewart, who was in hospital. I wrote a note and stuck it on the window: "If any burglar comes round here I'll give him a bunch of fives!" Grandpa Stewart died, aged 64, and he left a widow, Vicky, a South Walian Barmaid, much younger than he was. They had met at his local bar, The Hotel in Church Stretton. The hotel had recently been the scene of terrible tragedy where despite valiant attempts Alec's son-in-law, our uncle, Sub-Officer Alan Wildblood and fellow local retained firemen could not contain the flames. Five people lost their lives that night, including three brothers all under ten years old.

Our classmate Mark France, died aged just nine years old, knocked off his bike by a car down in 'the dip' opposite Broad Oak Crescent.

We moved up to Mr. Heath's class. He was an old-school stickler and was in his last year before retirement. I was caned several times, either across my knuckles or over a knee on the backside. He would put his arm round the girls when they went up to him with their exercise books. There were several male teachers – Mr. Heath was by far the oldest, and least typical. Mr. Turrell and Mr. Ewels were younger more progressive teachers: Mr. Turrell small, wiry and with a straggly beard and glasses; Mr. Ewels, tall and kind. Mrs. Kinrade was an older teacher who read us Malcolm Saville's 'Lone Pine' children's adventure books. Set on The Stiperstones, ten miles south of where we were in school, the warm sun shone through the window onto our desks as she read to us. Everyone's favourite, however, was Mr. Steven Butler. Mr. Butler was on our level; he knew how to relate to children. He played guitar and ran a guitar lesson once a week for the mums. He wrote, produced and directed a film starring his pupils. He smiled at everyone, and everyone loved Mr. Butler.

We had a good school football team that played schools as far away as Longden and Shrewsbury. Andrew 'Comprehension' Cooper would watch from the side-lines before filing his match report for the school newsletter. The cub packs had football teams too, and Saturday mornings was our time to play. There were local tournaments, although we never lifted a trophy.

Outside of school we would play and walk fairly long distances around the village, which was growing. Lyth Hill was not out of bounds; we would cycle up there and make dens in the bracken or swings down in the wood. I had a blue bike made for me by Gramps and given on my ninth birthday. He had made it out of spare parts and sprayed it blue, with the word 'Special' transferred on to the down tube.

School sports day marked the end of the summer term. Duncan Platford would win everything athletic but other traditional events included the egg and spoon race, three legged race and the sack race. Nick Preece did very well and was a very popular winner. I was one of the last, if not the last in most of the events, but it was all good fun.

An old cream coloured council bus came once a week and took us to the swimming baths in Shrewsbury. There we would splash around but I couldn't swim. Eventually, just before the last sports day, before we went up to senior school, I managed to 'doggy paddle' a width across the baths, a ferocious 10 metre struggle. Quite soon after that I hung on in to complete a length of 25m. At the sports day I was called out in front of everyone to receive my certificate and badge. Beaming from ear to ear as I went up to collect it, I returned to sit next to my mate Chris Berkeley, who had helped me to learn.

In September 1972 we were now in our final year of Junior School. There were two classes with approximately 40 pupils each – Wonderful Mr. Butler's class and Miss Simmonds' class. I was in Miss Simmonds' class. Miss Simmonds was jovial but prim and proper; she was also a guide leader and had taught my mum. The two classes joined together on a Friday afternoon for country dancing, sometimes after the school nurse had stood us in line and checked us for nits. Miss Simmonds had a record player. Those who did not want to, or were too immature to take part, usually us boys, would stay in class to read and draw.

Country dancing lessons gave boys the chance to dance and hold hands with girls. Jackie Parkes was the most beautiful girl in the class, also one of the most talented and clever. Emma Clarke, Amanda Yerbury, Sally Jenks and Jane Powell were all 'on the top table'. Tim Lewis, Nick Preece, David King, Stuart Willocks and David Hall were there too. These children were always on the top table, always the best, but screeching away during their violin lessons proved they were at least mortal.

And so it came to the great split. Our innocent merry little band was growing up. The results of the 11+ Exam were not particularly surprising: the grammar schools were in Shrewsbury. For these children Co-educational Wakeman School or Priory Girls' or Priory Boys' were their options. Mark Fisher, Nigel Emery and Duncan Platford were sent down to Church Stretton School, eschewing the Shrewsbury area Secondary Moderns in favour of the fresh air of the Stretton hills. The lumpen proletariat, about 80% of us went to Meole Brace Secondary Modern School under the Headship of Mr. Barnes.

In that summer of 1973 Mum and Dad took us to Butlin's Holiday Camp in Filey Yorkshire for a week. The Redcoats organised us, with competitions and entertainment everywhere we went. One competition was for young boys to be paraded in their swimming costumes. I stood next to a very athletic black boy. I had never seen a black person before. It was a mistake to stand next to him. In my swimming trunks and with my porky little body, despite my chubby red apple cheeks, I could not compete with such youthful vigour. He won, of course. Back home Mum had thought it a good fun idea to dress me up as a girl 'Miss Bayston Hill' or some such to enter me in a fancy dress parade. She had always wanted a girl it seemed. I unwittingly and innocently became the butt of many a joke wandering around the Memorial Hall gamely in a dress, a wig, lipstick and full make up unaware of how silly I looked but in a few weeks I would be up at big school - Meole Brace Secondary Modern.

Chapter 4:

Growing

We're so Secondary Modern

Meole Brace Secondary Modern School! Everyone knew the stories: heads pushed down toilets; whacked with Mr. Bailey's slipper; the terror of the fifth formers, whose *raison d'être* was to bully the new kids. We stood there at the first assembly, sitting amongst strangers while 'Beaky' Barnes laid down the law of what was and what wasn't acceptable. I cried in this assembly.

Meole Brace Modern School had 1,234 pupils at this time; a huge sports hall was under construction, several playing fields, and also, down the bank where we would sledge in the winter, rugby pitches. There were eight classes of first years, forty classes in the school, four storeys of classrooms. Some of the older kids were massive. The whole school crammed into morning assembly, to be lectured, preached and moralised to, and occasionally to be entertained. One assembly very early on in the term Mr. Cureton-Jones, Mr. Jones and Mr. Craig got up on stage. These teachers were musicians too! They played a banjo, a guitar and a violin. They played very fast Irish folk music, it was frenetic and vibrant and fun. I had never heard anything like it in my life. Suddenly I was immersed in a world of colour and sound. Sitting there in the main hall, tears ran down my face again, but this time they were tears of joy.

Notices that needed reiterating were relayed via the tannoy system directly into each classroom throughout the day, and when the bell rang you moved on to the next lesson. We were being trained to respond in the correct manner. It took a long time to find out where everywhere was. We had been big fishes in a little pond; now we were small fry trying to swim in this big sea. Split from your old friends, trying to adjust, you had to grow up quickly and grow a shell around yourself.

And then we had P.E. with Mr Barrie Sleath, who had recently moved up from London. This subject would become very important for me, which is testament to Barrie and his inspiring teaching.

When we had been at junior school we all changed in individual cubicles for swimming. Suddenly, in P.E. there we all were in a big changing room, all together, all getting naked to shower after our first lesson out on the sports field. Some of the boys were physically fully grown men with pubic hair and huge penises. I can't remember that I had seen anyone naked before. There was I, just eleven years old, suddenly in an instant massively aware of my body: my fat, my breasts, my flabby gut, and, most of all, my tiny genitalia: an innocent pre-pubescent Raphaelite cherub flung into Dante's inferno with 1970s apprentice pornstars! I could feel the ground opening up to swallow me. Surely there had been a mistake! This was not the body I should have been given. Where was my proper body like theirs? Why was I so different? I was also very aware of some nudging and whispering from other boys around me; their giggling and pointing were enough to confirm my suspicions.

I had always been a happy-go-lucky lad at junior school. Now suddenly I realised there was much that was not as it should be in my life. I had failed the 11+, therefore a 'thicko'; and now this. I felt terrible. Why hadn't I been prepared for this humiliation? What could I do? In an instant that outer shell that was being developed to keep me tough gained another layer, this would become the carapace to my sunny temperament. This outer show of 'happy resilience' found the character strengthened, at least on the outside, the side on show to the world. I tried to keep calm to cultivate an air of *insouciance*, of normality, I toughed it out. Above water the swan was serene; but under the water it was desperately flailing around. At least I knew now and understood my limitations. I became hyper-sensitive, acutely aware of my deficiencies and determined that no one would see through my defences.

I loved English. Mrs Hardman was our English teacher and she read the class an extract of my essay 'My Room', the first piece of homework we had been set. Maths seemed pretty straightforward too. Mr Holland said 'good' to me in front of the class when I was the only one who could express 24 out of 25 as a percentage. And Mr Holland didn't easily give praise. A regiment of teachers included lovely Miss Davies, History, and boring 'Skippy', Geography, Hairy Mary, Home Economics - we were a Secondary Modern School in the progressive 1970s after all. Mr Squire, cigarette in hand and 'Urco' Owen (thus named for his similarity to the character from 'Planet of the Apes') taught metalwork, Dean and Kaye taught woodwork, both subjects I was, at best, average at. Mr 'Benny' taught Biology: highly strung and small of stature, his pejorative epithet 'Benny' hinted at 'gayness' – much frowned upon then. Mr Janes and 'Gus' Ceha taught Physics. Gus lined us all up and asked someone a question, saying that if he got it wrong every boy would be slippered, and we all were. For equality's sake all the girls were slippered too! Mrs Buckley and Mr Ramsden taught Art. I loved Art, particularly making posters, drawing cartoons and big fat multi-coloured lettering in the bright and airy art room.

Settling in, I made new friends. Tim Corbett, a big, affable, intelligent lad interested in history and war games became a good friend. Geoff had blonde spiky hair, and soon a hip flask of whisky in his pocket at the tender age of thirteen. The girls, Tracey and Wendy were lookers. We were friendly, and they auditioned for Noel Edmonds' TV show 'Multi Coloured Swap Shop' as some kind of talent-free dance-song-fusion-duo! 'J' and 'M' were lesbians from day one. Little Mark S was dangled over the top of the science block stairwell by his ankles and bullying and fights were common; Big Andy K, although hard, was not nasty but was nevertheless given a bloody nose by 'Jamo', adjusting the pecking order as the 'hardest kid in the school'.

Attending Meole Brace School felt like a great big ongoing experiment into the effects of bells and whistles and tannoys on a large population of captive young teenagers. Pavlov would have had a field day. Kids came from out in the countryside, bussed in or dropped off by commuting parents, kids with names like Dagmar and Ackin and Brian. There were also a number of 'towny' kids, offspring of railway workers, postmen, prison officers. It was a bit of a zoo like being in a continuous video for Madness's 'Baggy Trousers', with everyone a Bash Street Kids Beano Comic caricature! Nearly all us 'country lads' had nicknames: 'Nelly' 'Flea' 'Rat' 'Mouse' 'Spanner', 'Beanhead', 'Jungle Boy' 'Buzz' 'Cogs' 'Fang'. I was still 'Scoob'. If you didn't have a nickname then an 'o' or a 'y' would simply be tacked on to the end of your name – 'Dave –o' or 'Jones – y'.

The school was now about 12 years old. 'Beaky' Barnes, the headmaster, was a stickler who always wore a tie – even when he came out with the school walking group of a weekend. However, Beaky could surprise us. He got a stunt motorcyclist to come to school one day, someone famous. We were in lessons when we saw this guy wheelying up and down the steps outside, warming up for a lunchtime show, with the underlying message something to do with road safety. Pretty cool really.

During the five years we were there, as a rule morning and afternoon breaks would see a massive gang of us playing football up in the top playground. Blazers would be put down as goalposts, and twenty - or so a-side would just go for it hell for leather. This was the unofficial proving ground to get you into the school football team. Being such a big school, there were five school football teams. I never made it anywhere near any school team, but I did enjoy letting off steam and I did get vaguely proficient at the game.

The older kids tended to congregate out on the field behind the new Sports Hall. At morning and afternoon breaks the building would look like it was on fire – up to 200 or more behind it. Smoking was tolerated by the school, policed by teachers and accepted, contained where it was. This tribe were into David Bowie, The Sweet, Bay City Rollers, David Essex and wore flares with patch pockets, tank-tops and platform soles, especially the boys.

Additionally to this constant hullabaloo was Bayston Hill Scouts. It was even more distilled craziness squeezed into two hours on a Friday night and a few camps spread throughout the year. Here we met with those who had gone other ways after the 'great divide', the 11+. One of the first big ambitious things we were involved in was a Scout Gang Show. The performances were in the Memorial Hall in January 1974. In one skit I was cast as a famous burglar, who, when the lights suddenly went up was caught red handed by TV presenter Eamon Andrews for a 'This is Your Life' presentation. Andy C was Eamon, and Spanner was my 'wife'! Other skits involved miming as a jazz band and singing songs in which we pretended to be down at 'The Old Bull and Bush', blackcurrant squash masquerading as beer in our tankards! I loved the smell of the grease paint and backstage it felt really special and atmospheric. It was a roaring success, and was a good fund raiser towards the new scout and guide headquarters that would be built on the Glebelands in the middle of New Bayston Hill later in the year.

Bayston Hill was growing rapidly; Poplar Crescent, Christchurch Drive and adjacent roads were being built. The area was now one massive building site and we would play there after school. There were no barriers to keep us out but our parents said it was dangerous. We climbed to the upper storeys inside unfinished houses with no floors, past roofing slates stacked up on the scaffolding, we just swung around them, disobedient monkeys.

Our older cousins Janet and Andrew from Liverpool produced children: Andy and Elaine had Kirsty Alex and Laura. Janet with husband Geoff had Kate and Sarah. Kate and Sarah were diagnosed with Muscular Dystrophy and subsequently became wheelchair dependent for life. Despite this Kate became a senior teacher and Sarah became involved in Paralympics and Sport to government advisory level.

Ever loyal Uncle Ron would visit every year from Denmark with Else and daughters Jean and Marie, our cousins. He bought me a 'Gray Nicholls' cricket bat for my birthday from Cockles Toy Shop in Milk Street.

The long summer holidays of the 1970s went on forever. We had many favourite places – the building sites became private houses and homes, so we headed out into the nearby fields. At Cavern Camp we swung on rope swings and we would cycle up on to Lyth Hill to play in the bracken and in the woods much as our parents and grandparents would have done. Imagination played a major part in these games: any stranger encountered along the way was a spy for the Russian KGB. The dog would run after the sheep and we had to run and shout after him. Occasionally we would get as far as Sharpstones Railway Bridge where we would be trainspotters – *Ingys, BoBo's, Deltics* – none of it really meant much to me, but occasionally I would become more interested when an old steam train travelled the line. Dirty kneed we crouched and caught frogs and lizards in jam jars, magnifying the sun's rays onto them with shards of broken glass.

Always we were home in time to watch telly before teatime: 'The Magic Roundabout' was psychedelic animation with a dog, a cow, Zebedee a jack-in-the-box, a guitar playing wigged out rabbit called Dylan and a girl called Florence. 'Captain Pugwash', funny cartoon pirate stories and the straight-down-the-line storytelling of 'Jackanory', read by a celebrity of the time. Then fish fingers, bangers n mash or beans egg and chips. Thanks Mum! After tea in our gang, off on our bikes again, not a care in the world.

Saturday morning television was 'Robinson Crusoe', 'The Lone Ranger', the French series 'White Horses', all in black and white – even for us with our posh colour telly until the shambolic 'Tiswas' brazenly gatecrashed onto our screens.

There was much adult discussion about Britain and the European Economic Union (EEU) or The Common Market at this time. We didn't totally understand it but teachers, and Gramps held that apart from anything else it kept the peace, and was very important.

At the end of my first year at Meole School, in July 1974 we went to see Mum's sister Ann and her family on Vancouver Island Canada. This was the first time for us, only Dad had ever flown. We met our Canadian cousins Cheryl, Dave and Pete and went 'up Island' in a rented camper van to Long Beach where we had a barbecue every night, singing round the campfire, religious songs learnt from Cheryl: 'The Wise Man Built his House upon the Rock'; and also a round song to include everyone sitting round the fire: 'The Purple Stew' – very hippy meets Jesus. We played on the beach and walked amongst the rock pools and flotsam and jetsam turned over by the Pacific Ocean: warm long relaxing days and gentle sunset nights. On the Tsawwassen Ferry we entertained passengers with our knitted frogs, a present from aged Aunt Hilda (who lived to be one hundred years old), arming them with felt penned cut out cardboard guitars to become 'Three Frog Night', a west coast schoolboy pastiche of the L.A. rock band 'Three Dog Night'. We travelled across Canada by train and plane, celebrating my 12th birthday on a flight between Winnipeg and Toronto, having been the first family to visit Dad's 'Uncle Bud' since Charlie Wellings, had waved him goodbye when he emigrated in 1919.

*****

Five thousand miles further south on that same Pacific coast the streets of Lima were teeming with life. Markets bustled; minibuses pushed through the crowded streets:

'Independencia!', 'La Molina!', 'Surco!', 'San Isidro!' shouted the bus boys monotonously and rhythmically to entice customers onto their speeding death trap unregulated vehicles. Pedlars pushed carts and trolleys to and from the hustle and bustle of the fruit markets; fishermen landed their catch and headed in to town; shopkeepers shouted their news, vying for attention above the din of "Naranjo! Naranjo! Naranjo!": the inane chant of the orange sellers. Pickpockets, ragamuffins, homeless beggars, policemen, prostitutes, street food vendors selling from clapped out re-jigged bicycles: a city on the move; a burgeoning city built on hard work, blood sweat and tears; and everywhere were lives of toil and strife and hardship and poverty and struggle. Corruption at the highest level filtered down, ingrained in the psyche: dishonesty, lying, stealing and cheating stitched into the fabric, a daily way of life – run, or be run over; elbow your way up; look out for yourself and screw your neighbour. In the heat and the humidity, in the pollution and the grime, in a one bedroom apartment with one toilet between twenty families Herlinda brought up her family as best she could. She and Jorge shared a room with eldest daughter Liliana and four other brothers and sisters all under eight years old.

*****

In September, back in school the teachers had noticed a difference in me. Had I picked up a new attitude, a more forceful challenging persona? I was put on report and a letter was sent home to my parents. Any more than three C's in a week, and I had to report to Mr Bailey, which would result in the slipper. Mum and Dad started to despair, wondering why I had changed. Was it their fault? Had they spoilt me? Why had I repaid their kindness like this? My name was heard on the tannoy more often, so now I was cultivating a reputation amongst my friends, sitting at their desks in different parts of the school. "What is he up to?" they would wonder and I didn't know either.

I was saved by my love of P E. The countryside was a source of inspiration to Barrie Sleath, who ran the Duke of Edinburgh Award scheme at the school. Kaye and Dean, woodwork teachers, operated a walking club, and the Scouts were always walking somewhere. Many of us travelled to school by bike. All this exercise was helping me grow and direct my energies. I enjoyed most things, and tried, but was hopeless at gym and could never climb a rope; it was the walking that I loved. I would pack my rucksack and get up earlier at weekends than in the week in order to fill my flask and get my lift, joining the gang to Mid Wales: the Arrans, the Berwyns, the Rhinogs; and also, nearer to home, the Long Mynd, of course.

About this time Auntie Puss asked us three boys what magazine we would like to read and got us a monthly subscription. Rob got Rupert Bear magazine, Chink got 'Tell Me Why'; but I asked for 'Climber and Rambler'. Now every month I avidly read articles on Scotland and news of expeditions to far-off places and also the adverts so as to be up-to-date with the equipment of the day. All very grown up, I wanted to join in the playground and Scout discussions about subjects including tents, sleeping bags, tubular aluminium framed rucksacks, Everest, Patagonia and Primus stoves. I also found some other magazines in Dad's bedside drawer around this time: Mayfair and Penthouse...

Chris Bonington's expedition to the South West Face of Everest - 'Everest The Hard Way' – captured the mainstream media attention in

1975. Everest had been climbed by what was now an established trade route over twenty years ago, and new challenges were sought. Bonington's attempt to climb, for the first time, one of the faces of Everest has been described as 'the apotheosis of the big, military-style expeditions.' Barclays Bank International sponsored the expedition to the tune of £100,000 (which in Shropshire terms was roughly the cost of 25 houses at the time). It was filmed for a documentary and it was a huge success. The key was the scaling of the rock band at about 8,200m/27,000ft by Nick Estcourt and Tut Braithwaite. Dougal Haston and Doug Scott reached the summit on 24 September and bivouacked at the South Summit.

Back on the ground in England Dad was in hospital. He was deemed strong enough and the surgical techniques had advanced enough that surgeons felt confident to fill in the hole in his heart he had lived with all his life. It was still a serious operation; nothing was a given. Mum cried in the Kwiksave supermarket hearing Roger Whittaker's 'The Last Farewell' and despite her lack of confidence she managed to drive herself to Birmingham to visit him. Dad came home to recover and soon he was back at work and with new vigour, he realised there were activities that he could now do that he had previously been too weak to do, hillwalking being one of them. He and Mum went for a recuperative holiday in Mallorca.

At school a circular went round about a skiing trip in Italy. It was £96 all inclusive. I wanted to go, and got myself a paper round to pay for it, earning £1.60 for a seven day week. The Sunday papers were so heavy that I had to split the round in half and make a double trip. If there was a walking group outing I would sometimes get up earlier to do the papers first; but Dad, with his new found energy, would do them when I was late, or Nige Emery would, for 20p. I put all my money towards the ski trip, with a little help from Mum and Dad I took £2.50 a week in to school, and Mr. Sleath kept a record of it.

School gave us our routines. One of these involved sneaking in to dinner. Dinner money was 60p a week – 12p a day – and a thousand of us would be fed in two main sittings, all regulated by dinner ladies who collected our little purple dinner tickets as we queued. Our plan – me, 'Jungle Boy' and 'Cogs' usually — would involve hiding behind the big curtain in the main hall and then jumping into the queue as they all filed in: simple and effective. I had to take it one step further, though, devilment got the better of me. Mrs Askey would count hundreds of tickets into piles on a table on the main stage for reconciling. As I went past I blew out my cheeks, and whoosh! Up went all the neat piles up into purple confetti swirling around her head! Outraged, she chased me out of the school building and all around the football pitches in a Benny Hill style chase – except she was an older lady wearing dinner lady stuff not a bikini! My name was called over the tannoy that afternoon to go to Mr Barnes' office and I knew why this time.

I had to reign in my behaviour or I wouldn't be going on the skiing trip. The resort was in the Dolomites in Italy. It was the first time on skis for all of us. After several crashes, throughout the week I developed my own style: very fast downhill, uncontrolled, with a huge snowplough stop at the bottom.

I came home to news that Chink had passed his 11+ and was accepted into the Priory Grammar School for Boys. He had done well without having to try too hard. Chink had been a popular member of his class, well liked, with girls in particular. He got himself a Saturday job with Ken the butcher, helping him out on the meat round. On the occasional Saturday if Chink wasn't there I would help Ken. He would stay at some houses much longer than others with strict instructions that we were not to get out of the van – Chink and I compared notes and decided it was 'for nooky'!

That summer we went to stay with Ron and Else in Denmark. They lived out in the flat countryside in an airy neat whitewashed house. Dad drove us up through Germany via Cologne where Mum's cousin Richard Astbury was a disc jockey for the British Forces Broadcasting Service. In his studio in Marienburg we watched him broadcasting his morning 'Housewives' Show' live. He gave us some 7"vinyl singles which we played to death on Ron's record player while we played table tennis or lounged in his garden. 'I Wanna Dance Wit' Choo (Doo Dat Dance)' by Disco Tex and The Sex-O -Lettes and 'YaYa' by John Lennon were our favourites as we lolled the summer away.

Around the mid 1970's our Scout Troop was like a big gang. There were so many of us that another troop had to be created: Eric Lock, named after the local World War 2 flying Ace, met on Friday nights, and the new troop – Darwin – met on a Wednesday. It was also only a short walk up on to Lyth Hill for Night Hikes and Wide Games – basically an excuse for the troop to split in to two and wage civil war on itself. The rules were fairly loose no serious violence was dished out: just the odd rugby tackle into a bramble thicket or someone pushed out of a tree. All friends again we walked back along Grove Lane together, singing lewd and inappropriate songs learnt from the senior patrol leader Andy:

'The first time I met her, I met her in pink, all in pink, all in pink, she made my finger stink – down a dark alley where nobody goes!'

Images of a rosy hued temptress skulking in some urban passageway proffering open illicit jars of pickled onions puzzled me but I knew it was naughty.

We would also join district camps and events. One of the biggest events of the calendar was the Annual Strettondale Hike in May. This was the junior version of the Long Mynd Hike. Scouts entered in pairs, carrying a two man hike tent, food, fuel and overnight supplies and navigated a course visiting checkpoints to have their times recorded. Starting and ending in Church Stretton, the first afternoon hike took us over Caradoc and The Lawley and on to the foothills of the Long Mynd to camp at Woolstaston. Next morning we went over the Mynd, down past the glider station before an ascent of Ragleth and back to Stretton to finish. This event became a rite of passage for Scouts.

The summer of 1976 was the hottest one on record. Chink and I were booked on to the Scout summer camp to Great Tower in the Lake District at the end of August but we were going away with Mum and Dad and Egger before it started. Dad towed the caravan to the Welsh coast and we stayed with Mum while he went off working, visiting Welsh doctors by day and camping with his family by night.

The coves and rock pools were enticing. Exploring one such secluded cove Chink and I stumbled across a group of older teenagers about 18 or 19 years old. One of them, a girl, was sunbathing topless. She left the group and came across to speak to us as we stood there transfixed. Coming closer she matter-of-factly started to tell us all about the creatures that lived in the pools. The water lapping our belly buttons, concealed our little stiffys! She might as well have been speaking Chinese, for all we cared; we were transfixed, in the presence of a virtually naked very pretty female in all her glory, sun-browned skin, long brown hair and hairy armpits, real boobs and nipples.

Back at home an 'Auntie' came up the stairs to the toilet as a parental party was in full flow downstairs. I had sneaked Dad's latest Mayfair out from his bedside table and became very involved in looking at the pin-ups when my very first ejaculation occurred, just a millisecond before she popped her head round the door to say 'Goodnight Stew'! 'Good night!' My reply felt disembodied as the warm oozing delight messed the sheets and my neural pathways fizzed with a new addictive vibrant pleasure.

Chink and I were 'the toast of the town' with the lads on the bus going to Great Tower Scout Camp, recounting the topless story over again to our mates.

The Leaders worked really hard to get everything organised for the camp – a huge stock of billy cans, ladles, patrol boxes, toilet tents, double gas burners, tables, benches, Tilley gas lights with moth attracting wicks, spare wicks, gas bottles, larders, muslin screens to keep the flies off, washing up bowls, sisal, rope, climbing equipment, canoes, bog roll: the list was endless.

I had my 14th birthday there, which could only mean one thing: The Bumps! For the uninitiated, the bumps involves being hoisted high into the air by a gang of scouts holding feet, ankles, arms, legs, boisterously throwing the bumpee up and down as many times as they have years, plus one for luck!

I was 'volunteered' as chief aerial runway tester, testing out a rope slide slung from a tree, starting about 8m high (25ft) and descending

40m (125ft) to the ground. Rudimentary safety gear "slowed" it abruptly. An expendable member of the Troop, that's what I was – but I loved it, bouncing up and down, swinging around grinning. A lot of knot tightening was done after I had tested it. A great week was had by all, kayaking on Lake Windermere to keep cool, climbing Helvellyn and having fun before school started again.

The heat had sapped us all that summer. We took shade down in Cavern Camp. Three of us together climbed onto the rope swing, breaking it and sending us crashing down into the 6 inch deep stream, adding to the collection of bruises, scars and scabs we constantly sported.

When the drought eventually broke huge spots of rain pock-marked the tarmac where we stood, slowly at first, then faster and faster, filling in the gaps and releasing the fresh smell that we hadn't realised was missing; but now it overwhelmed our senses as we danced and jigged in our soaking t-shirts and shorts as the steam rose and the humidity soared. We danced like fools into the night, joyous; and later, lying in a cool bed for once, I knew that another summer was coming to an end, and that we were growing.

Installed at the Priory, Chink found out that some of the teachers had been there since Dad's time in the 1940's, Doctor Proctor, the R.E. teacher, among them. There were some younger more forward thinking teachers too such as the great Al Hansen. Chink soon had a set of compadres including Paul Wynn (later to become a very good friend of mine), Nige Roberts, Jez Hopper and Bod. We had new neighbours in Broad Oak Crescent too: Kevin and Judy, a young couple in their mid-twenties. Kev was from Nantwich having grown up in a pub was gregarious and funny, and he had a big afro of hair. He had a huge collection of records – loads of late 60's early 1970's west coast guitar music: The Grateful Dead, Frank Zappa, Dan Hicks and His Hot Licks, Cheech and Chong, Wild Man Fischer as well as some Reggae music: Toots and The Maytals, Bob Marley and The Wailers – all amazing stuff to us youngsters listening to his LPs on his cool sound system. Their move to Broad Oak Crescent was a revelation to us. Prior to this we had just been moaned at by neighbours when our football went into their gardens.

Training began in readiness for our trip to the Ten Tors in Dartmoor the next year with the school walking club. 20 miles or more was a regular jaunt. However I had felt a lump and it was painful; I couldn't bend my left knee. Still, we completed the 35 mile course over the trackless expanses of Dartmoor in the heat. Nelly Richardson Tim Corbett and Darren Phillips completed the team with Dave Topping and me. A stipulation was that you had to camp so we walked 34 miles and camped, leaving a nice easy run in the next morning for breakfast.

The next month I was admitted to The Nuffield Hospital (thanks to Dad's company medical cover) to have the lump on the side of my knee removed. After a week I was on crutches and back at school trying to be cool, hamming it up, looking for sympathy from the girls as they listened to 275-285 AM Radio One on their little transistor radios on the big school field.

Scout camp that year was at Maentwrog near Harlech in North Wales. Chris Fryer our glorious leader was fully occupied running around dosing everyone up with kaolin and morphine as a bout of food poisoning ran rife through the camp. Phil Ritchie wrapped a bra up in the flag and it floated down gently as we all stood there in a circle in the field saluting and sniggering. Chris was not impressed. We had a mass ascent of Cnicht – 'The Matterhorn of Wales'. The Aerial Runway was tested and Andy C was able to get served in the pub up the road, sneaking us out the occasional shandy – blind eyes were turned, I'm sure. News came that Elvis Presley had died of a drug overdose whilst on the toilet.

Back at school it was impressed upon us how important our Certificate of Secondary Education Exams (CSE's) would be. Those at Grammar schools were doing the well-regarded General Certificate of Education (GCE), commonly known as 'O' levels. We were advised that a grade one CSE would equate to a GCE O level at about grade C. The highest grades were deemed beyond our standard. Things were starting to get more serious and adult. A girl had already left, pregnant at 15.

Two caretakers in grey coats carried a big machine into a small classroom and plugged it in. It was a video, and we were sat down to be shown a film about being a milkman, so this was what the future held! A good milkman was able to go to the golf driving range after work to bang golf balls off into the distance, or so the video led us to believe. I left this little event underwhelmed completely.

Egger was still at junior school. He was a good scholar and very intelligent. He had many interests – astronomy, guitar, cub scouts, The Beatles. His friends included Andy Deighton, youngest son in the first black family in the area. Maybe because we weren't very studious, Chink and I would annoy Egger, we would flick his ears and goad him and any annoyed reaction from him would be countered with us chanting 'Gettin itchy! Gettin itchy! Gettin itchy!' to his further annoyance.

Others at school were not as clueless as I was and had taken it upon them to research a career. How people could see a path set for them throughout life was a mystery to me; I was still reacting to the sights and sounds of a world I found full of wonder, skating away on the thin ice of a new day, every day. Flea was off to the Navy, following in his father's footsteps, as was Dave Topping. Nige 'Rat' studied on day release whilst working on the roads for the council. Some of the others were on the way to Shrewsbury Tech. Nelly Richardson set himself on a career in Outdoor Education. Puss worked at the Jobcentre and got me started with a job in Shrewsbury in the newsagent warehouse of Surridge Dawson and Company.

I spent the summer of 1978 there. The building, a tall slim red brick structure forms the junction of Castle Foregate and Smithfield Road. Built in the 1880s, with an ornate metal balustrade; it would not have looked out of place in Old Chicago or New York. Inside, using original cargo lifts we moved newsprint bundles and periodicals delivered by train from London, sorting them before onward dispatch to the small towns of Mid Wales and Herefordshire: Carno, Builth, Aber', Newtown, Llan'dod, Kington.

'Jolly' Rogers had been there a year. Acerbic and sarcastic, Jol's dry wit and observations on life were far too funny for one so young. A fellow Bunkenite (as those from Bayston Hill are known), Jol loved playing cricket and football. Down in the basement he and I tied up parcels of magazines, taking breaks whenever a new copy of Hustler or Mayfair was found to be in the shipment.

Although I was working full time at Surridge Dawson, I was not yet 16 years old. I was still in the Scouts. The summer camp was up at Tywyn. The highlight that year for me was a birthday visit from Kim and Fiona, both 14 years old. Fiona's parents had a caravan in Aberdovey. They managed to sneak into our patrol tent while it was empty but we didn't even manage to have a quick snog, all teenage awkward angst and in the eye of the storm of that bastion of a male preserve that was a 1970's scout camp! They were fairly soon ejected by the scout leader known as 'Vice Head' named so on account of the shape of his cranium.

When we got home from camp Mum and Dad had arranged a 'sausage and cider party' for me. A few mates, all lads, were invited. Mum had found an old 'gazunder' pot – a porcelain piss pot from a bygone age. She had filled it with cider and floated a load of cooked sausages in it for us to eat! It looked disgusting, we all laughed as we fished them out with forks, while tapping our feet to the two pieces of vinyl we could lay our hands on: Mum's 'Voulez Vous' by Abba and 'Songs from the Wood' by Jethro Tull, loaned by Tim Corbett. This fairly subdued gathering, in the playschool room marked a rite of passage, those in attendance were on their way to work or study elsewhere. Mum closed the playschool the following year, and the garage became my bedroom. I painted it bright orange.

With money saved I cycled up to Harlescott on the outskirts of town to spend £13 on a 'Blacks' down sleeping bag, quite an outlay at the time, but what I wanted for what I planned to do. The exam results came out, out of eight subjects I had managed to gain passes in just three - Maths, English Language and History. I had been expected to do better. All of my friends had done better, even Rat with his dyslexia.

Surridge Dawson finished me, so as a late applicant I was accepted in to the Priory Boys' Sixth Form in Shrewsbury, the only one there from Meole Brace School. Everyone else had either gone to the Wakeman, the Technical College or had an apprenticeship.

The contrast was huge. Here was a single sex Grammar School set on the banks of the Severn, populated mainly by local middle class boys. Apart from the dinner ladies there was only one woman in the whole place – the school secretary, Mrs King. Everything was in shades of grey, including the uniforms. There was an undertone of rebellion in the common room of the sixth form emanating from the bright young things, occasionally identified wearing their ties round their heads and punk safety pins in lapels. They were cheek by jowl with the hidebound establishment conformists already on their way to careers in industry or the military.

The school Combined Cadet Force lured me in for approximately two weeks before finding out that, in the likely event of a nuclear war, our task would be to keep Shrewsbury's sewers open. That was the only extra -curricular activity on offer. Some of the teachers were excellent, however: really on the boys' level – but I found it really difficult to break into the friendship groups that existed. My charm and charisma suffered a bruising during this year, and after Meole Brace I felt lost, out of my depth and unhappy.

I did have some friends from Scouts who I saw occasionally. Geoff Beaman was one, a keen climber. Tim Lewis or Chris Berkeley usually had a smile, as did Chris' brother Graham, who walked everywhere with a violin case in his hand.

Things were not too good at home either. Mum and Dad had always argued, and things seemed worse now. Mum had just been diagnosed with breast cancer and seemed to confront it with an anger directed at the world in general. She must have felt a strong sense of injustice, since her mother had died from the same disease. Here she was, one of three girls from a very feminine background, now with three sons, who were strong-willed, a handful, to say the least. One morning during a furious row I threw a cup of tea across the kitchen straight into Mum's face. I slammed the door and skulked off to sixth form. That day I found myself further alienated, as Chink told his friends what had happened and they shunned me. Life remained pretty miserable from then on. Mum had not been hurt physically; but I knew I had to do some thinking, and some apologising.

A couple of trips away and completing the 50 mile Long Mynd Hike at the age of 16 were the only things to brighten up a fairly grim time. February 1979 was one of the coldest winters of the 20th century: the A5 was barely passable, and Lake Ogwen in Snowdonia was completely frozen. Scout friend Snowy Taylor and I camped at Bochlywyd, under Tryfan Mountain, a spot I had camped at several times in summer conditions but this time was on the lake, not by it. I was glad of my decent £13 Blacks sleeping bag.

Another Snowdonia trip, driving up in a mate's mini we climbed in Llanberis Pass, dark rock, cold and damp, steep enclosed gullies, and the first time for me climbing a multi pitched route: 'Nea', graded 'Severe' standard.

What I was discovering was that the lads at the Priory hadn't just been taught about what was what. They seemed more able to problem solve and had ways of developing ideas to advance, more than the standard Meole Brace pupil may have done.

Towards the end of my year here a General Election was called for 3rd May. Margaret Thatcher's Conservative Party was up against the Labour Party of James Callaghan. Thatcher had tabled a motion of no confidence in the Labour government following the Winter of Discontent with high inflation and unemployment. Refuse lay in huge piles in the streets and rats crawled everywhere. The vote was just carried 311 – 310.

The Priory had a mock election: a clean-cut 'suit' stood as the Conservative candidate; a Liberal candidate was a lad in a grey jumper whose election posters were defaced with the words 'vote goat'; and the bright young things were all squabbles and pastiches of Che Guevara and Neo Communist youthful rhetoric and not much else. I'm not sure whether there was even an official Labour candidate. In the real world Labour and the left had walked on, blindly unaware that the mood of the nation had changed. The power of the unions, taxation and restrictive working practices had hobbled industry, and Thatcher set herself up as a vanquishing conquistador seeking to right wrongs and deregulate for small businesses. A sea change in politics was happening, I was growing and understanding a little more of how the world worked.

Margaret Thatcher took office on the 4th May 1979 with these words from St Francis of Assisi:

'Where there is discord, may we bring harmony, where there is error, may we bring truth, where there is doubt, may we bring faith, and where there is despair, may we bring hope.'

My year at Priory had not been very successful. I had managed to turn my CSE grade 1 Maths into an O Level and to get a B in Art.

Mum was admitted to hospital to have a mastectomy to remove the cancer from her left breast. Puss and Dad were able to impress upon us how serious things were. Dad booked us all a holiday to Canada to see Mum's sister Ann and her family, as he and Mum had been very ill since our visit in 1974.

Six weeks on Vancouver Island is an amazing way to spend a summer. The two families went 'up island' to camp at The Buttle Lake Campground in Strathcona Provincial Park. We wanted to enjoy the campfires and the Canadian fresh air again. I led Dad on an overnight hike up to a place called Auger Point, the first time he had camped in the wild. It seemed as though he wanted to make up for lost time and he was happy that I was starting work when we returned home.

I asked Dad if I could attend a week long course at the Strathcona Park Lodge Outdoor Education Centre. He agreed, on the proviso that I paid him back. The family returned to Victoria, leaving me to get involved with the Canadian Wilderness for a week. I was having the time of my life climbing and mountaineering and meeting Carla and Toyah, lovely girls of my age from Vancouver. We climbed Mount Albert Edward (2093m) and rock climbed and abseiled and canoed. The trousers were starting to fit at last, I had found my passion but the adventure was over, on our return home I was to start a new job. This was a 'proper' job with terms and conditions – I had passed the test and interview earlier in the summer for Clerical Assistant working for Post Office Telecommunications - and as such, I would be released back into captivity.

Chapter 5

Softly Trapped in a Social Experiment

Fuelled with Frivolity and Folk

Three days after my 17th birthday I started work for Post Office Telecommunications at Telephone House on Smithfield Road in Shrewsbury. The start had been delayed due to industrial action. I joined the Stores Clerical Group, housed on the 8th floor, the top floor of the highest building in Shrewsbury. I had my own desk and phone – Shrewsbury 53285 – and a view above the multi storey car park out to Caradoc, the Stretton hills and the Long Mynd. Within the first day or so, this being the 1970's, the new intake had a meeting with Charlie Brown, the secretary of the Union. Charlie emphasised the importance of a union, how it looked after its members and how it stood up for our rights, arbitrated in disputes and represented us for things like terms and conditions and pay. He also said that the vast majority of employees were members in Shrewsbury. I liked Charlie, understood what he said, and signed up straight away.

My first pay packet, cash in a little brown envelope, was over £30 – a very handsome sum, and then every Friday (after working a 'week in hand'). When I told Dad how much I got, as I handed over my 'keep' to Mum, he asked me not to mention it to Gramps, aware of course of the struggles he had had in his life.

The job was tedious. We all sat at desks filing bits of paper, joining like with like, sending out memos, filing, more filing, asking for budgetary job numbers from the budget group next door, filing, sending '*billets doux*' out to the main stores at Hereford, Shrewsbury Ditherington and Machynlleth as we tried to keep track of the stores needed to build and maintain the analogue telephone system for Shropshire and Mid Wales.

Dull. Through the window the hills taunted me. On our floor there was one calculator/abacus type machine. There was plenty of paper that needed shuffling around, though, all light blue and pink and white and yellow but I could do this quickly if I put my mind to it. A large percentage of the workforce was older women and men, some who had been working for the Civil Service or the Post Office for 40 years or more. There were also a fair number of ex-servicemen. The décor was various shades of brown and grey. Many people smoked at their desks and the occasional fire in a waste paper basket was not unheard of.

The works canteen was next door. Under 18s had a daily allowance of 15p – for that I could get a bowl of soup and a bowl of rice pudding every day for free. The major attraction of the job for me however was 'flexitime', an average 37 hours per week had to be done. I soon worked out that it was sometimes possible to do a minimum of 3 hours a day without having to 'flex off' – technically to be at work without having to ask the supervisor for time off: you could come and go as you pleased within these parameters. What I hadn't realised was that working too fast (or efficiently) would be detrimental. Time and motion studies had decreed how long tasks should take; there was no room for maverick misfits such as me. The unintended consequences of my actions were that I then owed the company time, time that burns for a young buck wanting to set the world on fire.

A great revelation though was the tea trolley. Exactly on the stroke of 09:30 the door would open and in would come Ethel or Sandra or Mary with tea, coffee, bacon or sausage rolls. After some testing of the system, I found out I could wake up at 09:00, jump on my bike, cycle like fury, three miles mostly downhill, dump it in the bike shed under the car park, run to the lift, and arrive, very sweaty, at exactly 09:30 just as the tea trolley arrived, where, thanks to more subsidies, these greasy delights were procured for a few pence, breakfast eaten at the desk as the sweat dried on my back. A bit of filing followed, or if I was really bored, I would go to another department and chat to someone in a similar role, lovely Lisa in Traffic department on the fifth floor, if I was feeling brave. Quite often I would go for lunch at 11:30 having done less than two hours' work. I would often have the minimum lunch break to save the flexi, but I would go before our ageing spinster supervisor, arriving back as she left for her break, therefore allowing me a second 'break' to read the New Musical Express or the Daily Mirror! Most people started early and left early; the office would be fairly quiet after about 4pm. This was the time I should have had to stay late to put the time in, but I would occasionally just sign out.

It really was that easy. This huge bureaucratic machine lumbering into the 1980's was a dinosaur in desperate need of technological advances and staff motivation. Many people sat unquestioningly at their desks; happy to accept their pay, but inevitably I ended up owing the company time. There was little motivation and promotion was pretty stagnant due to 'dead man's shoes'. It was another big social experiment. Sitting at my desk, it felt like being back at school. Every lesson was the same, though, as we went from one payday to the next. Had we been conditioned at school for this? How much work was actually being done, by whom and for whom? Massive overstaffing seemed like a hangover from the power of the unions, obviously still in full force at Post Office Telecommunications they had not been broken by Margaret Thatcher. But how had I become ensnared in this gentle trap?

The social side of office life was a major attraction to many, I'm sure. There were always collections being arranged for birthdays, marriages or newly arrived babies. There was a thriving Tele-Post Club that had not one but two social clubs. On Friday we would all go to the pub with our wage packets, returning to do the bare minimum before flexing off for the weekend: *P.O.E.T.S. day* – piss off early, tomorrow's Saturday.

Friday night was Raven's Night in Bayston Hill. I had now graduated into the Ranger Guide/Venture Scout Unit – RaVen Unit for ages 16 to 20. Most of us lads were in full employment now. This group was my social group; I didn't particularly mix with work colleagues outside of work. To be considered for promotion at work, five O Levels or equivalents were needed. Having four, I enrolled at evening classes, taking Geography and passed, mainly because I enjoyed it, it inspired me too.

One day at work I was phoned by Mrs King from the Priory School. 'Stewart, your brother Charles has been taken to hospital as he has been hit in the leg by a javelin whilst in a PE lesson!' Chink and one of his mates had been playing 'split the kipper', but with javelins! Safety regulations and risk assessments? There was a certain amount of onus placed upon school children to 'behave', but this still left room for incidents to occur when they were not being supervised.

*****

Jorge Escudero was working hard in Lima. He had started a business selling electrical goods – fridges, freezers and televisions were the new cache of an emerging Peru. Everything was imported from Japan and China. These appliances were changing people's lives, and he was able to offer repayment terms. Liliana was a bright child, hard-working and very pretty. She was always top of her class and her dream was to be a doctor. She wasn't quite 12 years old when her father Jorge broke the news to her. "Forget about that," he told her abruptly, "you are coming to work, to manage the shop." So after school she had to get on a bus and travel across Lima, change buses, travel and then walk to the shop. She learnt how to sell, to invoice, to keep the books, to cash up, lock up; keep things safe in one of the world's most dangerous cities. Her dream had been usurped by her reality. She had been a 'Brigadier'- similar to a prefect. She ran a tuck shop and gave the money to a teacher for her 'prom' but when the time came, teacher and money had gone and she was the only one of her friends who could not attend. The family had to leave their accommodation suddenly and find a room at short notice when the rent was overdue. Very difficult times.

*****

My unfulfilling work life in Shrewsbury was compensated for by having money and a lot of fun outside of work.

The Two Tone Ska revolution in pop music was taking the country by storm. This upbeat music originating from 1960's Jamaica now found new roots in Coventry where black and white youth sang in harmony amidst a backdrop of real racial tension and inner city inequality. The Specials, The Selecter and Dexy's Midnight Runners, three bands topping the charts, all riding high on the wave of this new idealism, played Shrewsbury Music Hall. Tickets were available for the princely sum of £2.50. I went with Karen, didn't even get a kiss but didn't care. It was my first gig; I loved the mosh pit, the atmosphere, the sweat, the camaraderie and the anarchy of it all.

For a young and restless lad there had to be more to life than a desk job with good terms and conditions. I bought a motorbike, a second hand Yamaha DT 175, an off road machine. At weekends mates Stu, Bri, and a small gang of us would ride off to explore the local lanes and bridleways, and further afield to Mid Wales: Strata Florida and The Monks' Trod or over The Berwyns via the 'Wayfarer' route.

Motorcycling was very dangerous at this time, just before tighter regulations were brought in. A couple of mates died in motorcycle accidents, one was decapitated. The motorbike test was very simple: ride round and round the block until the assessor said: "Next time I will step out into the road, and I want you to stop without locking the brakes." This I did, and was now able, at 17 years of age, to jump on any motorbike of any power.

Post Office Telecommunications was being streamlined, ready for privatisation, and as a part of that we were all dangled the carrot of having our pay paid directly into our bank accounts. If we agreed to this we would receive a handsome payment of £77. As a by-product of this, credit from the banks became easier to obtain in the form of loans and credit cards. The downside was, consumerism could reel in the unwary like me and so I became beholden to the company. The company was now known as British Telecom (BT).

I was a weekend warrior now, tied in to the daily grind because the money tap dripped into my bank account weekly. Leaving was not an option as BT was the best employer in the area, and I had not been trained for anything else nor had the wherewithal to leave. To leave would be financial suicide: I could have possibly picked up work as a labourer on less than half what BT paid, and for a considerably larger amount of effort and inconvenience. I realised that I would have to 'play the game' and went for promotion boards, since things were slowly starting to change as modernisation and new working practices were being brought in.

For a while now Nick Preece, Rat Lawson, Nige Emery and I and whoever else we could co-opt had taken to drinking over in Hook a Gate, the neighbouring village separated by the Rea Brook. We went there mainly because our parents didn't, and, being under age, it was easier to get a drink down at the Royal Oak or The Swan. Incredibly, you could ride a superbike but not be able to buy a drink! Rat and I even joined The Swan darts team where we would go on a Friday night and pitch up our darts with an old bloke who would throw sharpened 6 inch nails. On the way back up the lane we could sometimes roll into a house party somewhere consisting of fellow scruffy teenagers lounging around in dimly lit rooms nursing a can of cider and pretending to be 'out of it' or 'weird and interesting'. Finding a young lady for a snog was a very rare bonus!

At work I hadn't been in Stores Clerical Group for long before I was moved on to the Motor Transport department, a similar type of work. I also did a stint as a 'relief' worker. This was a great job: you went out to places such as Hereford and Machynlleth and Aberystwyth to be trained in other jobs so as to be able to cover when their staff went on leave. We 'reliefers' were on 'the lodge', claiming a nightly allowance to cover bed and board plus a mileage allowance for the motorbike. A lot of money could be made, the nightly allowance eventually reaching £50. I soon had enough money to go and visit Carla in Vancouver, with whom I had kept in contact since I met her at Strathcona Lodge in 1979.

Being far down the pecking order, I had to take my annual leave in the month of January. I had saved up for a year and bought a return ticket to Vancouver. Christmas, two weeks before I was due to depart, was the season of office parties. Ours was at The Riverboat, a bar in the 1960's concrete shopping mall next to Telephone House. That afternoon it was packed out with office workers drinking far too much, obviously myself included. I went outside to get some fresh air. It was dark; I leant against the wall, suddenly feeling an uncontrollable need to vomit. At exactly the same time a policeman passing on his beat noticed my unsteadiness and general drunkenness. As he approached I threw up, just as he put his hand out towards me. The next thing I remember was the cold steely bite of handcuffs and a police radio calling for assistance. Two officers bundled me into a little mini panda car and drove me to Monkmoor Police Station, where I was charged with being 'drunk and incapable' and put in the cells for the night. Released in the early hours of Christmas Day, I was bailed to appear at Shrewsbury Magistrates Court in March. On the long walk home, at least I had time to sober up and try to invent a story for Mum and Dad as to where I had been.

I landed in Canada in early January, still technically 'on bail'. I stayed a couple of days but there was little spark between Carla and me so I took the ferry to Vancouver Island and spent a few days with Auntie Ann and Alan and family before taking a long train ride from Vancouver south to San Francisco.

It was a pretty lonely experience on the train, but seeing the devastation from the volcanic eruption of Mount St Helens in Washington State that had erupted the previous May kept me in awe. For mile after mile everything was still coated in ash – eight months after the devastation. My destination was California: simply inspired from hearing Scott MacKenzie's 'San Francisco' on the radio. I went to Alcatraz, and took a tour round Chinatown; but what I had not understood was that San Francisco was the gay capital of the USA. Understandably I was still very naïve, but now a fledgling independent traveller.

John, a BT Engineer of some renown, was chairman of Shrewsbury Magistrates: 'Hanging Judge John', as he was not affectionately known. He did not accept my plea of 'Not Guilty' when I was up before him in Court after returning from Canada. I represented myself, and the basis of my argument was 'drunk and incapable... of what exactly...?' When asked, as an 18-year-old, if I habitually drank copious amounts of alcohol at lunchtime, I replied, "Yesh,"! I would have been fined £10 for a guilty plea. I was fined £16. I asked for time to pay – I had spent everything on the holiday, and was in the process of buying another motorbike which realistically was beyond my means. The offence of 'drunk and incapable' was later removed from the statute books, but remained on my police record for years.

The Duke of Edinburgh Award was available at BT. Younger staff from Hereford, Shrewsbury and Newtown attended on weekends to navigate around the Mid Welsh hills, The Brecon Beacons, The Lake District and The Peak District. The young ladies that came usually made a beeline for the (even better paid) engineers. I did my Gold Expedition at Easter down in Exmoor. It snowed and drifted up to 3 feet high in places. We found refuge in a pub that served good cider and we passed the expedition.

The summer of 1981 was a long hot one. Mum and Dad went away in the caravan with Rob, leaving me and Chink in the house alone. We didn't always get along. One particular fight started with Chink making himself a potnoodle sandwich. Just as he put the bread lid on it I came in and, in my compulsive idiotic way, slammed my fist on to it, sending noodles squirting out of the side and rendering the thing an inedible mess. Chink stormed off quickly returning with a bike chain with which he lashed out at me.

As the house was parent-free it needed livening up with a party. All the Ravens were invited, and pretty much anyone else they chose to bring, plus anyone from the pub. What could go wrong? Fiona opened the door to a stranger but found him the worse for wear and confrontational. None of us knew him so we tried to turn him away but he grabbed a screwdriver from the windowsill and threatened us. The police were called but would not arrest him until he had left the property. During this melee the power supply to the freezer was inadvertently knocked off. As an unobservant teenager I sensed nothing. Two weeks later when Mum and Dad returned Dad opened the freezer to find all the contents putrefied. Tempers were lost.

We had a lot of parties wherever we could. Nick always had his guitar, we would sing some Simon and Garfunkel or 'The House of the Rising Sun' before the night drew on and we started dancing to the record player; Nine

Below Zero, The Rezillos, X Ray Spex, The Rolling Stones, Bob Marley, Eric Clapton – an eclectic mix. By the early hours, often mischievous, a favourite trick was 'gate nicking'. Lifting any neighbourhood gate that could be coaxed off its hinges we would either swap it with a neighbour's gate or walk it down to the parade of shops and stack it with some others. These were pretty mild suburban pranks; there was no rioting in Bayston Hill.

School roof sitting was another popular prank: night climbing up on to the roofs of either of the two junior schools in the village. Nick and Tim took this a stage further when they climbed on to the roof of the Wakeman School with a couple of friends, Geoff and Joe, and fixed a plastic crow to the roof before abseiling their getaway.

The Ravens did everything together. 1981's annual Easter trip to Glencoe in Scotland was one such event. The sun shone, the hills had a great covering of snow and there were many cornices. Tim and I took great delight in jumping off and plummeting down the corrie headwalls before ice axe arresting safely. We all went to Aberdovey to watch the wedding of Charles and Diana on the telly in Fiona's Mum's caravan. We camped for a week at the Gower in the August. Geoff and I climbed at Three Cliffs Bay. Lounging around at the top of the cliffs were some stoned nudists, completely wasted and unable to get down. Geoff and I rigged up a lower off for them. These were the halcyon days of happy hedonism for us too.

Different factions of us would go across to Aberystwyth on a weekend – to crash out on the floors of our student friends; Roger, Tim and Kim were part of a big house share in Bridge Street. There always seemed to be a party on somewhere at which we were made welcome. Tim did bat and bird surveys as a volunteer and was also a member of the Caving Club and the X Aba Mountaineering Club – the latter along with his friends Tim 'Blutes' Pakenham and Tim 'Spadge' Sparrow.

Back home Stu, Gary, Bri, Nick and I banded together to buy a Citroen D Special between us: £62.50 each. This ancient French vehicle took us down into Switzerland to rendezvous with Melanie, Nick's sister, who had been working as an au pair. The old car never missed a beat, but was finally retired to a farmer's field somewhere near Eaton Mascot.

We didn't really realise the very fortunate position we were in. Elsewhere in the country things were very different. Unemployment, racial tension and inequality in deprived inner cities were rife in Thatcher's Britain. The Government instituted new powers for the police under what became known as 'the Sus Law', where anyone could be arrested purely on suspicion of having broken the law. The major flashpoints were inner city areas with high black or Asian populations. Very few job opportunities, housing issues and a young disenfranchised multicultural community with no prospects but plenty of energy, made the ensuing riots almost inevitable. Major riots took place in Brixton, London; Handsworth, Birmingham; Toxteth, Liverpool; and Moss Side, Manchester. Police and civilians, were injured, much property was damaged and cars and buildings were burnt and looted.

In the aftermath of the riots the Government commissioned the Scarman Report. Lord Scarman reported the condition of the situation and its effects on the lives of black and Asian youths and made recommendations, including positive discrimination and future community outreach programmes. The University of Strathclyde was preeminent in setting up Community based degree courses to look at pragmatic ways of helping to solve these problems, something that I did not know at the time but that I would later become very involved with.

*****

Before the year was out the police were after me again. In October I was riding my motorbike along the parade of shops at Bayston Hill when the car in front of me signalled right and then turned left. I went over the handlebars, over the bonnet and surprisingly landed in the road uninjured. Fortunately there were witnesses as there was a fair bit of damage to the bike. A few weeks later I was summoned to court for the offence of dangerous driving. My plea was Not Guilty, this time I felt unduly wronged. A couple of witnesses gave statements and I had legal aid. Magistrates overturned the case of *West Mercia Constabulary v Wellings* but I received no apology or any funds towards the cost of repairing the bike. I failed my work promotion too.

Approaching Christmas, friends returned from various places and there was a district event hosted by Shawbury Venture Scouts. This was a cross-dressing party, so all us lads dressed up as women, including makeup, and boarded a bus. The problem was that it was the coldest night on record, -27C. The hairs in your nostrils froze and other body parts under flimsy dresses shrunk. Prior to this I had been pleased to note that I was catching up with my late entry into puberty and confidence with the ladies had been slowly building.

On Christmas Eve in Bayston Hill we had all gathered in The Compasses Inn – our spiritual home, and the drink and the banter were flowing. The last I remember about it was having 'crossed swords' with Nick outside in the snow – basically peeing over each other, he was my closest friend, after all! I stumbled home; perhaps the disgrace from the previous year had registered somewhere. The next day Nick's Mum Judy was on the phone. My initial thought was 'Oh shit! She's annoyed at all the piss on his trousers…'

"Nick's in hospital," she told me. 'He was hit by the lad from the chip shop driving his Porsche back last night!'

Nick had been thrown into the air by the collision at the end of our road. His mangled leg would take years to heal. He was in and out of the orthopaedic hospital in Oswestry for long periods of time.

*****

An idea to go to the Isle of Skye was hatched. Nige 'Rat' and I went with Bri Turner who decided to stick to low level walks but Rat and I wanted to venture into the Cuillin hills. It was October, after the Longmynd Hike, and the weather was letting us know why Skye is called 'The Misty Isle'. Our first night was at Broadford Youth Hostel. We went to the pub and chatted the barmaids up. Rat referred to them as 'The Horse's Collar' and 'The Mouse's Ear'! We stumbled and rolled back down the road in a deluge, stair rods smacking the tarmac and streams running down the road. Back at the hostel, we had ignored the 11 pm curfew and, locked out, went round the back to break into the drying room. We broke a window and climbed in.

Needless to say, the next morning the warden was not happy. He presented us with a bill for £5 having measured up the glass which he had had to fetch from Elgol. We paid him this, doubling our accommodation costs in an instant before driving round to Glen Brittle to camp and sober up. Bri went for his coastal walk and Rat and I, armed with a rope and a map, managed to scramble ourselves to the top of Sgurr Alasdair, the highest point on the island in a good weather window, between bouts of rain. There was no one else around; it was magical, a peak won with a fight up and a run down the screes of 'The Great Stone Shoot'.

It was at The Shrewsbury Folk Club (before it moved to the Seven Stars from the Castle Inn) that I first met Chris Morgan. Chris was a couple of years older than me and also worked within the masses at BT, but on another floor to me. We both ended up working on 'Relief' later on. Chris had a brilliant unaccompanied voice, very deep, and he sang songs of old England, having learnt a lot about singing from his sister Isobel. Chris was a great character, he had an acerbic wit, an affinity for Northern Soul music, swimming, cycling and beer.

At the Folk Club, many of the attendant reprobates were outdoor types and walkers to boot. Some of these characters I had seen on Long Mynd Hikes. Dave Hoy was one. Dave was in his late thirties and a veteran of Halley Base British Antarctic Survey. I first saw him, or rather his T shirt, screaming at me to 'Have a Shitty Day!' as he galloped down the Lawley, already gaining ground.

Ken Hughes was the Master of Ceremonies at the Folk Club, and his record in the Hike too at this time was exceptional although Ken had primarily been a long distance cyclist. He would cycle 200 miles to Sidmouth Folk Festival in one go, sleeping briefly in a hedge, spend the week singing in the pub, cycle up to Whitby and return via Fylde. All powered by copious consumption of real ale.

The Shrewsbury Folk Music Club was vibrant around this time. Our friend Stu Altman was a musician of some note, played saxophone, bagpipes and penny whistle and would also sing like a nightingale. As his friends, we went down to listen and also to be a part of this event that had turned into 'The Human Jukebox' on a regular Sunday night. The venue was The Castle pub in Coleham, an old building set back slightly from the road. There was an upstairs room where the older more serious folkies would gather on a Tuesday for the Folk Club. But on Sundays it soon became our end of week destination. Usually we would go in after a decent hill walk up into Snowdonia and come to listen and drink and join in with the many singalong songs that were becoming more familiar with every passing week. The main man and Master of Ceremonies was Ken Hughes, an impish looking character in his early 50's with a grey beard and mischievous eyes: he was usually attired in a collarless shirt with rolled up sleeves, a wooden cross of St Andrew round his neck, below a red knotted 'kerchief; a waistcoat and green corduroy trousers held up with a leather belt whereon often, when not in use, would hang a pewter tankard. On his feet were leather open-toed sandals displaying his battered toenails. Topping off this old fashioned but functional garb would be a trilby hat adorned with a badge or a feather from a hedgerow. Ken looked like a character from another era and he sang lots of good old songs with a rousing chorus: some of them stories in verses that tried to make sense of the human condition like 'Sammy's Bar'; or sometimes a more ribald offering like 'Jolly Jolly Grog', or the great crowd pleaser, 'The Rattlin' Bog'.

Ken would ask around the room, a singaround, so singers could ready themselves, knowing when it would be their turn. When there was a beer break the 'band' would play some tunes – Taff Brissenden, cloth cap on his head blinking mole-like with his nose perched on a large red and white piano accordion while its bellows gently breathing in and out as his fingers deftly moved across the phalanx of black and white keys on both sides, jovially accompanied by Mal Brown, a brash Scouser, on banjo, Stu on penny whistle, Squeaky Nick on fiddle and maybe one or two guitarists or fiddle players that might have drifted in from somewhere or other, passing through. The bar would be full of all sorts of people – navvies, lecturers, students, a resident team of archaeologists, footballers still there long after their Sunday League match had finished, many beer lovers, a few drug aficionados with the odd dog on a string lurking under the seats sniffing out scraps of cheese sandwiches or a stray pork scratching wafted down from dog heaven, a ladies' darts team, possibly an Irish traveller or two, hippies who had come down from the hills of Mid Wales, the odd suburban professional looking for what was lost to them between Monday and Friday, office workers, accountants.

Many people would be smoking, and the drink would flow, as not everyone would wait for the singer to finish before squeezing up to the bar, cheek by jowl. Ken would shout: 'Lovely Order! Singer on the oche!' and generally there was good respect for those who were regaling us with their songs and giving of their souls to impart the glorious wisdom and beauty of their craft. Mick O'Keefe was the landlord: a no-nonsense burly bloke who kept order but also wanted to enjoy a good time himself; a good fair fellow, really his job was not unlike that of a headmaster, to Ken's ringmaster.

With such a disparate crowd there could have been trouble; but the heady mix of music, tobacco (and occasional whiff of ganja) smoke, banter, jokes and frivolity made for a great happy get-together – live and let live! The singers performed, in the main, unaccompanied. Dennis Hall was a very gentle character with a voice that betrayed no stress or strain: 'On an evening in summer – late on in July'; or a song about a travelling salesman with a roving eye; or 'Otago'. Dennis could also duet with George Soames, a Cockney, long resident in Shrewsbury, who had worked in the Granada Music Hall for years, and had been there when The Beatles played in 1963. Tears would roll down their faces at some hilarious episode they put into song.

'Tell' was a singer songwriter from Porthmadog who had drifted east years ago and stayed. His guitar strings were held in place by golf tees that he'd picked up when stumbling around Meole Brace Municipal Golf Course, maybe looking for magic mushrooms or on his way to continue singing at someone's house somewhere. Tell had a superb way of singing and had a big following, particularly among the drinking classes – Jim Croce's 'Time in a Bottle' was his signature song, but he would sing us his own compositions too – 'Pethgwyll' -basically 'Wild Thing', but in Welsh, and also a song called 'It's Snowing in Baschurch'.

There were several older men whose repertoire amounted to possibly only one or two songs, but Ken would keep them in the loop week by week, and everyone was afforded the same amount of respect: Ron Howells sang 'Napoleon Bonaparte', and Geoff 'Silver in the Stubble'. Maureen Cunningham, a wee Dundesian, had a song about 'Cholesterol' and also 'When the Heather's on the Broom'. Pat Sheard was the Folk Club Secretary and a lovely singer. Other characters included ginger-haired bespectacled 'Addled Nick' who would sing a bawdy tale, usually out of tune and often with the aim of offending someone. Peter Bamber, a calligrapher, would accompany himself on guitar and sing 'Sister Josephine' in a wry and whimsical way (as Jake Thackray had intended when he wrote it). The 'audience' were really a major part of the goings on – Cheesy Jack in his horn-rimmed glasses would pass round cheese that had been festering in his pockets, wrapped in a handkerchief. We would all take a small piece and enjoy the tang with our beer. Little old Lenny Roberts had a gammy leg, but was always cheerful. Alan Jones lived out towards Bomere Heath but was an ever-present and went hillwalking; he would join in, describing himself as 'the audient'. There were many characters there, and the place was joyous and vibrant; it was a great way to relax at the end of the weekend before Monday came around – always too soon. At 10:30 Ken would shout: "Last Orders at the Bar!" and would choose three singers to wind the evening down, each singing one 'for the road'.

The thing about the Folk Club was how non-judgmental everyone was. Everyone would wait patiently for the singer to compose himself if he forgot the words (as I often did, although I would more often than not just make them up!) or, if they knew the words, they might quietly utter the next line to help. I think it was the mix of young and old that was so special, with the lead coming from older exponents of the art. The older people would speak with us directly and take interest in what we said and our thoughts and ideas on things: much more open than the handed down paternal wisdom of other places I had been. I really developed an affinity with people here of whatever age: they all seemed to have something in common, an alternative viewpoint, open minded, a positive attitude… I gravitated towards them.

On one Longmynd Hike training run in September 1982 I sold my harmonica to a mate and decided to join some Folkies at The Miner's Arms at Priest Weston as a ceilidh was on. Armed with approximately £4 from the sale and not much else, I left Bayston Hill at dusk via Lyth Hill and stitched together a route through green lanes footpaths and byways through the back of Vesson's Farm up on to The Stiperstones and across Shelve and down to join the shenanigans. At the Village Hall the dancing was in full flow. There was a table with some bread and cheese on it so all my £4 could be spent on ale, at 65p a pint.

In the Miner's Arms at the bottom of the hill a great session was in full swing. John Fellows had been spotted under the see-thru plastic tarp he had fastened to the hedge in the back field. John had won The World's Worst Singer Competition several times and we soon found out why – very funny out-of-tune songs about elephant's bottoms and Chinese junk pirates. Rees Wesson was there too: an expert accordion player, Rees would sing, dropping contemporary punk lyrics into his performance, an example being 'Peaches' by The Stranglers. I slept under a pub table that night.

My musical knowledge was expanding – as well as The Doors and The Velvet Underground, I was exposed to the folk singing of Archie Fisher and Nic Jones' 'Penguin Eggs', plus The Dubliners, The Corries, The Chieftains, Christy Moore and Moving Hearts, Planxty, all on vinyl; and, in person, the never-to-be-forgotten Fred Jordan, who headlined Shrewsbury Folk Festival that year. Bachelor Fred was an unaccompanied singer from the Ape Dale, a backwater between Ludlow and Much Wenlock. Fred lived in the house he was born in and sang at clubs, concerts and festivals around the country. Fred had been awarded The Gold Medal by The EFDSS (English Folk Dance and Song Society).

During the long evenings of summer, a walk of up to twenty miles with Stu or Chris was not uncommon. With my feet under the table at the Folk Club, I managed to get invited to a trip Alan Jones and Dave Hoy were planning for Easter, to go up to the very far north of Scotland, to Sutherland. I had read about this magical mystical place in 'Climber and Rambler', but had not climbed further north than Ben Nevis prior to this. Sutherland is another 4-6 hours north. In true Folk Club style we left to drive north after the pub shut. Alan and his mate 'Bad Eddie' shared the driving, with me and Chris in the back as neither of us drove. We camped on the beach at Achmelvich in an old 8 man ridge tent and drank at the Culag Arms at Lochinver when not on the hill. We climbed. It felt like an undiscovered world to me, untainted free and wild; Ben More Assynt, Culmor, Stac Pollaidh, and attempted the mighty solitude of Suilven, but were thwarted by high winds and only Dave and I had crampons and ice axes. One of Alan's friends, Bill, walked along in a duffel coat, knitting as he went! Slightly eccentric was Bill: he continued knitting whilst sitting in amongst the fishermen in the Culag Hotel in the evenings.

Back at work, the year wore on and I was becoming increasingly restless at BT. It was a 'gentle trap': safe and secure, but hard to break out of without somewhere to go. My lifestyle was good, but I yearned increasingly for adventure and excitement: a rough and ready freer life.

One late afternoon in the office I became aware I was the only male in a room of a few women. The subject got round to sex. I cringed. A bit of a roll around on the carpet at home with a neighbours' daughter, a premature ejaculation in my pants was my only sexual experience thus far. 'I bet you're still a virgin, aren't you, Stewart!' The words, easily thrown by a girl a couple of years younger than me, produced cackles from the others. I went bright red, lost my tongue for once and just clammed up. In truth I had been dreading something like this but was unable to counter attack. "Hmm…" I thought to myself when I finally managed to get out of the building and take some fresh air. "I'm 20 years old. Everyone seems to be paired off except me. I want sex, I want what they have… but how?"

This embarrassing revelation prompted me to make a concerted attempt to find someone. A friend came up trumps: she had a girlfriend from her netball team, who lived up on 'The Grange'. One Sunday evening I went down to the Seven Stars to meet her for a date. It went well: she was lovely, with dark shoulder length hair, a cute smile and a good sense of humour. She enjoyed the pub, the music and was up for things like walking and maybe climbing. She worked in accounts and she had a car – an Austin 1100. All was good. We clicked. The weekend after celebrating my 21st birthday she and I went away for a few days camping in Mid Wales where, in a Vango Force Ten tent, I finally lost my virginity.

I was steering my motorbike increasingly in her direction now too. She was happy to ride pillion and I had bought her a helmet. And so things went on. Friends were increasingly partnering up and settling down. We were all turning into our parents: secure jobs, building a future and saving. Well, most seemed to be doing that. Not being 'like that' was my conundrum: could I cut this all off and run away and find adventure, live in the moment, not just when I had some annual leave to take? Every day could be an adventure, I was sure of that. My world was vibrant and colourful; but now things seemed to be fading just a little. What could I do to keep life exciting when I was too scared to jump?

There seemed less opportunity for mischief of any kind now. She was great company and would enjoy walking and camping but had decided to draw the line at climbing. We would go winter walking and I could go away on mountaineering trips with mates when I could.

At this time I had access to the X Aba hut on the A5 at Capel Curig Snowdonia. Spadge and Blutes and Tim were in the club, the Aberystwyth Mountaineering Club and I was their guest. This little hut was a strong but roughly built ex-shepherd's hut sitting along a track above the River Llugwy. The hut had a sleeping platform in the roof space accessed by a steep wooden ladder. Old mattresses had been thrown down and a spare sleeping bag – nicknamed 'the spunk bag' festered in one corner. Directly underneath was the common room. In the corner was a log burning stove on a slate hearth and a stack of wood drying. Moth eaten 'comfy' chairs in various states of disrepair were arrayed near the stove. To the right of the small windowpane, which permitted just a small amount of light to penetrate the gloom, sat a bookshelf crammed full of curled up climbing magazines and literature. Clinging to the walls were trophies of foreign adventures – signs brought back from Chamonix, The Frankenjura, Spain and Norway; fading pictures of young Turks climbing big and gnarly things. In the kitchen grimy burners sat on metal trestles along the plain whitewashed stone walls, gas bottles below. An annexe, with bunkbeds that could sleep eight, gave the hut a total capacity of about sixteen, although at the annual Christmas Dinner, many more would cram in and sleep wherever they could.

We went to the X Aba hut to be nearer the mountains and to climb. We explored, scrambled and climbed the Glyderau, Tryfan's east face, the Llanberis Pass, Dinas Mot, Cyrn Las, Devil's Kitchen, the Alphabet Slabs, Clogwyn y Tarw and many more. Big days out here of course, made us very thirsty. Drinking would generally be to excess. After a walk down to the pub for several pints of Castle Eden we would stagger back to the hut for whisky bottles by the fire.

At one point one night, climbing down the rickety hut ladder in the pitch black I lost my footing. Gripping the edge of the sleeping platform, in my addled confusion, I was convinced that I was hanging from a space station orbiting far above the earth and sure that if I let go I would be lost in space forever. It was a real feeling and one that filled me with dread, but also excitement. Was there an umbilical cord to tie me to the mothership? What was in that whisky?!

Despite these thirst quenching evenings we invariably rose and did something the next day. This could be in the form of a couple of us trudging up to Pen Llythrig y Wrach (slippery peak of the witch) and crossing the Carneddau in a snow storm, or walking the ridge from Capel Curig to the tiny lake Caseg y Fraith and over the Glyderau. On one trip I cycled up on my own from Shrewsbury on the Friday by way of Bala and over the Crimea Pass to Betws y Coed and then up to 'X Aba' and several reviving pints. The next day was a big day over the hills before many beers at the Annual Dinner. It was wet and cold and I suffered the hot aches (a physical reaction to the cold, usually in the hands causing intense pain). Blown around on the mountain by day, returning to a log fire in the hut to warm our bodies and to dry our clothes we would write up our exploits in the hut logbook.

I felt glad to be a part of this group of individuals, all of whom were competent, confident and independent.

'Stumpy' bore an uncanny resemblance to the ski jumper Eddie 'The Eagle' Edwards, down to the jam jar thick glasses; he was a good climber with a lot of stamina. Chris was a louche figure, self-possessed, well-monied and driven. He went out in winter with Spadge to do Grade 5 routes, hard routes which seemed beyond my capabilities. Chris was a going out with Alex, a lovely smiling physiotherapist. Tim and I taught her the basics of ice axe and crampon use during a damp and melting week in Glencoe. Rod was a sport climber, massively strong in a slim frame and, like them all, it appeared, very intelligent and a self-starter who knew where he was going. I felt out of my depth in some aspects, but happy to be included in this group nevertheless: it was so different from my 9 to 5. Several of these people had been to public school, and the difference was plain to see, they were already climbing and exploring overseas; but they liked me, I liked them and the banter was good.

By the 1980s things had changed in the way big mountains were being climbed. Gone were the days of Chris Boningtons' big siege tactic expeditions. Newer streamlined small compact teams would try new and hard climbs in remote places, sometimes comprising just two climbers and possibly a cook/camp guard and a pack donkey. In 1985 Joe Simpson and Simon Yates became one such team in Peru, finding the magic unclimbed line of The West Face of Siula Grande, deep in the heart of the remote Huayhuash mountain range.

Route successfully climbed, descending from the summit, Joe broke his leg. Simon had to lower him down the mountain. Down they went but Joe inadvertently lowered into a crevasse, was hanging free on the rope. Simon, unable to get an anchor, was in imminent danger of being dragged in too. The decision he made to cut the rope was an easy one: they would both die if he didn't do this. Simon managed to get off the mountain alone; but had he sent Joe to his death? Despite being severely injured, Joe managed to escape from the crevasse and crawl his way back to camp, where Simon, preparing to return to civilisation, was able to bring him safely back for medical help, after a dangerous journey back to Lima through a country devouring itself in civil war. This incredible story has been well documented in Joe's book '*Touching the Void*' but the backdrop to it is as harrowing:

Abimael Guzman, a philosophy professor at the University at Ayacucho, Southern Peru had been inspired by a visit to China where he learned of the Cultural Revolution. His university became a hotbed of unrest and a base for the Maoist group 'Sendero Luminoso' (The Shining Path). Their attempted revolution turned into a civil war which killed approximately 70,000 people. The war etched fear and heartache into the population of Peru in the villages in the mountains, in the towns and cities and over the mountains and into the jungles of the Amazon.

In Lima, Jorge Escudero's fledgling electrical appliance store 'loaned' televisions and video recorders to 'Academia Cesar Ballejo' a front for The Shining Path. An uncle who refused to pay extortion money was assassinated. Liliana's cousin had recurring nightmares after some terrible ordeal in the jungle.

In one attack 'Senderos' destroyed a bridge over a ravine ripping a community apart. Local people struggled on in fear and poverty as Mafia helicopters flew in and out with cargos of cocaine bound for Colombia, police unable to offer resistance. Another insurgent movement, Tupac Amaru, were resisting government forces as well, with the net impact that chaos reigned. Trust was gone now, the basic ideas of society eroded, as common people lived in ignorance and fear, unable to understand who their friends were and who their enemies were. Insurgents did not have uniforms and raided indiscriminately leaving police and government forces unable to identify their enemy and communities paranoid and helpless.

All through these troubles Liliana tried to manage the shop for Jorge, her hopes of studying now just a dream. She had left full time education and this new life was teaching her some hard lessons. Once she was so vexed that she left and went to work for a Bingo master, selling customers lucky bingo cards. She lasted three days before Jorge realised what he had lost and begged her to return. This action had a marked impact upon Jorge, who valued his daughter's hard work and diligence: she was able to attend, from 1984 at the age of 15, for three years '*Escuela de Salud – Cayatana Heredia*'. Here she learnt about apothecary, the basis for pharmacy and drug administration. This was as near as she could get to her dream of becoming a doctor, and it all had to be fitted in around her work at the shop.

*****

In Britain the miners lost their fight after a year-long battle, their capitulation followed by hundreds of pits then being deemed "uneconomical" and being closed, leaving communities broken, with families finding their main breadwinner out of work. The National Union of Mineworkers, led by Arthur Scargill, was in disarray. With the NUM defeated, the strength of the unions had now become severely diminished by laws restricting their powers.

Margaret Thatcher took further control now, rolling out her revolutionary economic changes. Among her targets was reducing the council housing stock. Our Aunt Puss was about to retire from the Civil Service when her offer came up. She had worked all her life, having gone from serving in the Wrens during the war to working for the Forestry Commission and ending her working life at The Job Centre. She and Gramps had been living at Lansdowne Road since 1937, paying rent for decades; now she had the option to buy the house for £8,000, as opposed to its market value of about £15,000. This she decided to do, already having paid for it several times over in rent.

By this time I was climbing, walking, settled in a relationship, doing what I wanted when away from the prison of work. Was it time for me to flee the nest, take some responsibility, put some roots down too?

Back at work things were becoming heated following fallout from the Miner's Strike which we had had solidarity with. Thatcherite changes after the privatisation of BT had inevitably ushered in a newer more assertive management but with that came opportunities. BT was a corporate supporter of Operation Raleigh, a youth organisation based in London. Raleigh offered young people aged 18-25 the chance to go on a three month expedition to a remote part of the world to learn and to challenge through scientific, adventurous and social projects before returning home to contribute to their own community. Opportunities like this didn't come along very often. I immediately applied.

Chapter 6

Moving On, Moving Out

But Not Moving Up

In the mid 1980's Mum and Dad decided that they wanted to move and start afresh. Mum had been to a friend's house out in the countryside on the north side of town, a place called Yorton Heath. The house was a semi-detached stone cottage over a hundred years old with gardens to the front and rear and a big wooden garage, fields all around cut by country lanes. A request stop north on the Shrewsbury to Crewe railway and then a half hour walk would get you there, but not before a pint in the unspoilt Railway Inn, run by Alice and Addie, old sisters, and Alice's daughter Liz. Between the pub and the cottage, a distance of a mile, was a tiny church: St Mary's, Broughton. Mum and Dad were captivated by the place. They put the family house in Broad Oak Crescent up for sale and made an offer for the cottage.

Chink had recently moved out. Egger was still at school, about to study for his 'A' Levels in Maths, Physics, Chemistry and Biology. I was still at home too, getting too old to be a cuckoo in the nest, but not jumping because I had not been pushed, although increasingly I was spending more and more time at my girlfriend's parents' house, or away at weekends visiting friends in Aberystwyth or camping up in the hills. Mum and Dad were looking forward to their move as they were becoming disillusioned with life in Bayston Hill. Mum wanted her interpretation of 'the good life', a rural idyll of domestic bliss. However things had not been good for some time; they were arguing more. Maybe Mum must have been worn down by the energy of us three lads, our behaviour or just by life in general, but on 1st August 1985 they moved to Yorton Heath, their idea of heaven.

Now this would have been the perfect time for me to commit to my girlfriend, who was ready to set up home and had a good nest egg saved; but something within me was resisting settling down. Stu Altman was buying a house in Cleveland Street, Shrewsbury and was looking for a lodger. I had always got on well with Stu, and he agreed that I could have the spare room.

Frivolities and fripperies continued. We were all game for a laugh, and we would team up with likeminded reprobates, Egger was one such and Chris Morgan another, of course. Weekend ceilidhs, or barn dances as they are sometimes known, were popular, and we would cycle out to the ones further afield. Often Saturdays would involve a walk with an early start. Chris and I had a favourite walk: we would get the train to Church Stretton then walk back to old Shrewsbury over the hills, up the Burway and out onto the Longmynd choosing paths through the heather and out across towards the Portway before dropping down into the fields and hedges around Pulverbatch and then onto and over Lyth Hill. If there was time, we would call in on Puss for a cup of tea and a piece of cake before loping down into town, and The Loggerheads pub, where a lunchtime sing along would be underway, the assembled throng, shiny faces beaming out from above the froth of a pint of good ale, market shopping tucked under the ancient pub pews. These sessions would last until about half-past two when everyone would disappear and the pubs would all shut until the evening time.

Mum and Dad took out a bridging loan to help them pay for Stone Cottage, Broad Oak Crescent having not yet sold. I wanted one last party in Bayston Hill. Mum and Dad were away now so the party was set. I invited all and sundry – bring-a-bottle, all night party, bring a friend. Many young people were there, Chink's friends I had not met before. Chris Morgan brought along some of his Northern Soul mates, including 'Alex the Astral Taxi' and other characters. 'Boozer' and some punks from town rocked up. This boisterous party rapidly descended into mayhem, music cranked up to maximum beer over the walls and ceiling; cigarette burns in the carpet. A Punk fight, a girl pushed against a wall, the studs in her leather jacket scraping the wallpaper into strips. Food fights, peeing in neighbours' gardens and frolicking in the flowerbeds. Mum and Dad's bedroom that had sensibly been locked from the inside was re-entered via the window, couples left bodily fluids on the sheets and vomit under a pillow. Nick copped off with a young lady from across the road, recently seen through her bedroom window dancing topless. A great party!

The next day things seemed very different. A clean-up operation was under way, and eventually we thought we had done a pretty good job, apart from the wallpaper the vomit and the cigarette burns. I hadn't realised what a big deal it would become. Mum came over to move some stuff over to the new house, and she hit the roof! The upshot was that the buyer pulled out of the deal. I moved out pretty quickly and moved in with Stu in Cleveland Street. I went over to Ireland with the motorbike – I now had a big Yamaha XS 850. Luckily we had booked time off from work and we hoped it would all blow over while we were away.

I celebrated my 23rd birthday in Ireland. We rode over to the west coast: we explored the Burren, visited Cork, kissed the Blarney Stone, and camped at Doolin, near Lisdoonvarna, where the *craic* was great in the pubs. In a pub near there we got a front seat to see the legendary John Martyn. We took a boat out to the Arran Islands, the last land before America; we climbed Brandon Mountain on the Dingle peninsula; and I sang Irish songs (learnt from Pogues records) at O'Donoghue's pub in Dublin as the Guinness flowed.

Upon returning I went over to Yorton to try to make amends. I was allowed to sleep in the caravan but I received a frosty reception and there was talk of costs and bills for damage at Bayston Hill.

I was well asleep when the flashlights rudely awoke me. "Come out, Wellings, we know you're in there!" Bleary-eyed, I grabbed my leather jacket and opened the caravan door to be dazzled by two police officers shining flashlights in my eyes. Mum and Dad were standing at the door of the house looking bemused, saddened, perplexed and angry all at the same time.

"You are being arrested on suspicion of attempted murder, following an incident in Pride Hill, Shrewsbury," the police officer informed me as I was led away. I didn't know what to say. I was taken to Shrewsbury Police Station. Whilst we had been away the English Border Front, the EBF, just local thugs, had been on the rampage in Shrewsbury. During this melee an old lady had been knocked to the ground and had received potentially life threatening injuries. Witness descriptions of the assailant were given. Allegedly I matched this description. As the seriousness of the situation crowded into my tired and confused brain I remembered the ferry ticket in my jacket pocket. I retrieved it and handed it over. "I wouldn't do anything like that. I wasn't even in the country!" I protested. The ticket was taken away for examination. "My girlfriend can vouch for me!" Despite this cast iron alibi proving my innocence I was still held in the cells for several hours before being let out without charge, or apology, or a lift home. West Mercia Constabulary held a list of 'likely lads', and since my pyrrhic victory after the bike crash in 1981 my name was on the list. My respect for those police evaporated that night.

Having moved into Stu's spare room' I started to enjoy life in the town. The Folk Club was within walking distance now, and a whole new world of pubs was opening up around me. I kept my pushbike in the hall at Stu's and stored my motorbike before eventually selling it. An Operation Raleigh selection weekend was coming up and I had managed to get on it. This was my big chance. It was out at Squilver, under the Stiperstones, an area I knew well. The selection weekend was based on military type training to observe how the participants coped with no sleep and very little food whilst trying to complete team building challenges throughout the night in the wet and the cold. A typical test was to build a raft out of barrels and planks and sail it across a small lake at night. We did this, and were rewarded with a raw swede to share between the team. Lots of walking and carrying heavy packs did not faze me. Each successfully completed task added to our ingredients to make ourselves soup over a campfire. The bigger the meal, the better the team had done. There were also individual interviews, and everyone had to deliver a 'lecturette' on a subject of their choosing. This was done in a barn, also at night to keep us awake. I enjoyed the tasks we had to undertake, but despite this I was not successful.

Back at work I had been moved around a few times, never being part of a section for long. I went for promotion but was again turned down. My first impression was made long ago and it appeared my die had been cast. I felt trapped and like I was going nowhere.

Life at Stu's was taking a bit of adjusting to. We had been friends although Stu was nearly 5 years older than I was. Now there was a more formal edge to it as I had to get used to paying the rent on time and buying food and paying my share of the bills. Stu and his girlfriend Jane went on holiday, and the opportunity to have a party presented itself, no thought for consequences, just a chance for fun. I was pretty good at attracting freeloading ne'er-do-well hedonistic partygoers and there seemed to be more of them in this neck of the woods. Always there was plenty of alcohol, and then a bit of food bought more as a sop to convention, but when we found some butter and pineapple chunks in Stu's side of the fridge we got creative. The hard cold butter was a substitute for cheese and was pinned to the pineapple squares by cocktail sticks. This was the start of the descent into the now usual mayhem where details are unnecessary. We party goers cleaned up to a standard that we thought was sufficient; but unfortunately we had failed to notice the butter smeared all over the ceiling. Stu saw it straight away when he came back, as he had decorated just before he went away. He had words.

My time there now was threatened and I felt my options closing in on me again. My girlfriend was more sensible than me, but for some reason she still believed in me, or she wouldn't have suggested that we buy a house together.

Stu was very patient, he didn't evict me straight away, but I needed to grow up. At least I was paying my rent on time, most of the time. I took a day off to work at the West Midlands Show as a car park attendant. £20, easy money was on offer. All I had to do was to stand in a field and as every car drove up I had to point to my 'oppo' on the far side and say: "Follow the bloke in the orange mac." That was it. Hungover, surreal thoughts clouded my brain. Fighting the boredom I adopted a new persona, I lay down on the grass and started slurring: "… follw blocking torinj mac!" in my best Eastern European accent, deciding I would feign ignorance of the Queen's English, if challenged. My rationalisation was that no one knew who any of us attendants were, and it was for one day only, and who cared? I got paid, and headed straight for The Nag's Head on Wyle Cop with my silly mood and the £20 already burning a hole in my pocket. Much later, staggering out, I succeeded in getting my leg over my bike and headed down the road, but at fair speed something flicked up and mangled itself into the front wheel tipping me straight over the handlebars, toes still in the toe clips. I landed on my shoulder and neck, with the bike still attached to me. The front wheel completely collapsed. I bounced well, I was not injured. Undoubtedly the amount of drink taken had relaxed me. I carried the bike back to Cleveland Street and left it in the hall before going back out to the pub.

At this time I attended a fair few bike rides with a group of cyclists who met on Sundays. Rides of up to 80 miles were the usual, taking in villages and towns of Shropshire and beyond into Wales. Most of these cyclists were older men: Hoppy was in his 70s, and Doug was 76. I took my camera along and processed my own monochrome prints in the darkroom of The Gateway Arts Centre in Chester Street. I enjoyed these bike rides and photography; inadvertently it became a way to avoid my major drinking excesses. Part of the reason I drank so much may have been subconsciously my way of dealing with my lack of success at work and the notion that I was 'on the outside', neither relating to my circumstances or to my colleagues.

Grandpa Wellings was not impressed to learn of my lack of success at work. I had always respected Gramps and what he had done, and this made me sad. He died on Friday 2nd January 1987, aged 88, with Dad, Puss, Ed and me at his hospital bedside. There wasn't time for Ron to come from Denmark. Accompanying Charlie's "Cheyne Stoking" death rattle, on the ward TV Bruce Hornsby and The Range played '*The Way it is'* accompanying 'Final Score' and the football results on Bank Holiday Grandstand. A very good man was lost that day but the world just kept on turning.

We were out on strike at BT that month, the first time ever for most of us. BT wanted to change working practices as part of a pay deal and we heavily opposed it. We were out for three weeks and as a union official, I was on the picket line. Very few crossed, and we stood around the braziers at the works entrance warming our hands against the cold. However it wasn't picket duty every day, and I could slip away on my bike for the odd local hill trip. People in the pub would buy me beer, which was a good act of solidarity, and I was grateful for this kindness in a bleak January which saw me delving deep into an overdraft.

The union presence at work was as strong as ever. I had become more involved and joined the committee, attending meetings about various issues related to Health and Safety sub-committees. A mix of men and women, we were a young branch committee. In contrast, our colleagues on the Engineering side were old, exclusively male and steeped in the ways of committees: clichéd expressions, tobacco, tea and expenses. I did, however, start to feel a part of something. A comrade Andy and I were selected to attend the National Conference in Blackpool, at the Winter Gardens. We were handsomely supplied with beer money, and our lodgings in a Blackpool Bed and Breakfast were found for us. All we had to do was to stay awake at conference and report back when we got back to Shrewsbury. There were many parties and 'schmoozing' pub sessions: branches from the big cities – Liverpool, Cardiff and London — were well represented; and they could drink. However, there was a day off midweek and a march was organised. I used this day to travel up to The Lake District and climb Helvellyn on my own – that flame was still alive.

Back in Shrewsbury soon after, being so frustrated, like a spoilt brat I walked out of BT. I wanted to bite the hand that fed me. I wanted something better.

I was brought back down to earth. "I thought we were getting a house?" the girlfriend said, leaving me to stew in my own juices, and now riddled with bile and doubt and guilt. I ate humble pie and went back into work to face a disciplinary panel. I felt like a broken little boy as I sat facing Mr Nice and Mr Nasty. Nice had been my boss previously, and was a fair man. Did he understand the boredom? Probably. A mark was put against my record and a sanction put in place, pay docked and my name taken off the promotion list. After that I just kept turning up to work and everything ran smoothly again in the soft prison.

With her scrimped and saved deposit we bought a house up on Crowmere Road in Monkmoor, an area of old Victorian housing and council houses, urban, with a couple of open-all-hours shops along the road. I knew the area and liked it. It was an end-of-terrace two bedroom house with a high brick wall that curled round on to the Bell Lane Bridge. Trains on the main London to Shrewsbury rail line rattled through the cut below our miniscule backyard. There was a cherry blossom tree to the side of the house and enough room to squeeze a bike or a motorbike through the gates at the back. It had been built in the 1880s. Prices were going up at the time, and we bought it for £23,250. This was the highest we could afford on my salary of around £8,000. We moved in in June 1987: I was 24 and she was 25.

Chapter 7

Aurora Borealis

North to Alaska

As new householders we settled in together and we got on well, intimacy and space was important to us both. Over a year now after my fall from grace at work I was trying to knuckle down and carry on. But I had been accepted on another Operation Raleigh selection weekend. I couldn't pass this up, try as I might. I saw this opportunity as my last chance to do something before my youth expired – the upper age for Raleigh was 25, which I now was. I went to attend the weekend with Anna from The Ravens. We understood what was expected of us this time and that much would depend on how navigating the orienteering section was handled. It was just as exhausting as the previous one but we both passed.

Anna decided on going to Africa. Cold mountains lured me though and the venues for 1988 included Alaska, somewhere I thought potentially very remote which thrilled me. I received a letter dated 9th July 1987:

'I am pleased to inform you that you have been provisionally allocated to the expedition detailed below (Alaska). This allocation will be confirmed when you have raised your target sum of money, but may regrettably be cancelled if you are unable to achieve the target by eight weeks before the departure date of the expedition (26 May 1988)...'

Operation Raleigh had been set up as a four year project and was due to finish in 1988. Suddenly there was something for me to focus on, a meaningful challenge, some way for me to test my potential. Before this, however, there would be the not insignificant matter of fundraising £2000 to secure my place, a huge task. The motorbike had to go if I was serious about getting to Alaska. It did, replaced with a much cheaper to run BSA Bantam 175, an oldie but goodie. It wasn't as reliable, but it got me from

A to B and sometimes back again. There were grants to be had from the Walker Trust at The Shire Hall, and Phil from the pub tipped me the nod to the Roy Fletcher Charitable Trust. A sponsored bike ride had over £100 pledged but to get big money I was thinking about staging a music festival.

Shrewsbury Folk Festival had been going for a few years now, and had remained a small event based around the pubs in Abbey Foregate. Blutes, Kim, Tim (aka Fang) and his 'friend' Ziggy, their hippy mate from Aberystwyth, came to stay. After a big lunchtime drinking session we sat around in our back yard waiting for the pubs to reopen. Paddy was playing fiddle, when Ziggy spotted my Bantam motorbike. Dreadlocked and deeply tanned, Ziggy had recently ridden a pushbike from Istanbul to Spain. Despite being well over the limit, laughing all the way I volunteered to give her a motorbike tour, suggesting tongue in cheek that every time I beeped the horn, as she was wearing a t-shirt without a bra, she should flash her lovely tits! This she readily agreed to, even when we were stuck in a traffic jam outside the Bricklayer's Arms and the pavement was full of cheering male drinkers!

Chris Morgan knew a band called Lee Marley's Rare Herbs and had started rehearsing with them. He had also been playing with Merc and Steve 'Vodka' Edwards, calling themselves 'The Badgers'. Soon we had a line up for my planned festival, featuring local Indy bands The Geekais, Sister JoJo and The Brothers Gretsch, and Rees Wesson's Devious Roots. We had put gigs on at The English Bridge Community Workshop in the past. Vodka worked as a printer, and not only printed the posters but came up with the witty title 'Scoob's Half Baked Alaska Party'. Many more people got involved; a folk session with Ken and Mal inadvertently featured a gate-crashing homeless lad who had a blue stripe across his face and played loudly and wrongly on a battered trumpet: surely an acid casualty. Roy Gadsden from work made a huge vat of chickpea curry. Bob Oakley, keeper of the Red Lion at Longden Common, brought his travelling bar. 'Wicked Sir Dav's Disco' and some disco lights cobbled together from somewhere got people dancing. Loads of people turned up, it was a great success and another £300 was raised.

There was still a lot of money to find. A concert, raffles, it was all good money for the Alaska fund. The deadline was approaching, and I was still £250 short, but with a loan from Alan (the Folk Club 'Audient') I made it in time and could pay him back later in instalments.

Despite being aware of a need to get fit ready for the Alaskan wilderness and anything it could throw at me, I was actually getting fatter. A gang of us went up to Scotland and climbed some great mountains. Tim and I did the Liathach Ridge in Torridon in full winter raiment on a gorgeous spring day. Running, cycling and hillwalking more often, I did the Shakespeare Marathon in 3 hours and 52 minutes. I was beginning to shape up. April 12th 1988 was the day I passed my driving test. Positive things were happening now.

Soon afterwards I was on Pan Am flight 123 to Seattle then a Delta connection to Anchorage, Alaska. Alaska is the largest State in the United States of America: the last frontier. Now I was finally here, the wilderness excited me with possibilities. I felt vividly alive. I kept a diary:

'I have arrived a few days before the main body of the expedition. The expedition base is in a State Parks warehouse on the outskirts of Anchorage. There is plenty to do in the way of checking supply inventories, airing and folding tents and equipment. There is time to walk in to town and soak up the atmosphere as huge Kenworth lumber trucks roll up the highway towards the wilderness. Chilkoot Charlie's bar is as Alaskan as it sounds. Up here the nights are drawn out, with dusk falling about 10:30pm at this time of the year.

'When the main group arrives we are bussed to the American Army base at Fort Richardson for four days of basic training.'

At US Army base Fort Richardson they played 'Louie Louie' by The Kingsmen over the tannoy and served us army food in papier mache bowls. The toilet bowls lined up next to each other without the privacy of walls, obviously an anti-masturbation policy.

'This is just like Sergeant Bilko's Barracks. There are over a hundred of us: English, Scottish, Welsh, Italian, Kiwi, Canadian, American, Australian. After *some physical training days run by American soldiers, our trainer, Sergeant St.Armour, keeps singing out repetitively: "1, and a 2, and a 3 and a 4, - run a little, run a little, run a little MORE!!" As we jog along in formation, suddenly it feels like we have landed inside a M*A*S*H* filmset.*

'After a few days we are split into groups to go out on our separate smaller expeditions. My group comprised Henry, from Blackpool, youngest group member at 19, Ron, and Lem from Raleigh North Carolina, Liz from New Jersey, Mandy and Ian from South England, John 'Heathen' from Glasgow, Steve from Sheffield, Phil from Oxford, Dan from Ontario Canada and Jane, a Canadian Cross Country ski team member from Vancouver Island.'

Our first stop was Black Rapids Northern Warfare Training Site, Delta Junction in central Alaska. Here we trained in navigation, glacier crossing techniques and crevasse rescue, snow shoeing, winter camping and climbing, belaying, before a few days out on a trial expedition carrying 60lb packs and camping on the snow.

'Tuesday 7ᵗʰ June 1988. We arrive at the Chena Dome campsite to do some trail maintenance before our trip into the Wrangell–St Elias Mountains. After the training we have just undertaken, the physical effort of digging, carrying and raking tons of gravel along our newly built trail is helping to get us fit.'

Jane and I used our rest day to hike the Chena Dome Trail on Sunday 12ᵗʰ June.

'…(We) are the only takers for a 30 mile walk to Chena Dome on The Chena trail. At 10:40 we are in the tree and vegetation environment so typical of this part of Alaska, the mist right down giving an eeriness and atmosphere from a forest in 'The Hobbit'. A large proportion of the spruce, alder and birch trees have bulges half way up their otherwise thin trunks; strange footprints and smells give this place an otherworldliness… we soon leave the woods behind and are in tundra. The landscape is very up and down and we take in 15 summits during the day… it's like a giant sized Berwyns, but underfoot moss lies on fist sized rocks.

'The sky cleared to reveal awesome views… no habitation, only mountains, trees and the odd pool. We saw nobody all day, the only wildlife a few birds. We did see grizzly and moose prints and shit. We plodded continuously, stopping for

about a total of about ½ an hour all day. The ridges peaceful, still and calm,… stopping after 20 miles for a quick tea on Chena Dome at 4421'… A 1950s airforce plane had crashed on a col, the prop some 100' from the fuselage. Clocks, dials, wires, its guts everywhere. Photographs and continue on. We started to descend at milepost 4, and the hot day started to close in. Picking up speed down the bouncy moss floor of the 'Hobbit' forest, the rain came, hammering down on us as we reached the Trail Head. One mile on the road, thumb out and a man in a truck with a husky in the back saved us from being dissolved. After being out for 12hours 40 mins we arrived back, footsore, knee jarred and hungry, where fellow venturers bore gifts of cheese-sarnies from Fairbanks and more of Ranger Tim's salmon. Informed that the trail had not been done in under 18 hours before! Sleep came fast.'

A few more days trail maintenance here at Chena and we were on the move again. By Thursday 16th June, after leaving the highway and travelling down a track, we reached McCarthy (pop:24), gateway to the Wrangell-St. Elias Mountains.

'…The rough track is pretty straight and a couple of planes are parked along it; it doubles as a runway! We cross a wooden bridge over a massive gorge at about 2a.m. It is twilight – a sure sign we have come south…a huge torrent flowing out of the Root Glacier, a massive steep ice-field about 10 miles to the right. The only means of crossing the 150 yard stretch is by a pulley system carrying a metal chair: despite 12 hours in a bus and no sleep, we are all keen to try it out. Tents are hastily erected by the bus …

'Friday 17th June. After our 5 hour kip, people are stumbling out of tents. The backdrop of the day's activities is made up of the Kennicott and Root Glaciers, Bonanza Ridge, Fireweed Mountain and Sourdough Peak. Root Glacier has an amazing ice-fall and to be avoided at all costs.

Ferrying loads over the raging glacial torrent via the pulley…

'…our base campsite overlooking the murky grey fast-running meltwaters of the Root Glacier. Directly behind that the glimmering peaks of the Wrangells – notably Mt. Adna 16,000ft and 20 miles away! As we only have 3 weeks here, tomorrow we are heading to the hills: Doug's group to Donohoe Peak, Nigel's to Bonanza Ridge and Ian's to Sourdough Peak. I am heading for Bonanza!'

Between 16th June and 6th July 1988 as a group aged between 19 and 25 we faced challenges of weather, snow conditions, environment, nature, commitment and energy. We gradually melded into three distinct teams in this unforgiving wilderness. Black bears habituated the trails (now overgrown with alder and spruce in the long days of the short summer) and this kept us alert.

'We found refuge in an old dilapidated copper mine office, brewed up our lovely raven meals (real English food – dehydrated), and threw the tent up on a sloping floor.'

Abandoned copper mines, old 1930's wooden buildings, leant at crazy angles ready to collapse. They served as our temporary homes as we trekked between the ephemeral staging posts of McCarthy and Kennecott and on to our project sites, nomadically we backpacked our tents and dehydrated rations to the glaciers and peaks. The locals initially regarded us with suspicion. The gun massacre of 6 people here was still a raw memory and a vivid reminder to us that we were out in the wild now.

Bad weather hampered our attempt to climb Bonanza Peak but...

'Tuesday 21st June – Mid Summer's Day. 2:30! We're hobbling up the hill at just gone 3a.m. Starting early has made a difference, the snow is a lot harder. We fill waterbottles at a little spring and carry on retracing our steps of Sunday... breaking new trail up to the derelict copper mine... The snow is crisp on top but once we punch through it we are left floundering.... We gain the NW ridge and see the sun rising across some beautiful peaks including Mt. Blackburn. From here is our first view of the summit proper...'

Mild conditions produced avalanche tracks and every step on the high ridge was unstable. We were out of our depth.

'The ridge is knife edge sharp, and cornices hang both sides. There is a massive one we can see right under the summit. Ian, John and myself roped up moving with great care, using foot belays and spike belays wherever possible. If someone breaks through a cornice or falls off, the other two have to jump off the other side. Progress is slow, and there are very few points during which we are all moving at the same time.

'...Towards the top it is so deep I am forced to crawl.

...there are some dodgy cornices and bad snow. There are 20 yd parts where you can't tell if there is anything under the snow. Progress is slow'.

About 100 yards from the summit we have to pass directly under the massive cornice. You can see where avalanches have slabbed off. We skirt round and then, as it's my turn to lead, straight up shitty snow and loose rock right at the top, to a tiny summit with a wooden pole from mining days, stuck in a rock pile.

...along the ridge we hear the roar of avalanches, see them pouring down gullies, and accidentally start one or two when footsteps collapsed. We go on like this for two hours, dreading a slip or a cornice. Eventually after lots of scares and prayers we reach the saddle, safe ground.'

'...over a cornice we retrace our steps... stay roped up right down to the track as the snow is melting fast.'

One at a time we gingerly stepped down before running the final scree slope. The long trek back to Jumbo Mine left us after a sixteen hour climb, safe, hungry, shattered, elated.

The poor weather eventually broke and the Alaskan summer we had hoped for burst into its brief bloom and combined with twenty three daily hours of sunlight it energised us. But back at camp Doug's team are overdue:

'...Ian is concerned and makes plans for a search party tomorrow morning. Just after midnight some slightly drunken bums walk in, having been asked in to the house of Tony Zak, an old pioneer, eager to hear their stories and ply them with his whiskey.'

The following days are spent ferrying more gear up to where we are to do a glacier study with Brian Whalley, the scientist. We have time to visit the McCarthy Inn, a 14 mile round trip walk from our advanced base camp. We noisily bang mess tins to let bears know we are here.

The next few days were spent resting, eating and helping Brian with the glacier survey up by Jumbo Mine. A chance to climb another peak was discussed. We pinpointed what we thought was an unclimbed a 9260' peak on the map. Henry, Nigel, Mandy, John, Jane and I left on Friday 1st July with six days food, staggering along the trail towards the moraine again under 60lb packs. Getting off the glacier caused some consternation tackling the crumbling cliff to reach the bottom of the mountain.

'*Hot weather the next day causes unstable snow and ice conditions. John slips and arrests within 20 ft; Mandy follows, but falls over rock and snow, about 100ft… we rush over to her, thinking she will be injured; but apart from cuts, scratches, more bruises and broken glasses, she is o.k.*

'*By Tuesday 5th July we descend, defeated but not too worried. We tried. We spend the rest of the day, and the next day playing on the glacier, climbing steep ice and abseiling into sink holes. We all feel mountain fit now as we return to McCarthy on the Wednesday night, acutely aware that our time in this amazing wilderness is coming to an end.*'

The next phase of the expedition was a very different proposition. We were going to the Nancy Lakes canoe trail to conduct fish stock surveys, board walk maintenance and also to construct a log cabin. Then…

'*…the rest of us are going to Eagle River, nearer to Anchorage, to complete some trail maintenance. We've found out about The Talkeetna Bluegrass Festival… it is on (near) the end of the expedition.*'

But first we are under the leadership of Jock Marfell a 30 year old bearded Kiwi who is running the camp and operations along the trail. Jock's teams have been overseeing trail maintenance, building basic bridges, culverts, gravelling, sign making and filling gabions with rocks to shore up the river bank. Many bears have been spotted in the area, mainly small black bears, and all food has to be stored in bear bags high in the trees. We ford the freezing rivers by crossing arm in arm facing upstream, once across we just walk and walk to try and get some feeling back in the legs. Only then, having flicked the glacial grit from between our toes can we change footwear. We have to time our trips to be able to wade across in the morning while the river is low.

'*The Mountaineering Club of Alaska is organising a trip across The Harding Icefield, on the Kenai Peninsula. After discussions and a vote, Liz McCoy and I are co-opted on to the trip.*'

We had been invited to cross this icefield as part of a team of local mountaineers. Knowing the history of the area, they reckoned this to be only the fifth crossing; the first one may have been in 1940 but the first recorded crossing was in the spring of 1968. They knew of no Englishman ever having done it. The team comprised – Dan (in charge), Ken and Steve- aka 'The Three Stooges', seven others plus Liz and I.

'*Sat. 23rd July.... An old man is waiting to ferry us up Tustumena Lake to where we start our trek; we can just glimpse Harding Icefield throu' the clouds. The boat is fast, spray breaks over the bows, but it is still an hour and a half's trip. Once assembled, we hike through trees and alder, all at least 11 ft high, with our skis on our packs. We make camp at the glacier snout and proceed to be sociable with the other members of our team. The team are pretty experienced Alaskans although they don't have the edge we have from living in the wilderness for 2 months, they are a good bunch who know what they are doing. Ken is a long haired hippy who asks: "Does anyone mind if I do acid on this trip?"! Mike has a pack that must weigh at least 100lbs, what he calls 'power lounging'.*

'A very steady plod brings us slowly off the Tustemena Glacier and on to the Icefield where we can change crampons for skis with skins and transfer some of the weight from our shoulders onto the little plastic sleds we will be towing behind us.

'...suddenly everything seems light, and off we trundle to our campsite on some snow, sheltered behind some rocks. It has turned into quite an arduous day; we don't make camp until 9.30. Glen and I do a water run, and by time we get back, cook tea & brew it is midnight.

'*Monday 25th July 1988. Our new style of transport makes everyone happy, skiers especially. A late start is planned; we all have to travel roped in 3's due to crevasse danger. When we move we're pretty warm and the sky clears for a beautiful day in wilderness seldom travelled. The views when we get up onto the icefield are staggering, loads of peaks to our right, across about 15 miles of ice field. To the left are the mountains that give us shelter and in a little lee we make camp for the night at 6pm –early– GOOD. There is a slope behind us and everyone is eager to practise telemarking skills, climbing skins attached to the skis then ski down without them in this curious bent leg, arms stretched style. It is so awkward compared to 'downhill' that I am arse over tit in no time... just before it rains to cook, spag bloody bol 'dehydrated' again and abuse neighbourly ears with the penny whistle.*

Tuesday 26ᵗʰ July. *we depart, and soon hit crevasse country. The mist comes down, and before long complete whiteout has set in. We press on, but soon decide to make camp. We have to probe the area for crevasses before digging a windbreak with the snow shovel, which until now has only been used as a lid for our pan. That done, the tent is erected. The weather soon decides to change and we are treated to a brilliant view of cold peaks, nunataks and ice. Dan reckons only the highest peak Tru – Uli has been climbed as these are 'forgotten' mountains. He also says, weather depending, that we may head over to our right tomorrow to ski round an area probably not visited before.*

Wed 27ᵗʰ, Thur 28ᵗʰ, Fri 29ᵗʰ July. *'..It is like walking on the inside of a giant table tennis ball. The bearing is N31degrees E, and we just follow it for a few hours, getting extremely wet as it is pissing down. Camp is soon staked; everyone pitches in to build a communal snow wall which works very well. My sleeping bag has become soaked, but with 2 bin bags, 2 ziplock bags (for feet) and waterproofs strewn underneath I try to sleep. Liz's down bag is slightly damp so we put that on the top – warm but wet. Catherine is completely snug in the Dick Griffiths goretex bivibag & sleeping bag…'*

Dick 'Black Ass' Griffiths was an Alaskan 'Sourdough', an old trapper who offered some help to us. Sourdough is the live yeast culture used as a pancake starter. It also refers to a long time dyed-in-the-wool resident of Alaska. He got the name 'Black Ass' after an extended solo trip up in the Brooks Range. The wind was to his back and his 'pants' got wet, resulting in chilblains and frostbite, hence the name!

'…My feet have got horrible black bits on them. Thursday is soggy and white-out again, but it has stopped raining by the time we decide to camp. A piece of horizon comes into view and I try to air my sleeping bag. A float plane flies over us, the first form of outside life we've seen; it dips its wings at us. A slightly more comfortable night, although Liz is feeling rough, she is sickening for something. Friday dawns brilliantly… Sleeping bag gets aired and Kenny calls a couple of square dances in the snow. Dan 'The General' organises a group photo and in great spirits we all ski off on our last day on the glacier – A Great Trip. Camp at

730 is near rock. Yes we've done it, made it over the Harding Icefield. Laughter and banter. Great sunset. Nick's birthday – 26 old boy!'[9]

We go back to the Eagle River Trail for a weeks' work

'…finishing off our section of the trail, felling a couple of de-barked trees for bridges. We spend a night in Dick Griffiths' cabin after a river crossing. 'Lem says goodbye to everyone and rafts his way down the Eagle River solo. He has to get back to civilisation for medical exams.

6th & 7th August 1988 in Alaska means one thing Talkeetna Bluegrass Festival! Sat 6th Aug Steve, Ian, Henry and myself scrounge a lift. A 100 mile drive brings us to a forested area with trucks and cars lining the dirt road. It's a drizzly afternoon, but this doesn't stop people bopping to the fiddle-crazy foot-tapping tunes and wedging a few tins in. See a few people we know: Ken Hippy from the Icefield trip, LeRoy, Pat and some of their Denali Crew, Ranger Rick and Angela from Nancy Lake. We meet some good ol' boys and girls and as the beer rolls and the music hots up and the rain stops some serious grooving is partaken of. Eventually off to bed at 5am. The sun is shining we lie out well into the afternoon. Barbwire Twisters, North Star Band and Spud Grass are all worthy of a mention, as are Grover Neely and Alan Wilson, who recites some Robert Service Dangerous Dan McGrew poetry.

One day I vow to myself, I will learn that poem.

Returning to Eagle River we have a few days before we can travel home.

'Over Crow Pass we can see Raven Glacier, and to our right we look down Crow Creek We carry on and make camp on a little knoll overlooking the stream. It's a lovely evening but I'm aching.

Liz, Jock and myself decide to have one last trek into the Chugach mountains for a weekend of reflection and a walk up to the glacier. We get up to the river crossing, Jock sees a Grizzly, it was the size of a moose. Not far from there we come to Eagle Lake. Rafts are inflated and I soon get the hang of it. We are really in the back country and sitting by the stream is magic, just right to think back over the last 3 months – truly majestic: 3 months difficult to put it all in perspective or even take it all in, so I won't, I'll just be glad. Time for another brew.'

---

9   Nick Preece's birthday

SAT 13ᵗʰ Aug We cook over a camp fire on the moraine by the glacial lake. After about an hours' travel we find ourselves underneath the foreboding flanks of Eagle Glacier. There is constant noise and movement as ice falls away and water drips in crevasses. An ice cave, I venture in to take pictures. It has an eerie aura and the blueness is dazzling. I paddle off across the glacial lake, through chunks of ice. Raft packed away we walk to the ford site, water as cold as ever. Brisk walking on the other side still takes a mile to get some warmth back into feet. We continue 'the long march' - civilisation is round the corner and will catch us tomorrow.'

It was all over. Happily reunited with my girlfriend we drove down to Oregon, camping in Crater Lake National Park. We continued down to see how nature was reclaiming Mount St Helens. I had seen it from the train in 1981 as an eighteen-year-old.

Now for the big come-down. Nothing had changed; it was just as if I had stepped back into monochrome after the most Technicolor adventurous fun time of my life, where I was given leave to find out who I was and what I was capable of, to work and live with likeminded people and to achieve amazing things. How could I use this experience to help myself and others? BT had very generously paid me a retainer as part of their sponsorship of Raleigh. I had supplied the energy and enthusiasm. Now, after all this, would they let me be in charge of the paper clips?! I was 40 lbs lighter than when I went; with a straggly beard and different clothes and changed values. I looked and felt even more out of place.

While I had been away I had been usurped as Union Branch Secretary. I didn't really care; I was in a day dream now, stumbling round, unable to adjust back into this life. I was moved to a job at Ditherington Telephone Engineering Centre in the contracts office, and was trained up by an older lady who was retiring. First thing in the morning engineers took paperwork and discussed their jobs with the line managers, Dave and Bernard, who would then go to site visits, leaving me alone in the office with the admin to do and phone to answer. As soon as they were gone my mind drifted back to Alaska: vivid memories; so fresh; so vibrant. Then back down to earth with a crash as the phone rang with an engineer with a query that meant nothing to me; and I was unable to listen properly about to how to deal with it. Floundering, nothing was meaning anything to me now; I was a fish out of water.

I had my photographs and gave slideshows about my experiences to groups of anyone who would listen. I presented one in the Telephone House canteen, titled 'Avalanche Hour with a Difference!' I was asked on to Radio Shropshire to talk about my adventures and what Alaska had meant to me, and what I now planned to do.

Raleigh knew how Venturers would feel once they returned, and had ideas and a network of support to help us do what we were supposed to do: put something back into the community. For me it was an admin job. Shropshire needed a 'Venturer Coordinator', so I volunteered. I became first point of contact for aspiring future venturers. There were national events for us to get involved with, cycling and conservation among them and the occasional selection weekend in the county to attend. It was fun being on the other side of it and instructing and being part of the judging team. During this time I failed the BT promotion board for the third time.

Alaskan friends, Steve, Henry and Nigel came over a few weeks after we had returned, in early October, to do the Long Mynd Hike, which I had often talked about. We all cruised round it easily in 15 hours but the next day I felt no twinge of pain of any description, such was my fitness. This was soon daily becoming eroded working in the office, though. I had to put up with it or leave but at home she and I were trying our best to make a go of it, so I grinned and I bore it. Dave could see that I was struggling and was a good manager. He took the time to explain that my job was important to the running of the office. I tried to be a company man, but, whilst it didn't hurt too much, there was a massive Alaska-shaped hole in my life.

On 24th March 1989 the Exxon Valdez hit Bligh Reef off the coast of Alaska, spilling 11 million gallons of crude oil into Prince William Sound. This was one of the biggest oil spills ever, and a huge wildlife disaster unfolded, with daily pictures of oily seabirds fighting for life and volunteers trying to degrease them. The coverage disturbed me; the pristine wilderness I had known had been violated.

The world was changing, and after my travels and the Exxon Valdez disaster I became more aware of world events: student demonstrations in Tiananmen Square in Beijing were brutally suppressed. In South Africa, Nelson Mandela was released from prison. Nearer home was the Hillsborough disaster, the Pan Am Lockerbie bombing. The Berlin Wall came down in November, bringing the Cold War to an end.

Twenty-four satellites were launched; these would become the basis for the World Wide Web.

*****

In Peru life continued. Liliana was now 20 years old and running the family business with an iron fist inside a velvet glove. Jorge was the real boss though. Business was good and they won an award as best import business for Sol Gas in Peru. Liliana's brother Julio was sent to a strict military school before doing National Service. The civil war continued. Liliana tried to find time to study, to try and find some reason for herself within the crazy world of Civil War in Lima. Always a bright and intelligent mind, she tried to juggle work with studies in Pharmacy at Escuela Superior de Salud 'Cayetano-Heredia' de Lima. She stayed the course and received her certificate as a 'Diploma de Bachiler' in 'Farmacia' on 24th May 1991.

*****

In our little corner of Shrewsbury we were bohemian in outlook, easy-going and up for a party whenever possible. A new friend, Cara, delighted in her self-proclaimed title of having the 'best tits in Shropshire'! Around this time we were meeting more new friends around the neighbourhood, including Paul Wilson, who was a seller of Oriental and African books and book collections and also a gig promoter and manager of Scottish band 'Swamptrash' (with whom his best friend, from his time in Sudan, Garry, played banjo. Later Swamptrash would meld into the Acid-Croft Dance sensation Shooglenifty). Paul lived on Monkmoor Road with his wife and their daughter Moya. Paul had lived and taught in the Sudan for years, and Moya had been born there. When they left the desert they moved to Shrewsbury. Paul was the most gregarious, charming, and witty, intelligent, intense and cultured man in town. A retinue seemed to assemble when he sat down to drink, and there was always a vibe around him.

Paul lived pretty 'high on the hog', dressed well, and had good self-esteem. Man, could he drink! And he could talk! Evenings, ensconced round at his place a few of us back after the pub, bottles of wine emptied before our very eyes; there he was, back-slapping and hugging and pouring more wine and laughing and strewing vinyl on the floor as he sound-tracked his magical existence on the hi-fi with the alternative American Rock Gods of the early 1970s. We would talk alcohol fuelled philosophical bullshit long and late into the early hours. I would wend my way home for a few hours' kip before the bloody alarm clock would send me scampering off to work at oh-my-god-silly-o'-clock!

One quiet balmy August Monday evening, a few of us congregated down at 'The Bell Inn', which was a good local pub and had a lovely little snug bar that neighbours Julian, Andrew and I and a couple of newly met young ladies got very cosy in. After the pub shut we decided that we should all get naked as Julian knew of an open air swimming pool in Much Wenlock which he thought would be a great place to go for a swim. Armed with only a bottle of sherry and a cardigan between us (the cardigan to put over the barbed wire to keep us safe in our trespass, the sherry to quench the thirst), off we drove, naked as jaybirds. We were soon swimming in the cool water in the moonlight. Driving back laughing and joking swerving down Harley Bank, we headed back to town where we paired up. Next morning, three hours late for work, I woke up in bed with a beautiful young blonde, all pert and luscious and keen to tell me how much fun we had had that night!

Embracing Shrewsbury life fully with japes like these actually confirmed that something was missing in my life: adventure and excitement to name but two. But then Operation Raleigh announced some new expeditions and another Alaska trip was scheduled for 1991.

I knew what I wanted in Alaska this time – to be a project leader out in the mountains somewhere. In 1988 the leaders were chosen for their experience and skills. Few of them had specific mountaineering qualifications, although one or two worked as Outward Bound instructors. I knew that I wanted to hit the ground running and that if I could get there I would need to be as physically fit as possible and to have climbed some big mountains.

In the February half term I teamed up with my Aberystwyth University Alumni (X-Aba Club) friends. I wanted to stretch myself and tackle some harder routes than previously, and to acquire some mountain competence. Spadge, Alex and I went to climb Tower Ridge on Ben Nevis. It is the longest ridge in the British Isles and a tough test of mountaineering skill, especially in winter. It was at the end of a good week, and we 'had our eye in'. Spadge was always the best climber in our group, but I think he held me in slightly more favourable esteem now with my Alaska experience and connections.

The three of us started off up the Douglas Boulder in less than brilliant visibility but calm conditions nonetheless. We weren't early but we did slow, as being a team of three there was some 'faffing about'. By time we had cleared the notch known as Tower Gap and then wandered around the Eastern Traverse, we decided to stay where we were, hoping the white-out conditions would lift: perhaps we would get a starry night? We huddled together, sitting in our rucksacks with every stitch of clothing on, shivering away on our little ridge ledge on the side of Britain's highest mountain on a February night.

We were not alarmed; we thought we could just sit it out until light crept up on us, when we would then shake off the icy fingers of a winter night and continue on our way. No one was waiting for us and no alarm would be raised, so we felt happy in our decision. Things gradually got brighter; but there was no magical sunrise, just a white-out. We had been there for hours trying to slough off the chilling indolence that was clawing at us, draining us. Upwards, trying to stamp some warmth into our very cold bodies we were soon on the summit plateau and very aware of huge drops around us as the white-out continued.

We must have walked past the ruins of the observatory and the summit shelter as we started going downhill again towards Coire Leis. Retracing our steps, we chanced upon the shelter and opened its door, crawling into a metal freezer barely large enough for the three of us. Inside, the walls were half a foot thick with ice. At least we had shelter now, as the wind was starting to rise. Sheltering helped us to grasp the reality of our situation, and we decided we had to take a compass bearing to get off the mountain. We were not as well prepared for Ben Nevis as we thought we were. Not long after leaving the shelter, we were cramponing on iron hard snow ice above the treacherous Five Finger Gully. Realising our mistake, at last we had some idea of where we were. A traverse right got us back on to the path towards the zigzags where we could find our way off. Every step involved a hard kick into concrete ice. We finally got off the mountain after 27 hours, all intact.

As it was our last day, and Spadge a teacher was due back at work, a long drive south was necessary. We took it in turns to drive for an hour each. I was nearing the end of my stint when the tree went underneath the bonnet of the car with a hard banging noise that woke me up! The black Ford Escort slid down the bank and snowploughed to a halt. So lucky were we: it had slipped between two much steeper drops, snow banking up over the windows. We climbed out and raised the alarm. A tow truck came up from Killin, and with much effort we were towed back out with a long winch onto the icy A82 by Rannoch Moor. Sub frame damage and twisted and bent metalwork meant that we had to be relayed home, another 24 hours! I made a couple of trips down to Spadge afterwards to help with panels and trim, and our friendship remained intact too.

Every ten years there is a national census in the UK. In 1991 I did it as a second job to raise money for the Alaska expedition. As a third job I worked at Condover Social Club as a Bar Steward too, as there would be no money coming in for over three months while I was away. Fitness, money experience and motivation had all been addressed. I was ready to return to the wild.

There seemed to be more Brits in Alaska this time, and a certain 'je ne sais quoi' was missing. Deep in my heart I wondered if Alaska '91 would offer the same intensity of experience I had had in 1988. Like going back to a lover after an enforced absence perhaps, things are never going to be as they were: we were both more worldly-wise. McCarthy wasn't on the itinerary this time but Alaska is Big, and the opportunities are many. I was detailed to run a trail building and maintenance project at Coghill in Prince William Sound. This was obviously linked to the Exxon Valdez disaster, although maybe more as a public relations stunt than a tangible piece of aid work, and I had to convince the venturers.

Matthew was the Expedition Leader, a precocious 24-year-old, barely older than the venturers themselves; we were an eclectic mix of young people. In my Coghill group was Gavin, a photographer from Essex, living and working in London. By contrast, Bernie was a shepherd from Port Howard in The Falkland Islands. A seventeen-year-old Tim was taking time out before starting out on a career that would ultimately lead to him becoming an astronaut. Darcy, a 'valley girl', with the golden tan and peculiar language of that tribe, hailed from Hawaii. Keith, who would go on to become one of the pre-eminent outdoor climbing film makers of his generation, was also among our number; similarly, Joe, not as a leader but as a photographer who would later become famous for his landscapes.

Coghill includes College Fjord and Esther Island, an area now infamous after Captain James Bligh and The Exxon Valdez. Our group sailed out of the town of Whittier to land at our base with food and supplies for weeks and to enable us to set up a base camp and survey the area to build the Coghill Trail. Communication was by means of a military radio system that involved setting out an aerial and then hand winding to power a transmitter to contact the base near Anchorage. We had no luxuries with us just basic army ration packs 'ratpacks'.

The group moved all the equipment above the high tide mark finding just boggy muskeg where we set up camp as best as we could. The next day went for a group walk to see the lay of the land and get an idea of what was to be done in this very isolated area. Eventually we came to a cabin, the only building for tens of miles in any direction, where on the porch laid out to dry, were all four paws of a bear cub. The hunters were away; we never saw them. Back at camp I had to answer difficult questions from the venturers; why we were here building a trail that seemed to be for the sole use of hunters to massacre wildlife. Then it started to rain. It rained and it rained for a solid four days night and day. Then it stopped. For twenty minutes. Then it rained again for another seventy-two hours straight.

Motivation consisted of mainly saying: "We're here, let's do our best!" or "All this work will keep us warm!" or "Cheer up, you'll soon be dead!" or words to that effect. At least we weren't being shot at like bear cubs, although the rest of the area looked like the Somme. Wellies were the only effective footwear but they got sucked into the bog, the texture of a giant brillopad submersed in mud, deep enough to come in over the boot tops and induce a foot condition like trench foot. We camped on higher knolls under trees in twos in hike tents. I shared a tent with a female doctor, a lovely young lady and the small rations of pleasure she meted out alleviated the tedium of constant cold wet damp clothing, basic food and the need to motivate a group that could become despondent.

Keeping morale high was my most difficult task. When the weather allowed we got together around a smoky campfire with a cup of hot chocolate and a sing song which cheered people up a bit. We never saw a bear, and the rifle I had been issued with and taught to fire stayed damp, rusting and unused in the corner of the camp. Everywhere were tarpaulins strung over branches, corners continually having to be pushed from underneath with a branch to splosh the overhead puddles away and prevent them from collapsing and making further problems. Progress on the trail did happen, though. There were huge trees to fell by hand axe and a double saw with a venturer sweating on either side, then to fashion into bridges spanning gulches and rivulets prone to flash floods. Gavin and Bernie were very helpful with these projects, Bernie knew much more about it than I did, although I had had some experience of this type of work.

Joe spent a long time in the rain posing us all for a photo. When it did stop we had views across to the Chugach Mountains away on the mainland and small icebergs sailing out down the fjord with the tide. Post came as a treat. Letters from home were read as we bounced back over the sound first to the weird enclave of Whittier and then out to other projects, including a night out on the Harding Icefield.

The best part of the Expedition was the eleven day trip out into the Talkeetna Mountains. Here I had a good team of youngsters all tuned in to living in the wilderness. Eleven days' worth of supplies on the back is heavy, but we were all strong now. We camped on glaciers and made ascents of peaks in the area, mostly between 5 and 6000' high (1,500 – 1,800m) and snow covered. I made friends with another medic, before she departed to the ill-fated Eklutna Lake Trip.

As an inexperienced roped team, when one slipped, they were all pulled 60 m down the flank of the Eklutna glacier. Several were injured and one female remained in hospital for a few weeks with severe head injuries, having been initially in a coma. I was deployed at base at the time and was involved with relaying messages, but travelled to the hospital in Anchorage. One was in a very bad way and had to be flown back to the UK on a special flight and spent many weeks recovering. Back home, the 'Shropshire Star' cobbled a story together called 'Glacier Fall Rescue Hero', and I was the main story of July 18th 1991, sharing the front page with Kylie Minogue. But I was not the hero, I was 200 miles away at the time. The expedition lost its momentum after this accident.

I departed for The Picos de Europa soon after I returned from Alaska to backpack around the limestone gorges and peaks of the area for a couple of weeks before the inevitable return to work. This time there really was a change on the wind and all talk was of redundancies, which I immediately volunteered for. It wasn't happening immediately, but the tension was palpable.

Spadge, Blutes Phil and I went up to Scotland and on a calm May evening we left the car and walked up to bivi on the side of the hill in readiness to attempt the Skye Cuillin Ridge Traverse. We moved well, abseiling the Thearlaich Dubh Gap and navigating easily across the tops. The rough pink gabbro rock is perfect to climb on, offering great friction, its crystals winking in the sunshine. We climbed the fabled and sensationally exposed Inaccessible Pinnacle and then abseiled off to sleep below its nautical prow, which still signals to ancient seafaring time travellers. Next day's scrambling required a pause for the Basteir Tooth and ultimately on to Sgurr Nan Gillean (Peak of the Young Men) marking the end of the traverse.

It was here that Blutes produced from his rucksack his wisdom teeth and flung them symbolically into the void, announcing that Kim his wife was to become a mother to their first child. We had another day's climbing around The Cioch, a flat-topped stone set amongst the sharper peaks. And then the long drive home, which for some reason (perhaps after previous escapades) I wasn't involved in!

Back at work I had tried to keep my nose clean. I was sent over to Aberystwyth for a week and based in a portakabin in the car park at the TEC (Telephone Engineering Centre), near the seafront. My task was to fold some technical diagrams up and get rid of any duplicates, something a dog could have done. But for this I could stay the week and I could claim the £50 nightly lodging allowance. Tim Lewis agreed that I could have his room in Bridge Street, as he was away. After work I made my way back to his place, upstairs to the room and the big soft double bed, bathed in light from the dormer window. There was a knock on the door. I wasn't surprised, as this was a shared student house. I opened the door to a lovely young woman of about 19 years old with long brunette hair. A husky voiced 'Hi' emanated from this exotic creature as she undid the cord of her dark blue dressing gown, let it fall to the floor and stepped naked from it. She pushed me onto the bed with one finger. I took her out the next night but I never saw her again after that.

My relationship in Shrewsbury seemed to be creaking at the seams. My partner had strayed and I had too.

Redundancy was a lottery. No one knew until the day who would be leaving, but on Friday 31st July 1992 I was called into the office and handed a cheque and told to clear my desk immediately as my services were no longer required. I turned my back and never returned there. I went in to Telephone House a few days later to be given a bottle of whisky from John on behalf of the Union. He also gave me a telephone number for 'Release 92', the BT department that handled redundancies, they administered retraining allowances for life outside BT. If there was a course that would help me readjust after spending the whole of the 1980s in the employment of what I would eventually consider to be a social experiment, through Thatcher's reign, then I was in; you could not say fairer than that! I had escaped, released from captivity at the age of 29, after nearly thirteen years of being unable to find my niche, looking in the wrong places. The two expeditions to Alaska had given me an inner resilience but as for having a career I felt I was a nonentity, a complete failure. Now I could dust myself down, start again and reinvent myself. Now the adventure could begin for real.

Chapter 8

Preparing to Fly

New Life Starts Here

'Gonna break out of this city, leave the people here behind
Searchin' for adventure is the type of life to find
Tired of doing day jobs with no thanks for what I do,
I'm sure I must be someone, now I'm gonna find out who...'

Eddie and the Hot Rods

After long discussions, my partner agreed that she would leave her job and come with me. As partners we would mend the rift; we would rekindle the fire and try again. This seemed the perfect thing to do; after all, we had been together for nine years and had lived together for five.

The payout had been a good one – over £16,000. The sensible thing to do would have been to have paid the mortgage down and then found another job and had little to worry about. Measured and level headed wasn't the way I approached things though; I wanted out, I wanted fun and I wanted it now. This money allowed me to take charge – we would travel the world for a couple of years, and then decide. She worked her notice and I found a few cash jobs digging holes and painting windows. Kev my old friend from Bayston Hill agreed to house sit for us while we were away.

The phone call to BT 'Release 92' was exceptional: "Yes: if you want to retrain, just find a course and, once we have validated it, we'll pay for it," they said. I wanted to attend a week-long course to be a Mountain Leader, and they would also pay for the assessment once the logbook period had been completed – this would take a minimum of a year. My plan was to do the course before we went travelling, then get logbook experience, then go for assessment afterwards. The award is valid for working with groups anywhere in the UK and has to be accompanied by a current first aid certificate, renewed every three years. The course taught map and compass skills, with emphasis on group management, roped security on steep ground, camp craft, night navigation, emergency procedures, weather and related topics, covered whilst out on the hill and also lectures in the classroom. This was what I had been missing for so long; I had awoken from the dullness of office work and was able to use my body and brain and make dynamic decisions to look after groups safely on the hills and, assuming I passed the assessment later on, I could actually get paid for this!

I went on a week's climbing and cycling trip round Snowdonia with Gavin from Alaska. With all our camping and climbing equipment on the bikes, we toured around and climbed classic routes such as Direct Route on the Milestone at Ogwen, several routes on Tryfan's East Face and then out into more esoteric corners of Wales. As a free man now I was 'happy-go-lucky', but wanted to spend as much time in the hills as possible, partly to avoid spending the travel money, but also to gain more logbook experience ready for my Mountain Leader Assessment.

Another trip with Chink was quite eventful. By the time he could drag himself away from his current squeeze it was late afternoon as we left for a brothers' bonding trip before I departed to South America.

It was early evening by time we started up Grooved Arête on Tryfan. We were obviously going to run out of daylight; but we didn't care. We courted a challenge, but we decided to turn back halfway up as it was getting dark, so we made our way along a ledge to try and find our way off Green Gully. Without warning, the rock I was standing on broke off the mountain, sparks flying as it hit others and I jumped off as it bounced away into the darkness. Wrapping the rope round a huge chockstone, we abseiled down a gully but another giant boulder was dislodged, grazing my arse as it fell. Millimetres closer and I would have been dead. It shredded the rope, and we had to tie a knot around it and carry on, getting back to the tent at midnight, laughing just a bit too nervously. Chink and I were now well-bonded brothers. Now it was time to say farewell to all and to travel.

We flew to Buenos Aires and then flew over the Andes to La Paz, the capital of Bolivia and the highest capital city in the world. We would travel up into Peru and then south along the spine of The Andes. After that we would go to Australia, and then New Zealand, Hawaii and into the USA, landing in San Francisco before driving across to a wedding in Atlanta. The trip was to take six months.

*****

Giant white teeth hung above the city piercing an iridescent blue sky, their snow-capped peaks and ridges, some over 6000m high, steep and beckoning. Draped in a caldera basin below the shanty town of El Alto, spilling out and away into the highlands, La Paz pulsated, glinting through the dust in the harsh sunlight. La Paz is different in that the poor people live upon the heights and the mansions are at the bottom of the hill.

We did not stay long in the city. A day or two slowly trying to scuttle around the shuts and passageways, our bodies sucked the air for its limited supply of oxygen but with its excess of vehicle fumes. We dreamt crazy dreams in our hostel as we tried to acclimatise, strangers alone in a city teeming with business and activity. Markets and roadside sellers were everywhere: women with bowler hats, layers of cardigans and several brightly coloured woollen skirts squatted and huddled together along the dusty pavements to sell their wares, dogs and children running around. Bikes and mopeds and big old repaired repainted American trucks hurried to and fro, delivering Bolivian necessities as noisily as they could. The occasional displaced gringo would pass by, ignored by all but the blind or limbless panhandlers, or beggars burned by drugs and booze in empty doorways, tins held out, perhaps in hope, more likely in despair.

The brightness and the bustle was at odds with the cold and the rasping air, the bright colours of the people, clothes, buildings and vehicles glazed in patinas of dust swirling dervish-like through the streets and passageways where rags overhung as canopies blotted the sun into a shadowy patchwork, allowing dubious dealings and nefarious activity to flourish. We cautiously felt our way around like the un-regarded newly arrived Martians that we were.

In September 1992, Abimael Guzman, the leader of the *Sendero Luminoso* - The Shining Path guerrilla movement of Peru - was captured. Eventually this would lead to its decline and downfall but at the time Peru was in turmoil, expecting recriminations, tit-for-tat executions and random strikes: the country was on tenterhooks. A curfew was in place, and a high military presence on the streets. Guzman was discovered hiding in a ballet dancers' house in Lima. He was known to have psoriasis. Discarded medication bottles found in the household rubbish gave him away.

Travelling overland into Peru in October 1992 in my naivety I had imagined the streets lined with people celebrating 500 years since Columbus 'found' America!

From my diary:

'Once out on to the altiplano en route to Titikaka lake, the true scale of poverty starts to sink in. Everywhere are tin roofed, windowless 'hovels', for want of a better word. Some have muddy thatch instead; loads are unfinished, or seem to be. Slogans are painted everywhere – mainly MNR – a political party? Bolivia has averaged a coup every 10 months, since 1823… Outside the houses animals roam in the mud – pigs, dogs, cats, mules, donkeys, and, looking very surreal, llamas, alpacas everywhere. People just seem to be sitting around, or walking in the middle of nowhere, along the road from nowhere to nowhere, or so it seems. The great altiplano stretches away endlessly to our left, and to our right is bounded by snowcapped mountains of the Cordillera Real. The rough road bumps us along toward Puno, our destination for the night, over the border in deepest, darkest, dustiest Peru. The track eventually gives way to a mountain road, twisting, turning and lurching its' way round hairpin bends and sheer drops. Needless to say the driver takes it all at speed, passing on the brow of a hill, overtaking trucks and buses already travelling at speed themselves.

The bus is reversed onto a raft and we all have to get in line to push Bolivianos (currency), through the crack in the glass of a very temporary looking shack in exchange for a ticket for a motor boat trip. The motorboat follows in the wake of the raft 20m to the other side, where we step off onto an even seedier quayside.

'…tension creeps into the proceedings due to the recent media coverage of the Sendero Luminoso – Shining Path guerillas operating in Peru and the only pure Maoist Organisation still in existence. According to fellow travellers, they are still active in the western part of the country and we should be ok. Anyway, the Peruvian Inti is currently worth 1/500,000th of a dollar. In 1990 there were 62,000 Intis to a dollar, and the year before – only 47!… The Peruvians have introduced a parallel currency – the Sol. 1 Sol = 1,000,000 Intis. All this money changing and the corresponding commission rates can soon put a hole in your cash, until you realise the room you just booked cost £1.00!

Mon 19th October 1992 *– South American trains have become something of a legend. The right attitude towards this wonderful type of travel is essential. You have to embrace the journey as an entity in itself. 12 hours for perhaps less than 250 miles – a stately pace. Through the window life looked harsh: the tussock grass, the huts, the miserable little cultivations, the scratting animals, the people. The altiplano gives way to the mountains, and slowly the scenery changes: the vegetation more green…houses: the odd window and even a tiled roof here and there. Evasive young men in dark ponchos move along the aisles of the train, one nursing some kind of rifle, very unnerving. We slink down in our seats. Canyon walls close in on us and then open out into a huge bowl as dusk falls and the lights of the Ancient Inca City of Cusco twinkle in welcome; until stones start to patter on the windows which are quickly closed and blinds drawn.*

I feel as though I am in the wooden horse of Troy as we pull into the station. But we venture from our hostel in search of food – we have only eaten bananas and crackers for the last two days. The streets are narrow and cobbled and well-lit, and, after rounding a couple of corners, we find a huge cathedral-square with bright lights and music coming from an assortment of bars and eateries. The little pizzeria we choose smells of the X-Aba hut in Wales; it has a huge clay oven. The speakers blare out R.E.M. and Nirvana – the contrast from the altiplano is complete.

'Five a.m. on Tuesday 21st Oct: wide awake. Six a.m. at Cusco's other railway station, bound for the mountain top domain of the lost city of the Incas – Machu Picchu, travellers and Peruvians together – it feels like a school outing – not that we had many Peruvians in our class on the bus to Berkeley Castle in 1971! The train journey takes 4 1/2 hours winding through 110 km of stunning scenery. We drop down to 2000m a.s.l. and in this time we go from pampas into narrow gorges, woodland and eventually dense jungle. A bus takes us up the switchbacks. Suddenly there it is. Our first sight is of the classic view seen on the postcards and posters: a small city lying in a high col between 2 mountains with almost vertical drops to both sides. The city has been terraced away to our right, the higher part being the sacred shrines for worship, and the lower terraces the living/working areas.

…The Incas were a very scientific and religious people, and these two (ideologies) were inter-related, especially at Machu Picchu. Their world was underground, on ground and the sky, especially the sun, which they worshipped. Ancient Inca myth said it was borne from the Titikaka lakes, so Machu Picchu, on its lofty perch was as near the sun as could be got. The focal point is the Temple of the Sun. Machu Picchu is a geometrical phenomenon. Just below the Temple of the Sun (where, incidentally, a party of American Sun worshippers were performing a strange ceremony – in the rain!) is the Temple of the Condor. This temple has two windows. The sun shines through one on midsummer's day and one on midwinter's day. This was 300 years before Brunel was doing similar things with British railway tunnels. So how was Machu Picchu built? The Incas were very ingenious and observant. They knew about ice water and expansion. They had piped water from a hill, so in cracks in rocks they inserted wooden wedges and trapped water which froze at night. Eventually, and with a little practice and patience the rocks cracked and broke into the shapes and sizes they required to build this masterpiece. The condor features heavily in Inca mythology. It is their link between themselves and god – The Sun. Even the huge cordillera mountain ranges, the black rock, white snow and mountain – wing shapes suggest condors… all these things make sense.

It rains all day at the Temple of the Sun, but it is still magical.

'The slow train arrives eventually to haul us back up the tracks to Cusco. As dusk descends we walk around outside, talking with Peruvian fellow travellers. Eventually the train starts again, only to break down half an hour later, this time for two hours. We gamble for 'Intis' by candlelight, drinking beer, telling jokes that no one can understand and whistling silly tunes.

*'**Wed 21st Oct**: A day to look around Cusco, originally built by the Incas, looted and seized by the Spaniards and destroyed by earthquakes (twice). Only a day. But this was how we had planned it, not knowing (did anyone?) of the stability of the country in the wake of the capture of the leader of the Shining Path only a few weeks earlier. Cusco is a beautiful city, even higher than La Paz. It has a lovely clean central square with a highly decoratively carved stone cathedral at one side and shops under arches on the other three sides. Cusco has many cathedrals, but most can only be visited with a tourist pass, which we didn't have, but we did get in to see Santa Domingo and La Merced. The latter has a few treasures which weren't looted, the best of which is a gold and silver jewel encrusted crucifix which, for a bribe, the janitor will let you photograph.*

Dosed up with tablets due to stomach problems, the next day on the train I hardly notice the scenery, and a terrific thunder and lightning storm bids us adieu across the border and back into Bolivia. Tucked way up steep steps we find an agent who ran trips out into the mountains and we sign up to be picked up from our hostel in the black and cold of a pre morning. Our destination is the mountain range of Condoriri, where my first experience of being guided will be on Illusion Cita, a snow and ice peak of 5,330m (17,490ft).

– Excerpt from my diary:

'…We rope up, the overnight snow making it very difficult to see the fault lines of snow bridges and crevasse lips. We are creeping around as if on a fragile roof in the dark, never knowing when we might crash through a skylight… very tense and nervous. Our torturous twisting route is traced out below us, zigging and zagging and still nowhere near the steep headwall – the crux and key to the mountain. The sun is brilliant by now, the altitude makes me gasp and bend double, leaning on my axe at every opportunity. At last we start up the headwall. Ice-runnels fluted like buttresses lead up, three small pitches to

ice-mushrooms which hang under the summit rock, dripping already in the heat of the sun. We move together quickly.'

'Once at the rock, we traverse up snow ramps to our right and at 12 noon we are on the summit. The day is spectacular: clear, hot, no wind. Behind us, our first sight of Huayna Potosi – over 6000m. But we tower below it at 5300m. Across from us lie peaks so steep and high that hardly any snow clings to them – then the 'left wing of the condor', 'condor' and 'right wing'. These three, by legend and imagination, create a mythical condor figure, and I can just spy a real condor wheeling about their pinnacles. 'Black Alpamayo, eastern most of the group, sends her buttresses thrusting into The Yungas, the forest between the mountain and jungle which stretches far away to the north and east. Our gorgeous little pinnacle perch teeters in the sky like the perfect peak – the short rock pitch we scratch up in our crampons. I cram an egg sandwich down and a yoghurt drink, and before 10 mins are up we are reversing our steps- rapidly, as the sun burns us. The steep headwall slows us. I cower under an ice flake, belaying Juan, who kicks slabs of ice my way as he descends. Soon we are over the difficult crevasses and out onto the glacier again. The sun burns me through my sunglasses, causing my eyes to weep and my lips to blister. Staggering and gasping, we reach the moraine at 245, crampons off and jogging down the track to Base Camp.

'The horse seems even more overloaded. Off we go again; we are late. A quick glimpse back at 'our' mountain before we round the corner, and then it is out of sight. The truck loaded, the horse unloaded we bump off to rendezvous with(Israelis) Ari, Jason and Nesmetsio, who have been waiting 2 hours on the freezing altiplano, having trekked over two mountain passes from base camp that morning. My highest mountain by a long way. Climbing as a pair, Juan and I have made good progress. The track is dusty and atmospheric as dusk descends and we reach the highway. Zeni uses his horn more than his lights, in common with the other traffic which builds up but does not slow down as we hit El Alto/La Paz shanty town on the rim. Over the edge, the lights of La Paz, like stars and diamonds captured in a crater, twinkle their welcome.'

From here we are heading south into the driest desert on earth.

The *ferrobus* was comfortable. It took us to Arica on the Bolivian-Chilean border where we visited Señora Gladys Hulse at the British High Commission. This old lady represented the last vestige of British Colonial influence in South America, an anachronism. Sea level now at the port of Arica, refreshed by the greenery lush crops grow thanks to terraces of piped spring water, so welcome to us after weeks of aridity and altitude.

Arica was seized by Chile from Peru in the War of The Pacific in 1879. Bolivia lost its Pacific Coast, and ever since then the Bolivian Navy have been confined to patrolling the freshwater waves of Lake Titikaka. The Pan American Highway took us to Calama in the Atacama Desert. Calama is a mining town whose copper rich hills under a burning azure sky glow russet red, silver, turquoise beige and cobalt; here the worlds richest seams of minerals. It never rains, and it is the sunniest place on earth.

Sixty miles south lies San Pedro de Atacama, a tiny staging post surrounded by mountains and volcanoes – Lascar and Licancabur among them and some over 6,000m high, but it is so arid that they are completely without snow cover. Here we wanted to be part of the burgeoning transient traveller community.

San Pedro has a pre-Columbian history well represented by its museum. Corpses of little Inca girls, abhorrent, mummified and preserved on mountain tops as sacrifices to the gods were evidence of brutal life borne of superstition and sun worship.

The cape of night drops quickly in the desert. Hung with obsidian stardust jewels, its cold fingers send us in search of fire. The night's exquisite tentacles extend where no cloud has ever existed, breathing, for now, a purity into the soul. To stand outside in the desert is to feel the perspective of the heavens and the real fragility of the traveller, a mere speck in time and space.

The geysers of Tatio erupt their steam as night cold morphs quickly into dawn, igniting seismic activity. The driest desert has water, and there are even swimming holes. Too soon we had to leave San Pedro. Another overnight bus ride disgorges us into Santiago, the historical colonial capital of this long skinny country.

Santiago de Chile, a city of five million people, lies wholly within the central valley. The *Londres Hotel* with shuttered windows, crisp clean bed sheets and wood panelled airy rooms belied the dust, the dryness and the desert we had been a part of. Continuing further south we boarded a freight steamer, the '*MV Evangelista*' out of Puerto Montt.

Sailing to Coyhaique by way of Puerto Chacabuco and Puerto Aisen, sitting on deck amidst the containers, watching the glaciers drift by, stopping off on Chiloe Island, with its wooden buildings and churches, before sailing on down through the fjords and inlets of Chilean Patagonia where it felt like we could be in Norway. At a carpet factory we stopped and saw a swastika being woven into a design, a shocking reminder that the Nazis fled here after the war.

The volcanoes of the Chilean Lake District, Villarica and Llaima, Llonquimay and Osorno, tail off here into the Southern Patagonian Ice Cap before The Torres del Paine, unrelentingly steep granite fortresses scoured by vicious winds whistling up from the Southern Oceans. We thrashed our way through dense undergrowth and over huge fallen tree trunks to get as close as we could to the hanging glacier of Queulat.

I teamed up with a British travelling climber named Richard. A local boatman ferried us in his dugout outboard motorboat across a lake to a mountain known locally as 'La Tete', the highest point in XI Region of Chile. Fortified with only mutton and bread and a bottle of local red wine Richard and I scrambled over scree gullies and undergrowth to a col allowing us to scale the snow-capped summit.

Friday 27th November 1992: a 16 hour ferry journey returned us to Puerto Montt. From there we set off over the Andes to cross the continent, entering Argentina at Bariloche, a town of Bavarian charm, then across the southern Andean steppe by bus once more to the cosmopolis of Buenos Aires, from where we would fly over the South Pole to Sydney in New South Wales, Australia. Ten weeks in South America: I had loved everything about it and vowed to return.

*****

Liliana, now 24 years old, had been running the daily operations of her Father Jorge's business six days a week for half her life. His company, Continental Associates, had been recognised and she dressed up like the glamorous model she could be to accept the award.

Liliana's uncle Alfredo (Jorge's brother) ran his *Pomabamba Restaurant* in the Fepip area of the city. With the business and the restaurant, the family flourished but temptations were always near. Trying to keep the infamous Peruvian narcotics out of their daily lives became a struggle for some family and friends, which led to turmoil and strife and deep family divisions. The angst and hurt and violence and mistrust scarred deeply but forgiveness doesn't mean understanding.

*****

On New Year's Eve 1992/93 my girlfriend and I arrived in Auckland, New Zealand. We travelled down through the North Island, seeing the sights of New Zealand and walking around volcanoes and bubbling mud pools

We 'tramped' several famous tracks, as the Kiwis call them: the Routeburn, the Keppler, the Nelson Lakes, the Milford Sound. The scenery was incredible and the greenery lush and dense, all this because it never stops raining. The tracks could follow mile after mile of duckboard and there was no deviation from them. The huts we stayed in were very tidy, and there were always wet clothes drying and boots stuffed with newspaper. We spent six weeks this way; it was good and wholesome.

In Queenstown 'The Adventure Capital of New Zealand', I went for a day hike up the local hill, Ben Lomond. We went out to do what Queenstown is famous for – bungy jumping from a bridge over the Kawarau River in the Otago where gold was panned. I squealed as I plummeted from the bridge. The bungy stretch is calculated and adjusted so that you just dip head first into the river with arms fully extended. My neck was sore for a long time afterwards.

The airline route between Auckland and San Francisco refuelled in Hawaii. We were going to stay there for a week with Darcy, whom I had been with in Alaska. Her parents Gaylord and Carol lived on the island of Oahu, but worked on Maui Island during the week, so they asked us if we wouldn't mind house sitting their beautiful beachside house with a coral reef adjacent and a trimaran tethered up at the bottom of the garden. Well, at a push, we thought we would cope. Always in a bikini Darcy turned up one day with some friends and we launched the boat out into the Pacific, scraping it as we got it over the coral reef. Out in the deep ocean it started to fill with water as we realised we should have opened the self-bailers to let it drain whilst sailing.

There are sharks in the area, and we hung on to the boat and bailed as fast as we could, about a mile off Waikiki beach before sailing back and scraping the hull again as we re-entered the safety of the garden cove.

We walked and camped up on Diamond Head before we again had to say our goodbyes and thanks before flying to America.

From San Francisco we headed up to Yosemite, where four of us rented cross country skis to hike the trails. A cougar approached but didn't threaten, just loped slowly along its cold lonesome trail.

In Carmel, (Mayor: Clint Eastwood) we signed up to deliver a car from California to Atlanta Georgia, where the wedding of Lem and Laura was to take place in 10 days' time.

'Drive-aways' are a system whereby Americans buy a car from another State and have it delivered. The most direct route should be taken and the vehicle should be delivered clean and without damage. A look at the map gave us a thrill: our route went through Southern California. We saw the Hollywood sign and drove down the Boulevard, then across into Nevada, stopping to peer into that huge hole in the ground, the Grand Canyon. We drove through North Texas and into Oklahoma. Wherever we stopped for breakfast in the great American Diners of that land, we looked out of place, wearing neither Stetsons nor spurs. Arkansas passed by our windscreen, and we were into Mississippi. At Tupelo we visited the birthplace of Elvis Presley: a tiny shotgun shack with barely enough room to open the door. Over the border in Tennessee we visited Elvis' mansion home of Graceland. From there we headed south into Alabama before delivering the car in Atlanta, Georgia and were welcomed by Lem and Laura for the wedding.

As an usher at the wedding, I was honoured to escort the bride's mother down the aisle. The Anglican Church in the middle of Atlanta sat cheek by jowl with modern American buildings.

Newlyweds Lem and Laura left on their honeymoon and we were soon due to fly back home ourselves, but were within striking distance of having driven the entire way across America. From here we only had to drive out to Cape Fear on the Atlantic, and everyone was pretty relaxed about us borrowing the car.

As we were heading down the I-20, the Interstate Highway the lights of a patrol car flashed in the rear-view mirror and we were pulled over. "Do you realize you were exceeding the speed limit sir?" The officers' bilious face filled the driver's side window. I began apologies in my best British accent, trying to endear myself to any better side he may have had, explaining that we would be on the plane 'tomorrow' (and thus out of his country and jurisdiction). He remained unswayed. "Step out from the vee-high-cle!" He drawled like the deep southern cops I knew from TV. "Ah need some een-for-may-shine from you". I was ushered into his car, sitting in the passenger seat, four rifles stacked in a rack directly behind us. "Please lean forward and place your hands behind your back," he directed, and as I complied he snapped 'cuffs on me.

Kenansville County Courthouse was filled with young men in orange overalls, cuffed like I was. I managed to whisper to the court superintendent who miraculously understood my language and predicament and, upon payment of a US$85 fine I was freed. The violation wasn't that we had been speeding as much as the fact that I hadn't been carrying my passport or driving licence.

The trip was over and we crashed back to Earth in Shropshire. Kev was still renting our house. We stayed occasionally or slept on friends' floors or spare beds. The wanderlust was still strong and we had been pretty good with the money and had somehow kept a fair bit saved.

It was April now, and we went to Scotland to the Cairngorms to climb some snow-covered hills. This enabled me to get some logbook experience for the mountain leader award, still my aspiration.

I got some labouring work, and by June we were ready for another trip. We were going to cycle to Spain, and on 12th June 1993 I bought a brand new 'Dawes Sterling' for £320. Dad took us down to Portsmouth and we got the ferry on 17ᵗʰ June to Cherbourg.

Cycling in France is relaxing as long as you keep to the minor roads. The French embrace the bicycle and all its culture, and we were soon in a routine, packing up and leaving a campsite by about 9:30am, cycling through a few towns and villages, stopping wherever the fancy took us, eating bread and cheese and drinking wine. A few more miles in the afternoon and, after a study of the map, we would find somewhere to camp again, pitch the tent, fire up the camping stove and make the evening meal. We had books to read, cheap local wine and once or twice a week would we treat ourselves to a meal out. This was a great lifestyle, stress-free and healthy.

On July 20ᵗʰ we reached the Spanish border, proud of our achievement. We were camped at San Sebastian (Donostia) twelve miles beyond the border in the Basque region. All sorts of ideas about cycling on through the centre of Spain down to Morocco filled my head, but she was in her sleeping bag with a heavy cold, so I went in search of provisions. I wrote in my diary:

'I chain the bike up to a huge noticeboard bollard, in the foyer, below a video surveillance camera. Store security guys are patrolling. Half an hour later I return and POW! The bike has vanished!... I did once have a bike stolen in Shrewsbury! But at least I could walk home! I walk back to break the news, she had been worried. At least I'm ok. Then back at the supermarket a policeman takes us to the station, heavily guarded, where we fill in a police report.

'We walk around until we find the first 'GB' plates. These belong to a contingent from the South-West; they offer us lashings of wine, port and, yes, pot noodles! We all have a good laugh at my expense. Yes, they can take us to Bilbao tomorrow. No, it's not a problem! More port? Yes please! Even pot noodle tastes good.

Next morning we're up with the lark and soon sitting in Neil and Kim's car. They have CB contact with the others. Neil's 'handle' is 'Pot Noodle' as his roof rack has cases of the stuff strapped to it. I can imagine a huge downpour bursting the lids and the amorphous gloop giving the car an instantaneous Rastafarian wig, the windscreen wipers going full pelt to keep the gravy off the screen! Neil and Kim have towed their caravan, as far afield as Russia, Turkey, Czech Republic Spain and Norway.'

By Sunday 25th July we were back in Shrewsbury. That week I had to fill in some forms at the DSS, but on Saturday I scrounged a lift with Chink, who was going to London, and then hitched a lift from a motorway services with a family of travellers from Blackburn who were going to Sidmouth. I read 'Willy Wonka' to the kids, and the first person I bumped into in Sidmouth was Taff from the Folk Club. I pitched my tent hidden up on the cliffs behind a hedge, went to loads of sessions with Taff and Ken, read Isabel Allendes 'Tales of Eva Luna', cooked curries in a bus shelter and sang songs with new hippy friends on the beach. Involvement with this festival was as an outsider. I returned home in four hitches to 'sign on' and then on to get some more 'ML' days for the mountain leader logbook.

And that was the way the summer continued, and on into the autumn: blissful travel and doing what we wanted to do. I went up to the Fisherfield Forest in the North-West Highlands climbed some peaks there, notably Slioch ('Spear' in Gaelic) and also around Beinn Eighe in Torridon. Other 'Quality Mountain Days' (QMD's) followed for the logbook, often solo –the full Snowdon Horseshoe; walks and scrambles in Y Glyderau and Y Carneddau; and many long solo-cycling miles to keep fit in between bouts of serious drinking and fun with friends.

There was terrible news after I got home, ready for Puss's surprise 70th birthday party. Our Danish cousin Marie had died at home of an epileptic fit. Ron, Else, Jean and her children Nina and Martin, were already here, expecting Marie to join them when the tragic news was disclosed. The celebrations were obviously muted and we all rallied round, devastated at the loss of such a beautiful life at just 34 years old.

On the way home quietly later that evening I was attacked by four thugs. Barring our way for no apparent reason they just confronted us. I was kept in hospital with a suspected fractured skull and very sore ribs from the kicking we had taken. We had no idea who they were. The man who was admitted to A+E at the same time as us had been attacked in sleepy Bishops Castle. Sadly he died. We had travelled around the world without being assaulted once, then got beaten up in our home town. Violence lurks unseen just below the surface of even a sleepy provincial town.

We had decided that what money we had left would best be spent on one last trip – and India was in our sights. The money would go further there, after all, buying us more time, time spent avoiding going back to 'real life'. Marie's death helped galvanise us. She had lived with epilepsy and lived for the moment, and we took a leaf out of her book.

On Thursday 18th November 1993 we hitched a lift to London and found our way to the Indian Embassy in Aldwych. The stamp in the passport made everything seem real, and we booked our flights with Aeroflot for £330 to Delhi via Moscow, leaving on 5th December.

After an unscheduled nine hour stop in Tashkent, we reached Delhi and the madness started. In New Delhi and Old Delhi people pushed relentlessly, trying to sell you anything, the streets a macabre dance of snake charming, sacred cows, rickshaws, tuktuks, jostling chai wallahs, smells of spices, urine, diesel, grime-ridden humanity, jasmine, bales of cotton, jute. Sound and noise were everywhere: shouts, song, bicycle bells, tympanis: even a scratchy recording of Enrico Caruso emanating from a rooftop somewhere!

We found our way out of the city, destination Rajasthan, and the town of Pushkar. Camels can throw the inexperienced rider as they rise to their hooves, but their serene gait carried us away and out onto the edges of the Thar Desert where the sunrises and sunsets are the only clock you need. The saddles creaked as our train of farting camels advanced, guided by Rajasthanis resplendent in their exquisitely coiled turbans. Desert camp cooks fed us with boiled eggs and honey and flatbreads and sweet black spiced tea. In our sleeping bags we slept on thick hessian blankets topped with carpet, happily round a campfire under skies with familiar northern constellations.

The buses and trains to Ahmedabad could take almost as long to book and pay for as the journeys themselves. A bus took us away from the desert with an accompaniment of Hindi music, high pitched wailing from the tinny speakers, middle aged men acting like school kids on a day out, delighting in smudging the freshly painted seat numbers onto each other's clothing, play fighting, squabbling and laughing as we careered through the night. As we queued up in train stations witnessing the hidebound bureaucracy that, courtesy of the British Raj and the caste system now strangles India, a sacred cow would amble surreally through the constant mass of humanity. Public transport works well for the long distances in India, and initially we opted to pay a few rupees more for the luxury of first class travel and the chance to keep humanity at arm's length for a few hours. Later as money dwindled, we would travel standard class with the locals, their goods and chattels and their inquisitive natures.

It was Christmas Eve when we reached the Portuguese enclave of Goa, planning to stay by the sea to relax and imbibe the culture, play some chess in a beach hut and eat, drink and socialise. Like a young couple many centuries before, we could find no room at the inn, or the next, or the next; so eventually we settled for an enlarged under-stairs cupboard. It would have to do. Goa has a Christian history and is busy at Christmas but is only slightly less frenetic than the rest of India.

Soon we fell into a loose group of café friends that were good company. Partying on the beach was great fun, but more expensive than the rest of India, and we wanted to find our way up to Nepal.

The train we took went via Varanasi (Banares), holy city of the burning ghats on the Ganges and birthplace of the Buddha. We stopped here before carrying on towards Nepal by bus, reaching Kathmandu. Amoebic dysentery took over for a few days here, laying me so low that I had to seek out medical attention. We walked slowly round the sights of Kathmandu as I staggered back on to my feet the Palace of the Living Goddess, Durbar Square, stupas and temples, and mad dogs and mayhem on the streets and in the market squares.

The Annapurna Circuit was our goal. Shouldering packs, we headed out through the villages of Kagbeni and Jomsom along the steep-sided gorges separating Annapurna from Dhaulagiri, both 8,000m peaks. Staying in tea houses, we trekked with local people and other travellers from around the globe. We walked with an Australian girl who was overweight and, as we approached villages, children would come out in droves laughing and pointing and shouting at her: "Very fat! Very fat!" She took it all in good humour, as apparently to be of this body shape in Nepal is a sign of wealth and is thought very attractive.

We climbed up and down high passes, in our own search for a Shangri La. From Poon Hill we watched the sunrise over Annapurna Dhaulagiri and Hiunchuli, the biting wind in stark contrast to an afternoon in the hot spring waters below. The north wind cut through us as we trekked up towards Muktinath and Kagbeni, where the thumb of Mustang points out towards the plain of Tibet. Staying a few nights, every evening we would warm our feet by the hot coals laid under the tables after we returned from a cold walk. We tried to climb over the Thorung La, a pass of over 5,416m. It was blocked with snow, and we had to return, and left the next day to find our way back via Jomson and then to Pokhara using a different route. Maoist graffiti daubed on walls reminded us of Peru. We remained wary feeling a distinct unease. People seemed less friendly here.

Back in the warmth at Kathmandu we arranged to travel back to Delhi, reluctantly in my case. I wanted to stay and trek in other areas and travel more; but we had arranged to return in the spring ready to start another chapter of our lives. The money was dwindling, but we were seasoned travellers now.

Charlie Wellings 1898 - 1987

Bob and Marg's Wedding 1961

Ron and Else's wedding day 1954

Egger, Chink and Scoob

1970's Scout Camp: Paddy Jenks, Nige Lawson, Ian Davies, Peter Fieldsend, Neil Richardson, Unknown, Mark Emery and Nick Preece   *Photograph: Nigel Emery*

Another fun night with Paul Wilson

Liliana with sister Mabel and brothers Julio and Jorge Luis Peru

On Pequeña Alpamayo, Bolivia 1992

Liliana Escudero Vasquez - The Flower of Ancash 1998

Outdoor Education in the Community BA course 1998

Shooglenifty featuring the late Angus Grant on Fiddle

Winter bothying at Hutchison Hut, Cairngorms

First ascent of unnamed peak (5213m), Quimsa Cruz, Bolivia 1997

Liliana in Traditional Costume

Liliana, The flower of Ancash

My Office! Cordillera Blanca, Peru

Pisco summit step 1999

Ishinca, Tekking Peak, Cordillera Blanca, Peru

Our Wedding 2001

Our Honeymoon. On Curved Ridge, Buachaille Etive Mor,
Glen Etive

Ali and Liliana, Edmond Road Sheffield 2001

Ali and Matty, Pomabamba 2017

Photograph: Henry Iddon

Stewart

Liliana

Ali

Matty

On Kennecott Glacier, Wrangell-St.Elias Mountains, Alaska 1988

Chapter 9

Slipping the Bonds

Experience

We returned to sadness. Ashley Preece, brother of my old best friend Nick, had died in a skiing accident in Italy where he had been working as an instructor. He was 25 years old. The funeral took place at the Shrewsbury crematorium and the place was packed. I don't know how Nick managed to give a speech about his beloved younger brother; resilience, bravery and love shone and we found comfort in his words as the sadness descended.

*****

Egger came over in April; it was his 26th birthday and we were due to head to a party. Chink lodged with Paul Wilson now. We drank and we drank and then headed back to our house where I gave him his birthday present, a bottle of tequila. This idea came from a film called 'Betty Blue' but I hadn't understood the irony. We slammed some shots, and some more, and some more, then moved on to whatever else was lying around the house: ouzo, raki, rum, even a bottle of sherry.

"What's your name, Stewart?" The ambulance man started with an easy question. 'Where are you from?'

"Footwear Cheese!" I replied.

"Footwear Cheese?" he asked.

"Yeah, Shoes –Brie!" I cackled, and then threw up all down the hallway before they rolled our wheelchairs up the ramp into the ambulance.

At the hospital IV drips were inserted with long needles splinted in place, and we were put in adjacent beds. I was hallucinating and screaming, and my heart was palpitating as I looked up and saw several stern and worried faces staring down on me as if I was looking out of my own horror film. I was going to die. I knew it. I had to be restrained and sedated and kept where I was. Chink and Egger came to fetch me. Egger had been discharged the previous night and had had to be taken straight to McDonalds, where he ate five Big Macs.

We silly boys were to attend Mum's retirement do. She was retiring at 56 as arthritis was making things too difficult for her. As we drove there we heard news of Kurt Cobain's death. He was 27.

To escape from this crazy wayward homecoming I wanted to hold onto the positive energy we had felt in India and Nepal. Busying myself I attended a weekly first aid course and more logbook experience in readiness for my Mountain Leader Assessment, which was booked for 26th June to 1st July 1994. This was so important to me as it represented not only a positive focus for my energy but also a way of getting qualified to help people and to be able to do it in an enjoyable way, although I realised that it would involve a lot of time and energy and some money (which was now at a low ebb). A couple of trips to Scotland: the first a solo trip around the mountains around Taynuilt – Ben Cruachan, Ben Eunaich and the White Mounth then more peaks in Glencoe and the Cairngorms.

As well as mountain walking I had the chance to climb in some interesting local quarries and crags with a new friend, John who looked like Frank Zappa with his long curly hair and moustache and skin-tight pink leggings. He was working towards his ML too, and we added a TLA (three letter acronym) to our aspirations: the SPA – Single Pitch Award. The SPA[10] allows the holder to take groups climbing on single pitch crags and in conjunction with the ML and first aid certificate the holder of these awards becomes much sought after for this type of work. We wanted this.

My assessment started on the Monday, navigating around Tryfan and the Glyderau. On Tuesday we scrambled up North Gully, Bristly Ridge and the Gribin. Wednesday was a test of navigation around the Horns,

10   Now known as the RCI – Rock Climbing Instructor

Cwm Glas and on to Carnedd Ugain, carrying packs and in the mist. We camped at Cwm Lechog for night navigation. The next day rope work for security on steep ground in Cwm Tregalan, Bwlch y Saethau and environs before more rope work on the last day at Moel Barfedd. I was delighted to be awarded a 'Good Pass' for my efforts by Louise, senior instructor at Plas y Brenin.

The following weekend in Shrewsbury we awaited the arrival of thirty cyclists from Operation Raleigh, raising money as I had done. I had organised this as I still had connections with Raleigh. They were very keen to hear about my ML, and some potential imminent work was in the offing. This was perfect timing, as all the money had been spent: it was dole and climbing now.

At last I faced up to the inevitable truth. As partners my girlfriend and I had been together for 11 years of hard living, fun and adventures but the fire seemed to have eventually died out. I didn't want to go backwards now. She and I had been together a long time and had some great times and had also given each other space along the way; but the travelling together had really been close, too claustrophobic, our relationship had been smothered. We had both changed over our time together we had grown into different people from those two innocent young office workers of a decade ago and neither of us felt the compunction to rake over the embers of our relationship.

I moved out and went to live in Monkmoor Road, in the spare room of Paul Wilson's now estranged wife. Paul had moved out up on to a top floor flat in Kennedy Road, the posh part of Shrewsbury and Chink was lodging with him, having split from his girlfriend.

I had time to think about what I wanted to do. I liked meeting people, helping people, I liked being outside and I liked to travel.

I had the travel experience; now I wanted a formal qualification, a Bachelor of Arts degree I thought, and this would give me a chance to move on *and* up with my life. There was no time to sit and stare. Operation Raleigh contacted me about planning a route for the home coming of Ffyona Campbell, who was shining brightly in the media spotlight at that time. Ffyona had been walking round the world, the first woman to do so. Her route had started in John O'Groats some years back and taken her to Land's End. Then she had walked across the USA, Australia and was currently in Southern France, having walked the length of Africa and up through Spain. Time was of the essence, as Raleigh wanted to tie in with her publicity and boost their recruitment as a result. So a young lady from Head Office and I were dispatched to check the route from Dover up the East Coast to John O'Groats. Most of it would be done by checking maps and driving, and also there were local Raleigh support groups to contact along the way to make preparations.

In a logoed-up Mitsubishi Shogun, a great big 4x4, travelling up the country there was chance to get out and physically walk sections. One such 'recce' was to find a way through the north-eastern parts of Scotland without the hassle of having to go up the fast and dangerous A9, to the west of the Cairngorms, in the area around Dalwhinnie, the remote Monadlaith Mountains. I was dropped off, and a rendezvous was arranged along a minor road further north. I ran, navigating over gloriously wild terrain, as free as a bird. Cresting a ridge, I bounded up a small rocky tor, feeling fit and agile bouncing my way along it and made to jump off back onto the hillside heather. As I did so I jumped straight over an eagle that was feasting on a lamb, totally unaware of my approach. My sudden presence spooked it and it immediately rose and swooped away, an incredible moment of union with nature. I carried on, my heart pounding, and reached the rendezvous point with time to spare.

The job finished. I received pay for my services. It was late August.

I signed up for an Access Course at Shrewsbury College which commenced on Monday 12th September 1994. If you were in full-time education, you could sign on and get Housing Benefit. There were loads of us: the oxymoronic 'Mature Students' sat gathered round tables in the college canteen. Mick was our Sociology Lecturer: stereotypical small wiry leprechaun of a fellow with de rigueur odd-socks and wire framed spectacles, he conformed to the norm of nonconformity, but he was a brilliant lecturer, setting my thoughts down paths I had never imagined.

His mantra was "leave your preconceptions and agendas at the door"; and it worked. It changed the way I looked at the world, the way things happened in the establishment, religion, power, politics and education. Maths, English Literature and Communications, History and Computer Information Technology were all in the curriculum. The course aimed to bring mature students up to an academic standard to allow them to compete on even terms with young students fresh from 'A' levels.

Lectures were most days and assignments and exams and books to read and seminars to attend. Towards the end of the course, though, I realised I needed remedial lessons on the basics of computing. The reason was that the lessons were on a Wednesday, and every Wednesday I had been in bed with a bored housewife. She was blonde quirky and interesting and fun and vibrant, sexy and captivating.

One evening I was invited around to her house for a meal. She answered the door wearing just a collarless night shirt and served a pleasant meal on a small round table. 'Would you like dessert?!' she purred. She brought a huge gateau out of the fridge and plonked it down on the table then lifted her shirt and sat in it! She was gorgeous and it was great fun but I was determined not to get trapped 'on the rebound' and kept the heavy stuff at arms' length to make time for my studies.

One of the first things we had to do at College was to apply for UCAS –University and Colleges Admission Service. We were slightly taken aback by this as many of us were pretty academically raw. With tutor guidance and a computer-generated questionnaire that used your responses to match your personality and ambitions, most of us could work our way through it. I thought seriously about following my interest in English but eventually decided on Outdoor Education. On the course I became friendly with Mark. Mark had been a motorcycle mechanic and was a canoeist, a kayaker, a skier and a general outdoorsman and we got on well. There were courses at Bangor University (with Science) and The University of Strathclyde – Outdoor Education in the Community. Mark and I applied to both places and were both accepted by both. We went to Bangor and found the course interesting, but, for me anyway, it wasn't far enough away. I knew Snowdonia well, and I knew I would be tempted home too often. Strathclyde offered me a break with the past and a chance to reinvent myself. I was serious and this was my chance. Since leaving BT any time at home when not travelling had ended in serious drinking and partying, all good fun, but I wanted to see what I was really capable of; I needed a 'reincarnation', a challenge.

As the year of college progressed, so did the workload. Immersing myself in it helped me formulate ideas and start thinking about a future, and to drink less. The academic rigour was something I rose to, and I had to be organised with my time so as to be able to fit climbing in. I was aware that the course in Glasgow would be populated with climbers and, as I didn't think of myself as typically gifted, I knew that I must gain a lot of logbook experience by time I went there in the September of 1995, as there were higher qualifications to be worked for after the ML and SPA, and many of the others would be climbing harder than I could: they would be the natural climbers for whom it would be easy. They I surmised would subsequently be first in line for the good jobs afterwards. That was my how I thought it would work, and how I sold myself the challenge.

Andy, a teacher friend of mine, had been helpful with technical details as I had been preparing for my ML, as had Edwin, a neighbour and guru of knots and carabiners. Andy offered me the chance to assist leading a group round the Cairngorms on a Gold Duke of Edinburgh Award. I really enjoyed the trip, and we camped in the hills and under the Shelter Stone one night. Back home there were a couple more farewell parties before I left to head north.

Chapter 10

I Belong Tae Glasgee

An Academic Journey

The Ford Escort overheated as I drove down Great Western Road in Glasgow, but I had arrived, carrying all my worldly possessions with me. Entering Jordanhill Campus, University of Strathclyde felt a bit like the first day at school. I took a deep breath and went in boldly. These Halls of Residence were purpose-built, an Edwardian era red brick building that had originally housed female trainee teachers from all over Scotland. The remit had changed slightly, as now we 'Outdoor Eddies' were also permitted under its roof. We were one part of a triple degree – Sport, Arts and Outdoor Education in the Community. We all had our own lectures in our specialisms, and then we came together *'en masse'* for the joint 'Community' parts of it - modules such as Community Education, Psychology, Sociology, Marketing, Management, Computing and related subjects.

University finance had changed; grants had been replaced with student loans. On the plus side, I was entitled to the 'mature students' allowance'. Dad was very pleased that I was to continue my education, even after a 15 year break, and he very generously promised me £300 a term, and also helped me when I bought Mark's old Mk 3 Ford Escort car, the first car I had owned. Now with transport, and money coming in, I could concentrate on the course.

The majority of the students in the Halls were young ladies from around Scotland preparing to be Primary Teachers under the auspices of the Scottish Education system. In Scotland most start University at 17 years old. Many of us Outdoor Eddies were mature students, and Mark and I were the oldest, along with a grumpy Dundonian who had been in the Outdoor industry for a long time already. Mark decided to rent a static caravan away up on the shores of Loch Lomond over the winter and commute in from there. That suited his personality. I decided to take the offer of halls of residence, I wanted to be among people. There were a few of us older students in halls. Aged 33 I was coming late into outdoor education (I didn't realise how valuable my life experience would be). Most of my new colleagues had experience of working in an outdoor centre or at some sort of residential establishment. There was a buzz about the place from us, a crowd of likeminded people who had come together in the hope that we could be doing something good and useful. The thing was, although, my ML qualification was well respected, I had not realised at the time how important it was: probably a good thing, as I hadn't taken any stress along with me when I did it, just a thirst for knowledge.

There was another 'ML' on the course: Chris, mid-twenties, from Northumberland. Chris was a paddling guru and had many qualifications to his name – NGBs, – National Governing Body Awards. Many disciplines: windsurfing, kayaking, archery, canoeing, skiing, mountain biking, climbing, orienteering, hillwalking are individually governed.

These awards were sought by students separately from the Degree, which was an academic 'standalone' course that had been introduced in the 1980's as one of the recommendations of The Scarman Report. Commissioned after the riots of 1981. The report noted the involvement of disaffected predominently black inner-city youths disenfranchised from society, some of whom were behind the unrest. Our goal was to find ways to reach out to these and other groups, working with social agencies, listen to their issues and look for ways to assimilate: from a fractured society into a new multicultural Britain. Attaining this degree would prepare us to work with people in these communities, other 'at risk' people, people with disabilities, or anyone interested in the outdoors. Peter, our German friend on the course, encapsulated it in an early philosophy seminar, using, in the words loved by Outward Bound, a Chinese proverb:

'Give a man a fish, you feed him for a day; teach him to fish, you feed him for a lifetime.'

This was the first time I had heard this proverb. Metaphorically we would be teaching people to fish. Much was going on, and there were many issues to try and understand and to address. I loved the sense of purpose, and also how many of my new friends, although only young, were seasoned hands at this game, and how things were nearly always conducted with good humour, intelligence, integrity and fun. Heavy concepts were carried with a lightness of being. There was also an element of 'challenge by choice', and, as long as you tried, you could go as far as you wished with an activity, and to reinforce learning we could all try and teach one another along the way.

As a qualified ML, I took some of my class out on the hill to do navigation, security on steep ground rope work and related mountain skills on Curved Ridge, Buachaille Etive Mor (Gaelic for 'The Great Shepherd of Etive'). This mountain guards the head of Glencoe, and would become a place we would return to time and time again, always to find a different ascent of its labyrinthine walls, gullies, faces and slabs.

To reciprocate I was kitted up in a wet suit and taken out with the kayaking group. I tried, but I was hopeless. I found the rivers frightening. I wasn't a very good swimmer, and when the boat capsized, as it inevitably did, I was not good at climbing out underwater in the freezing cold and dark, the shock taking my breath away and panic closing in. I did try, and I went down some great rivers and I loved the view from the cockpit. The riverbank is a wonderful thing, but I asked myself the question: could I ever see myself being competent enough to lead a group on this type of water – and the answer was a resounding NO! The kayakers who looked after me were great and patient, non-judgmental and skilled in what they did. Afterwards I did gain some competence in an open canoe, but only on lakes, lochs and easier rivers. I learnt from my kayak instructor mates, their style of coaching - but I knew I wouldn't be following them.

Orienteering and climbing and gaining more logbook experience for higher mountain awards was the direction I wanted to go: it seemed a pretty clear pathway, as long as I could attain the standard; and it was great fun going out to gain this experience. Gaining these awards might allow me to work in many different theatres, even to work in the bigger mountains overseas, with a diverse range of client groups – that was my plan.

As a driver I was in the minority with Mark, Gavin and Chris, out of 20 plus of us. I was happy to take people in my car, and I could also drive the college minibuses, which was a bonus. I organised a winter trip up to Torridon where people teamed up to climb and learn new skills. Trips were also organised to the Cairngorms, and on one occasion I skipped a few lectures to fill my logbook up with some climbing around the Glencoe area and Creag Meaghaidh with Spadge, who had come up north for a few days. The climbing was always for a reason now: to try harder routes, to become au fait with rope techniques and placing anchors, to navigate, to discuss group safety, and build stamina, although that was not how our dedication sometimes came across. Of those who observed from afar, some thought we were just having lightweight fun and games, which was not the case at all. Serious technical skills were being taught and learnt.

My main climbing partner was fellow student Big Al. Twenty-four years old, Al had been in the Navy and had been on the front line in 1990 in the Gulf War. He had seen men die in front of him when aged just 19. But Al was a big, gregarious, competent, intelligent friend. He loved mountains and like me, held no ambition for any water-based awards. He was aiming for his ML and SPA and wanted to take things further. He was serious about it, and this attitude would help him overcome the fact that, again like me, he wasn't the best; but he more than made up for that with ambition energy and drive. Al was a good influence and, although still gaining qualifications, he was vastly experienced and a good teacher to some of the younger fellow students, and he took care not to patronise them.

During this first year at University there were many many trips away; every weekend we went somewhere. Al, our friend Brendan and I drove up to the Cairngorms as the mercury hit -27°C in Glasgow and the place ground to a standstill. We carried supplies into Bob Scott's bothy, using our ice axes to hack chunks from the frozen River Dee to melt for water. We stayed there four nights, and climbed on Coire Sputan Dearg and Beinn Bhreach.

Paul Wilson was up with a crowd in tow when we returned to Glasgow, and he had tickets for a Shooglenifty gig at The Fruit Market in Glasgow. It had warmed up considerably by time we got there. We jumped around; stage dived, jigged and reeled. The band were imperious.

Gigs were the exception now. The focus was on university work and exploring the Highlands, including midweek sorties if the schedule allowed. Al, Nina Sylvia and I found the Secret Howff, the mythical bothy hidden away high in a glen towards Beinn a'Bhuird. Another couple of nights were spent in Ben Alder Cottage right in the centre of the Highlands. Peaks around Loch Tulla were climbed from a base of Gorton Bothy, hidden treasures tucked away above Glencoe, and more out of the way places: Stob Coire Nan Lochan, Stob Coire nan Beith, Liathach Ridge Torridon, Streap Ridge, Glenfinnan, and many more, eagerly sought out.

First year placements were organised for the spring. Classmate Katie and I were to attend the Calvert Trust, near Keswick in The Lake District. The Trust specialises in outdoor activities for special needs groups, especially those with limited mobility. We learnt about abseiling people in wheelchairs, zip lines and sailing twin canoes down Bassenthwaite Lake with modifications for wheelchairs. The Uphill Ski Club used the centre, and there was a group of guys who had all been paralysed in motorbike accidents. They were fearless. We pushed them up to the top of Dodd, the hill behind the centre, and they just let their brakes off and hurtled down the slope until they bounced out or turned the chairs over, laughing all the way! To them there seemed nothing to lose, and they could regain some of their love of adrenalin. We were there for five weeks before returning to Jordan Hill for more lectures and assignments.

Gavin Burke came to visit. He, Al and I went to Ben Nevis and nearly ended this story with the rock fall on Raeburn's Arete described in the prologue. We returned to Jordanhill with a mixture of renewed respect for the dangers of mountaineering. On the noticeboard at Jordanhill was a job advert for a summer camp. The work was outdoor instructing at Concord College, Acton Burnell, Shropshire. I had never heard of the place, but Mark and I, as locals, were obviously very interested; so, with a year's worth of experience under our belts, we went to investigate and we both got jobs there that summer.

As we drove up to the intimidating Doric columns of the entrance and walked in to a wood panelled study we wondered if we were in the right place. Concord College is an International School that runs a summer school for students to learn English. Our job was to provide outdoor activities for them in the evenings and also during some lesson times so they could start to gain a basic command of English. At weekends we would organise local trips out to climb hills or go rafting on the Severn or caving at Llanymynech. Despite a very hectic schedule there were chances to fraternise with the other teaching staff.

Back in Glasgow, if I wanted to go south for the weekend I found the best way was to leave after lectures on a Friday afternoon and get the bus down to Bothwell services on the M74. A short walk and a quick sidle over the parapet into Bothwell services, thumb out, and, hey presto! I was heading south with the rush hour traffic. Once in the motorway system, it usually didn't take long to get a ride. The best way was to look clean and tidy, have a sign stating a hoped-for destination. A rope coiled on the top of the pack helped too. I couldn't afford to go up and down in my own car every time, although I had worked as a labourer on a building site after the Concord work finished and had managed to save a couple of hundred pounds. This got me to many places to climb. I was up and down the country as there were also three weddings, within weeks of each other, to attend: I was best man at Chink's wedding and Spadge married Rhi, a music teacher colleague.

Gavin Burke had met Nimmy at a Buddhist retreat in Taplow, Oxfordshire. Gavin, from Maldon in Essex, was a charmer: open, handsome, louche, but with an easy laugh. Nimmy was quite possibly the first black person admitted to the nobility of Britain, the adopted daughter of the Duke and Duchess of Richmond. She was making a career in the theatre and television, and she was that unusual mix of raucous and principled. Together they were a golden couple setting the world on fire. Gav had invited me, Chink and Rob, plus partners, Paul Wilson (Paul and Gavin had got on like a house on fire from their first meeting), Paul's daughter Moya and many friends. The wedding was held at Goodwood House, the ancestral seat, near Chichester on Saturday 21ˢᵗ September 1996. I had driven down via Shrewsbury picking up passengers, and we stayed with an old bookseller friend of Paul's who lived nearby. We stayed up until the early hours, Paul and friend coaching me with the lines I was learning for the ceremony.

On the morning of the wedding I set out early and, as I parked the old Escort, I looked up to see Goodwood House in all its glory. I felt insignificant walking up the driveway and the butterflies were really starting to kick in. A Buddhist ceremony involves a lot of symbolism and presents of love from one partner to the other. Nimmy's friend, Sharon D. Clarke MBE, sang a song to Gavin as Nimmy's present to him. Over the years Gav had heard various poetic recitations of mine, mainly vulgar, but nevertheless, undeterred had asked me to read a poem to Nimmy. I read 'Phenomenal Woman' by Maya Angelou. Reciting poetry in such a setting, in such esteemed company, gave me great pleasure to be so honoured. The meal, the speeches, the drinking, the dancing, taking place in one of the premier stately homes of Britain, was almost surreal. Famous people were there, with plenty of showbiz panache mixing with the great and the good and the highest and the richest. And us!

We camped in the quadrangle, and the next morning a polite cough indicated that heads should be pushed skywards through opened tent flaps.

"Would Sir care for some bacon and eggs?" the Butler enquired; served on gold leaf china too!

I sold the Escort and bought an old Toyota HiAce Van for £250. It had a red and white striped pop up roof and looked like a Punch and Judy show when parked up. I envisioned it being used a lot over the winter, as now I could take a few more of us away at weekends, and we could split the fuel costs.

Joanna had dark hair, a 'Minnie the Minx' attitude, and was a 20 year old music student at Jordan Hill. Sitting in the library one day, she decided the next two people that came in would be her flatmates for the next year. And that was how Lee Kelly (20, a tough Geordie, funny, kayaker of waterfalls and drinker of anything) and I came to be sharing a flat with her just off the Byres Road in the west end of Glasgow, near all the pubs and clubs. Whatever could go wrong?!

We had a themed fancy dress party, dress up as something beginning with 'B'. Joanna was 'bubble wrapped', Lee was a Buddhist monk, and I was a Bee. Paula and two of her friends came up from Shrewsbury to visit. I felt a *frisson* of tension with her as we had only recently met and she had driven 300 miles to visit. We all trooped to the end of our road to the Volcano Club (as featured in the film 'Trainspotting'), and were up most of the night before climbing aboard the van and heading out towards Rannoch Moor. Disgorging ourselves, the first hurdle was a night crossing of an in-spate tributary flowing into Loch Tulla. Al and I crossed it eleven times; making sure everyone was safely across. Then it was a five mile walk to the bothy in the dark, the wind and the rain for a soggy night's sleep and then back again the next morning, still wet. As we drove south a gust of wind blew the pop up roof up, and those in the back had to hold it down with climbing slings. The visiting girls were not impressed, and this was a reminder to me of how far away I had moved from my old life. They were convinced I was very eccentric.

Studying had to be done late in the library, as there was little chance for this in the flat. I found out about a job as a bouncer working at the Lime Club off Sauchiehall Street. They paid £5 an hour, which was good, although the hours went on until 3 or 4 in the morning. On the first night there was a fight and, with just two of us working, it was hard to control, especially since I had no previous experience. I took the violence personally. I shouldn't have, but with a massive Glaswegian face to face, telling me he was going to kill me I was taking no chances. After a nervous walk back through the dark streets of Glasgow, I slept with my ice axe under my pillow.

About 3 hours later, Al, Chris and I went to climb Ben Lui, and I was warned about how easy it would be for a black mark to be on my police record as a result of being involved in some ruckus such as this, and, if that happened, how it would then be very hard to find work as an instructor. Those comments made me think on, but Al applied for a job at the Lime Club too and, perhaps given his military background, soon found himself chief doorman.

We were always on the lookout for work to help pay for our travels to the mountains, beer, food, rent and to replace worn climbing gear and equipment. Tom, one of the senior course directors, came to us one day with a proposal. There was an ongoing project surveying the primary schools of East Renfrewshire Council with a view to producing orienteering maps. Al, Sylvia, Peter and I got the contract. We called ourselves PASS mapping services. Sylvia and I would go out and survey the school buildings and grounds with a measuring device, and then Peter and Al would turn this data into a map that the school could use for teaching orienteering. We did a fair bit of orienteering at this time; but second year Winter Placement was coming, a time where everyone would go their separate ways for a few weeks. Mine was arranged from 15th February until 21st March 1997.

I had contacted Mountain Craft of Glenfinnan, a small company run by Simon. Simon organised week long courses teaching winter skills, use of ice axe and crampons, and also more advanced climbing courses, either as an introduction or guiding on some of the classic winter mountain routes. Being on placement, my main role was to observe and write a logbook, reports and assignments for Uni. I did not possess the requisite qualifications to lead, the minimum being the Winter ML. I could be a 'mock student', though: I could be towed up and down by 'short rope' aspirants; and there were chances for me to do this and demonstrate techniques for step cutting, ice axe arrests, avalanche slope and profile assessment, navigation, belay construction and other skills under supervision.

University friends Aaron, Mike and I shared digs for the time we were up in Fort William. We lodged with an old couple. The three of us stayed in an attic room. They were skiing and snowboarding, and I was mountaineering, so every evening we would come back with soaking wet gear to drape about the place, soaked to the skin. Scottish winters sometimes have lovely dry clear sunny cold days, but mainly it's day after day of sleet, rain, hail, snow, wind, cold, battering wind, ice and perhaps the occasional glimpse of blue sky. Either way, our placement was always memorable.

Hit and miss days with the weather included a great day on Dinner Time Buttress in Glencoe; then a *'foul, foul, foul day'* at the CIC hut, compounded by having toothache. After a few days going west to get the better of the weather, we were short roping, stomper belays and glissading – sliding down, sometimes in control. I was allowed to lead some sessions under the watchful eye of a qualified winter instructor. Doing this allowed me to deliver a curriculum, something that had to be done, be witnessed, supervised and reported on for the university. There was also a Marketing assignment that had to be completed, questionnaires to be compiled, photocopied and distributed, collected, collated and decoded, all done without missing a day on the hill. It was full-on hard work, but exactly what I wanted to do. I decided to try for The Winter ML and to do the compulsory training. Al, now a qualified ML, and Chris joined me.

I had been working with instructors Tim and Will, who were generous with sharing their expertise. The placement ended on 21st March and I went to Knoydart for a solo trip to wind down and climb some of the Munros there. The day before the winter course started there was news that Tim, the generous instructor, was dead. Tim had been with clients on Point Five Gully when he slipped and fell. The next day, Saturday 5th April, there was much better news: Chink was a Dad, and I was an uncle to Dan, a healthy bouncing boy. The yin and the yang of life.

The Winter ML training course was compulsory before going for assessment. The weather was much kinder, but the warmth was stripping the snow from the mountains around Glencoe so we travelled to the Cairngorms for short roping, night navigation, safe snow-holing and attendant skill acquisition and instruction. I hadn't been able to work whilst on placement, so back to bouncing I went to refill the coffers (earning £74 for the week ending 9th May). There were assignments to do for Placement, Tourism, Research Methods; and a group of Norwegians were over on a university visit, and we had been 'volunteered' to take them gorge scrambling. There were Environmental Education lectures, and a Health Related Fitness assignment to complete. I was learning to windsurf for a module, and also managed to do some day coastal navigation on a yacht. In addition Al and I guided a group of Gavin's Buddhist mates on the Three Peaks, going south to north – Snowdon, Scafell Pike and Ben Nevis, on which they chanted all the way up. There was so much going on that studying and essay writing had to be done whilst travelling; but we all seemed determined to squeeze as much out of every opportunity as we could.

In the Jordanhill canteen the slogan 'Cool Britannia' was everywhere. I had not had the time to rue or reminisce on my time as the union man, as politics had slid off my radar completely. On May 1st Labour won a landslide majority in the General Election. This was the New Labour of Tony Blair and Gordon Brown, Blair having taken over as leader following the untimely death of John Smith.

I had noticed a gap in the timetable of our third year. Placement was scheduled for the autumn, and there were no lectures from late October until the Spring Term started in the January. I told Al, Tracey and Nina of my idea: I argued that if we could all arrange summer placements, then the late autumn would be free for us to go away somewhere and do something exciting for several weeks. Al and I now had the skills, and we thought South America would be great, if we could afford it. None of us had signed up for third year accommodation, so we found a static caravan park in Stepps, near to Glasgow that we could rent by the week. From there we could attend the few lectures that we were slated for in September and October; store our stuff in Al's loft and away we would go. Additionally Laurentian University in Sudbury, Ontario had a study programme reciprocating with our University called Adventure Leadership (ADVL). I signed up to go there in early January through until April, convincing myself I could afford this too if I worked hard over the summer.

Joanna had a Canadian friend, Marcie, who came to stay: blonde, young, and of course lovely. Al, Brendan and I took her along on a trip to the Rosa Pinnacle on Arran to climb its multi-pitch granite. Despite never having climbed before, she was a natural, and got on well with us, even buying her own round in the pub. A Glencoe trip started in the King's House on Rannoch Moor below Buachaille Etive Mor. Al and I were intent on climbing Shackle Route, a multi-pitch route on the mountain at about 'Severe' standard. Marcie was happy to join another group who were going to find their way along the Aonach Eagach Ridge which defines the northern side of Glencoe, a mighty ridge with bits of airy scrambling along the way and plenty of exposure. It wasn't every night that we drank so much, but on this particular occasion we did. Probably we were showing off. Early next morning Al and I found the bottom of our route but, despite the walk-in, we were still drunk, and Al had forgotten his rock shoes.

Extract from my diary:

'Ever resourceful, I said that I would lead the first pitch, remove my boots, drop them down on a bight of rope, and then he could second. This worked, but the boots pained Al so much that he had to remove them and retrieve his training shoes from the rucksack he carried before we could continue. Doing this in our eyrie of a sentry box proved uneventful if a tad comical. But then he pulled the ropes up. In doing so he accidentally punched me in the face, causing one of my contact lenses to fall out. How I managed to catch it on the breeze whilst jammed and roped into a 'sentry box' hundreds of feet above the ground I do not know. Not only that, but I put it back in again! We had to give up on our original route and veer and scramble our way up.

The day was gorgeous, and by time we were on the summit the beer was sweating out nicely. We jogged on and descended by way of Laggan Garbh to the A82 where we hitched a lift, dropping us at the start of the Aonach Eagach. We carried our rack and ropes all the way along it, catching the other group up, then down for a thirst quencher in the Clachaig Inn before hitching back to get the van. Being the driver meant longer hours of concentration, and I insisted that anyone (although it was usually Al) sitting in the passenger seat should stay awake and talk to me. It was good for stamina, but also meant that I had to really focus on my assignments and try and stay awake to find time to study.

There was no let-up, and we rose to the challenge. I wasn't aware of anyone in our gang using anything other than the natural sustenance of coffee to keep awake. There was even a 'Mr Jordanhill' to attend on Friday 23rd May which involved some streaking as several of us joined in the fun.

My current squeeze at the time was one of the Community Art students, and her first climb was Great Ridge on Garbh Beinn on the Ardtornish Peninsula. The climb is a vegetated multi-pitch climb of 'Very Difficult' standard, 410 m/1350ft in length, not the best idea for a beginner; and, being scared, she cried all the way up. I led most of it, finding protection sparse, but Al was there with her. They both cursed me together. After the climb she and I continued down to Ardtornish House on the end of the peninsula overlooking Mull. Paul Wilson was there holding court at his annual May retreat.

Then it was thumb out hitching and back to nightclub bouncing. The run-up to the end of term was relentless: exams and essays and deadlines. The Course Triathlon the day after the May Ball; with the 28 km run was hard with no improvement on my second place of the previous year. The next day the van died in Aberfoyle. I just left it there and hitched home.

Results were coming in and there were a good smattering of Merits. Dad was happy to come up and help me move out of the flat now I was without transport. Brendan and I took him up to a bothy in the woods above Ballachulish where a great amount of ganja was being smoked by the inebriates therein. The following day we fairly floated up Curved Ridge. I was impressed with Dad's ability, now retired and recently down to one kidney. Back in Glasgow we said goodbye to Marcie and Jo and drove south for another summer working at Concord College.

I had no outgoings and could save my money for the forthcoming trip to Peru. Mark was working elsewhere that summer, and Tracey got his job. Everyone loved Tracey, such a bubbly vibrant person. Luckily for me she had water qualifications, so we could work together well. Tracey was coming to South America with us. Although there wasn't much of it, any down-time we could find together I spent with a fun young English teacher.

Things were set for a summer of hard work. We organised the kids' activities. Logbooks would be filled in for University, and assignments drafted; reports would be written for Concord, and all would be good. Stu and Jane came and brought the Morris Dancers so these International Students could appreciate something of our British culture. On August 12th I paid for the Peru trip, and the Concord work finished on the 17th. Coincidentally Ms. English Teacher was leaving that day to go to Ecuador for a year to work. I headed down to Pembroke to climb with Spadge and Rhi for my birthday. A few days later Princess Diana was killed in the car crash in Paris.

The month of September was spent pretty much camping in and around the hills of Scotland, footloose and fancy free, to save money: climbing on Ben Nevis; soloing Tower Ridge in an hour and a half; Glencoe; the Inaccessible Pinnacle on Skye; the Southern Rough Bounds of Knoydart; sleeping on friends' floors in Glasgow so as to be able to do some more bouncing work at The Lime Club. On Monday 29th September we all moved into the caravan park at Stepps, and our third year at Jordanhill started again the next day.

Beinn Artair or 'The Cobbler' is an anvil-shaped hill a few miles west of Loch Lomond in the Arrochar Alps, and it was on this hill that Glaswegian shipbuilders in the 1930's would come and climb, travelling up after work on a Saturday and sleeping rough. One of their number, Jock Nimlin, was the first to climb Recess Route, a five pitch 'severe'. Now, below it I made myself a harness out of slings, having forgotten mine, and Al and I climbed it with our friend Niall. The central summit of The Cobbler is a rocky tor with an 'eye of the needle' to be threaded to gain the peak. Some well spoken English school boys appeared up on the higher ground with us. By chance they were from Shrewsbury School, and their teacher was Martin and we got talking and arranged our ropes so as the lads could gain the summit proper in safety. There and then Martin offered me some overseas work with the school the next year: synchronicity in action. But first it was time to leave for South America.

Chapter 11

Unclimbed Peak

Soaring with Condors

Riding now on a tide of energy independence and enthusiasm as we were, the stage was set for a trip into the unknown. Although Al and I had been to Bolivia before on separate trips the area we wanted to explore was unknown to us and rarely visited by westerners. Al had read articles about the fabled Quimsa Cruz (Three Crosses), a climber's paradise of vertical granite walls, remote and difficult to access. We went to the IGS – a military establishment in La Paz — where we found maps of the area. A public bus, in true South American style took Al, Nina, Tracey and me to the town of Viloco to begin our climb. The story is condensed from my journals of November and December 1997.

3ʳᵈ Nov. Nina was ill. Well, it was her birthday. We had all been celebrating to the max. Al, Tracey and I managed to stagger up Curved Ridge yesterday. Despite this I still felt hungover. At 3:45am the taxi arrived. I'm sure I left my crampons somewhere in Al's loft, but I had his spare pair. Tracey packed some stuff for Nina and we carried her downstairs to the taxi and away we went into the dreich Glasgow night.

5ᵗʰ Nov. Peru. The Badlands were passing the bus window: cactus, desolation, desert. Eventually we reached Arequipa. Sitting in the 'Nigth Video Pub' the menu offered Cat's fingernail, Burnt Octopus, Biting Cream, Fungus Cream, Alligator Pear Packed. We had a picnic on the grass outside.

9ᵗʰ Nov. Mad dreams. I'm running and grasping on to the street furniture and being very energetic, and still people walk casually by in the same direction but I can't keep up with them.

12ᵗʰ Nov. In the Torino Hotel, La Paz, Bolivia, 3500m. By chance Al bumped into his German friend Jens, who is an authority on the Quimsa Cruz.

Jens was really helpful and gave us pictures of the area – it is impressive – rock spires, granite walls, vivid green lagunas. I awoke in the night with hideous stabbing chest pains, lack of breath, shallow pulse. It persisted all night, but I suspected it was only a blockage from some food.

14ᵗʰ __Nov__. On the bus. Two little kids sat with their mother in the aisle next to me. They were snotty-nosed and rosy-cheeked, encased from head to toe in woollens. The oldest, a boy of about four, managed to get some chewing gum caught in his hair. I got the small scissors from my pen knife to extract it; the boy sat calmly, but an old lady nearby (probably his Granny) looked worried. We stopped for lunch.

A small crowd gathered, pointing at my huge yeti-gaiter encased plastic boots. They were the cause of much mirth and merriment. I pretended they were 'electronic boots' and acted as though they controlled my movements. Much clowning around and laughter. A pair of condors circled overhead. After four more hours of bumping and screeching brakes along teetering mountain roads we neared Viloco – the end of the road.

Viloco is a mining community and appears exceptionally poor – desperate almost – but clings faithfully to its two churches. We managed to contact a local man who was willing to drive us up to the estancia of Coyamacayo at the end of a very steep and torturous track, for a fee. Maybe half a dozen tin miners stay there. The communally owned American Jeep was a vintage c. 1950. We jumped from the back and shouldered our humungous packs. An hour later we were bivvying, brew on, at 4500m with a stunning sunset. Warm drizzle through the night.

15ᵗʰ __Nov.__ We were remote. Out there. In the Boonies. The slog up to the old miners' track took its toll. We were galvanised by views towards 'Pico Penis' (Pico Obelisco), a one hundred meter granite obelisk that marked the second pass we had to climb over. Walking through Torrini Chico and Gross Mauer humbled us, as if discovering a hidden Yosemite. This natural architecture is stunning, and the rock is beautiful granite with quartz crystals. The sun shone and did its damage; we were wilting. By the time Al and I dropped into the 'Biwak' site – across a boulder field by a tiny laguna, we were shattered.

We went back about an hour later to see how the girls were. They were not good. We crawled into a cave (our bivouac site) and brewed up nonstop for four hours. We were all in our bags by 7:15 pm, exhausted.

*16ᵗʰ **Nov.** Tracey was awake all night with symptoms similar to those I had suffered in La Paz (perhaps there was something in this 'altitude sickness' after all). Nina vomited but felt slightly better. Al was not good either. I was the only one who felt okay.*

I went on a recce to look for a route up Cuervo Diablo (Raven Devil), which Jens assured us went at about 'Severe'. I couldn't see a thing. The sky hadn't cleared, but the temperature had dropped. I scrambled for an hour above camp and saw a view towards another peak at about 9am. Was there a way up it?

I am sitting on an old moraine, on my own, the most amazing rock spires imaginable are all around. I arrived about thirty minutes ago. Since then cloud has enveloped everything. Large rocks crash down nearby, but I feel strangely calm.

In the cloud, back down at the tent everyone was still ill. By the afternoon Nina was well enough to slog up a scree slope with me in the hope that we would see some more of this incredible landscape. Back at camp I persuaded Al that he should come and look.

*17ᵗʰ **Nov.** The scree was not easy. It took the four of us three times as long as it took me yesterday. Still misty. We played charades for an hour waiting for a break in the cloud. Eventually Al and I went to the bottom of the cliff to spy a route. The mountain unveiled itself; a brief glimpse but it was enough. I actually made a decision! Climbing it was possible. Only two of us could do it; four was too many. It was a harsh decision, but Nina and Tracey gave us water and chocolate and said goodbye. We went to the rock and got on with it.*

Al led the first pitch – about 4b – in trainers and with his pack. He had no spare clothes or torch and very little food. The next two pitches were a rising traverse into a basin, easy enough. Then I lead a chimney, a mixed pitch. We then moved up leftwards to gain our gully. By now it was already early afternoon; we had started way too late. But the mist had lifted and we could see a route.

The next two pitches took us up a gully. Loose rock, melting ice, slings on spikes for protection, quite a bit of flak coming down. We had an axe and a hammer between us, but only my plastic boots for progress on ice!

I brought Al up the last of the mixed ground before the col, and he led easily up to it. Now we had a conundrum. It was 5pm. The route to the summit looked very complex – do we go for it? To descend now would put us in the firing line from loose rock and ice melted by the afternoon sun. Abseiling at night with one headtorch was not a good idea. It was going to be a cold enforced bivouac at 5200m: neither of us had sleeping bags.

The next two pitches weaved around precariously perched blocks and across ribbons of ice. It was no fun for Al to follow me as I couldn't organise much protection. As I had boots I failed to realise the fragile nature of his progress in cold wet trainers. He grimaced, then followed me to a sentry box belay from where I could see the summit.

'It's easy from here,' I told him.

He wasn't convinced. I tried a line that stayed on rock, albeit up very thin ledge… we were on the summit area amid jagged thirty foot pinnacles, easy enough to solo. As Al came up, the most magnificent backdrop was captured on film. On the summit rocks I shivered, partly with emotion and dry-retched due to the sun and lack of food and water. We toasted ourselves, Nina and Tracey, and our safe return, with whisky from the hipflask my brother gave me.

We decided to bivi at our last belay site. We laid the ropes, slings and harnesses down and topped it snuggly with a tin foil blanket. We donned all our clothing. Right on cue a thunder storm rolled in. Spectacular bolts of lightning flew across the sky. Two inches of snow fell while we shivered, ate some chocolate, a peak bar and stale bread and cheese.

__18th Nov.__ By 5am it was light enough to distinguish details on our black and white platform. In the early morning light the mountains we saw now appeared ethereal. Our mountain fell away below us more steeply than I remembered from last night.

Abseiling onto a small gap by the sentry box involved some strange manoeuvres. From a superb block we could abseil through a crack and back into the main gully. Al went first, but it was an awkward off-balance situation. I was falling asleep. Eventually Al called that he was safe.

I tied a prussik, but as I went over the edge I realised it was one of those that jams. Struggling to contain the panic that was welling up inside me, I remembered that my knife was under two layers, out of reach. I just managed to keep it together long enough. Al understood my gesticulations and I hauled his knife up on the slack rope, cut myself free and abbed into the gully. Having regained my composure, after the next abseil the ropes jammed. I prusiked back up 50m, cut some tat, threaded it and abbed back down again.

Al had just abbed pitch four of the route when a massive stone fall tore past us, missing us both by inches. Cowering, with hands over helmet and the smell of cordite fresh in the nostrils is a lonely, scary feeling. We were both frustrated and nervous by our slow progress across the traverse, exposed to the elements.

By the corner we had some route finding problems. It was snowing hard and we had been abseiling for seven hours. As Al leaned back the tat started to roll off the rounded spike. I grabbed the ropes. He was safe but we were in bits, shot to pieces.

An hour later we were back where we left Nina and Tracey. We packed the ropes and headed down the moraine and boulder field in a gathering blizzard.

I didn't really contemplate that we had achieved a first ascent in less than favourable conditions. I was thinking about a Sunday afternoon pub lunch…'

Within a few days of our climb, my first-ever 'first ascent' we were away again, this time down to the salt desert of Southern Bolivia: the Salar de Uyuni, near the border with Chile. Organising a lift into the wild in a jeep, no roads, just dust we pitched my very dated 'Phoenix Phreedome' tent fly over an old dry stone llama pen. From here we went out and climbed Cerro Caquella, a very remote peak (5947m, 19,510ft). We saw a few local llama herders, but nobody else. The mountain was interesting as it had snow ice formations of 'penitentes', strangely shaped natural phenomena so called as they have a similar shape to monks at prayer. The penitentes slowed our laborious progress further, but the view across the desert was incredible. We were as high as the summit of Kilimanjaro. Around us we could see, way off, several peaks of similar height.

*****

In Lima there was a beauty pageant and each of the twenty-five departments that made up the country had been invited to send its favourite, most beautiful young female representative to the final. Although she did not win the pageant, Liliana looked amazing and aroused a lot of interest. In Lima a young buck called Ricardo started coming round to the family shop.

Family links with Pomabamba had always been strong, and Uncle Alfredo's restaurant 'Pomabamba' hosted many events for ex-pat *'Pomabambinos'*. The day-to-day restaurant is the typical long thin tin-roofed room entered off the street. Tarpaulins and wobbly wooden boards separate the kitchen from the diners. The long wooden tables stand on grimy tiles, and are spread with white table cloths and the 'de rigeur' pressed metal napkin holders, salt and pepper pots found in every restaurant in South America. Every meal is accompanied by bottles of beer and music from an ancient jukebox. 'Cuy' (Guinea Pig) is popular as are the other Peruvian dishes of 'Lomo Saltado' (Strips of marinated beef) and 'Ceviche' (Marinated raw fish, chillies, herbs and spices).

Next door to the 'day to day' restaurant is a small hall reserved for Sundays and special occasions. Immaculately dressed old friends and extended family would while away an afternoon, sitting on plastic chairs under the harsh old fluorescent strip-lights, by an unused stage with a fading façade and damp yellowed whitewash walls, but their kingdom nonetheless. Gathered there, eating guinea pig and potatoes and runner beans accompanied by crates of 'Cusqueña' beer in dusty bottles, the laughter and the joy of real family echoed as they relaxed in the knowledge of togetherness; but with someone always posted as a look-out out in the street outside, eyes alert.

*****

In Lima our climbing team went our separate ways. Al was flying home, he advised me to be wary, and then he was gone. Nina and Tracey were going to Machu Picchu, and I was going alone overland to Ecuador to visit my Concord girl friend, who was teaching in a town called Baños. I spent a last night in the Hostal Europa, faded colonial opulence, with a roof terrace and an old parrot on a perch for company, and not a suit and tie or a crate of beer in sight. Two parallel universes lay just streets away from each other: me in mine and Liliana in hers – oblivious to each other, unknown to each other unknowing of each other's existence, encapsulated as we both were in our own lives, our own hopes, our own dreams.

The bus was comfortable and it pulled away on time, taking the coast road north. I had been travelling for days, and still there were two more days to come on public transport. The most northerly big town in Peru is Tumbes, popular with whaling ships and crews a hundred years ago, where, according to an old sea shanty; a matelot could buy a whole brothel for a barrel of flour. Now it remained a Peruvian outpost for the ongoing mineral resources row with Ecuador. Leaving Tumbes alone in a big old American sedan from the 1950s, heading the few miles out of town to the border, I felt very alone. My taxi driver chewed on a cocktail stick and just slowly said the words: "Amigo, amigo, que pasa amigo?" I paid him in dollar, shouldered my pack and walked the lonely few hundred metres down the strip to the border post. Things were more tropical here, and poorer. The strip was lined with tin roofed shacks; I was being eyed from behind every cracked window or dark alley. I was the only gringo. How easy it would be for me to just disappear; no one would ever find any trace of me.

As calmly as I could, I pushed my passport towards the soldier on duty and my lips curled up in a fake nonchalance that I knew he could see straight through. In that languorous way of the outposted government official with so much time on his hands, he inspected every page, turning them slowly, one by one, methodically, before finding a random one to his liking. Then the stamp inked; and slowly again my lifeline was slid back across the table away from his rictus of contempt. I was in, there was no going back. I walked on another few hundred metres through the same grinding poverty, everywhere piercing eyes followed me.

All buses were going the same way – Quito. I paid and hunched down as inconspicuously as I could, not even bothering to think how I might extract myself from this death trap in the event of it plunging over a ravine. All my energy used up; I just had to be a passenger and let it go and sleep the sleep of the dead. Piles of rotting bananas lined the road as we twisted and turned under canopies of trees, but the air was sweeter now, and on through the night we went.

Quito is the second highest capital city after La Paz. I caught the connecting bus to Baños, and I was out in the main square, the Plaza de Armas and looking for my friend's guest house. I had travelled four days to see her, (but having moved on she wasn't impressed) so a single room nearby was rented. A saint's day parade next morning: I went outside to be part of it, the colour and the noise of marching band after marching band. People gathered and food stalls and beer stands sprung up. I had been vigilant on my travels, but on this night I had been spiked. Next morning, the smell of urine in my nostrils, my head pounding, kidneys aching and bruised I felt a massive head rush, as specks of gravel gradually came into focus. My watch had been taken. I tried to get to my feet among people going about their daily business. Disorientated, somehow I found my way back to my room. I slept fitfully, only to wake, grab my possessions and walk away.

Tungurahua towers over the town, an active volcano of over 5000m (16,400ft). A straightforward track led eventually to a mountain refuge where I stayed that night. The next day a disparate band of us made an early start, although I had no way of knowing the hour. We continued to the top where the ridge narrowed and we were in the snow above the cloud forest.

It was time to go home for Christmas. I bummed around, staying with friends where I could.

Chapter 12

Destiny Calling

Reaching Potential

Toronto in early January is cold. Up the highway in Sudbury -40C° is not uncommon on some nights. Sudbury is a mining town: not pretty. Algonquins of the Ojibwe tribe used to survive here, travelling the lakes in birch bark canoes in the summer months. Large deposits of nickel were discovered here in the 1880s; then the railway came. In 1960 Sudbury became home to Laurentian University, whose Adventure Leadership Course (ADVL) is twinned with The Outdoor Education in the Community course from the University of Strathclyde. I was met by Professor Bob Rogers, founding father and head of the ADVL program. During our first meeting Bob told me he had been a good friend of, and grown up with the singer Leonard Cohen. For a fleeting moment I was reminded of another world I used to inhabit, a world of music and instruments and voices, a world invariably accompanied by smoke and alcohol, pubs and parties. That world seemed removed from my more recent life; the main music to me now seemed to be the sound of the wind in the mountains and through the trees, the flapping of the tent fly, the hiss of the camping stove and my own solitary singing.

It was a modern purpose-built establishment spread out in its own grounds that stretched for miles and encompassed five lakes. Settling into the halls of residence was pretty welcoming. A couple of students from ADVL had been over to Scotland, and now called by to reintroduce themselves. Lectures were mainly in a big theatre for major topics like Ethics and Philosophy and Sport related programs. Other opt-in modules were taught in more intimate classrooms: subjects like Bases of Law and the History of Ontario. We had regular email contact with our supervisors back in Glasgow, and a shared syllabus framework kept a check on our work.

A self-contained campus gave every opportunity for study, with a good library and resource centre. The ADVL program had a good outdoor store of equipment including cross country skis and camping equipment. There was a bar on site, with visiting bands and comedians. There was rarely a need to leave the place and after the travelling that I had been doing recently I was happy to dwell here.

I met 'Kate', a tall willowy blonde in her mid twenties, passionate about experiences, food and fashion. Very intelligent and studious, she had her own unique way of looking at life. We became lovers.

I tried to keep the relationship in context with studying and continuing with outdoor activities. ADVL had given me two sets of skis; the quartermaster just said: "Bring 'em back when the snow goes, end of April." Surprising myself how quickly I mastered the cross country pair, I would go out daily first thing in the morning on my own to ski the undulating trails around the campus. These were well-maintained and ran for many kilometres. I loved the repetitive schussing noise as the ski stride glided to the end of its run. My arms completed a double poling action, and the skis schussed away again, carrying the momentum. Skating style took me a little longer to master; the alternate slip and slide technique got a rhythm going but this seemed to use more energy.

Much energy was needed at all times of the day. 'Kate' and I were lusty and having fun. We met a few friends who were going to New York on a 'Spring Break Road Trip', a rite of passage, and we were invited too.

We managed to get our assignments in on time and email them over to Glasgow, sending them at the end of the day, overnight, as the internet speed was very slow. We squabbled and we had heated debates and we studied and we frolicked night and day but really this was developing into an unhealthy relationship as we were unwittingly excluding ourselves from the wider social and scholarly networks, all in the name of lust.

By early May, after a few days' hiking and camping in Killarney Park, my semester at Laurentian was coming to a close and it was time for me to return to Glasgow. Kate was staying on to work on a summer camp further south in Ontario after travelling up into the Yukon.

There were offers of floor space for me in Glasgow, and it was good to get back and see old friends. We were all there studying and tying up loose ends for the end of the year, but, as always, burning the candle at both ends. First trip out was to Curved Ridge, the round trip being done in three hours, happy to have kept the fitness. Marks were coming in for assignments; the most pleasing was a 90% for the Independent Practicum, a write-up of the climb in Bolivia.

One of the last modules we were to undertake was an Expedition as a group, our complete class of 19 people. This module had been eagerly anticipated since our first year: we had held fund-raising events such as a triathlon, and here at last we all were: together for the last time. This event should probably have been done at the end of the first year, as by now there was a wide disparity in the abilities of various members of the group, and also some schisms had appeared between the doers and the theorisers – yes, there was a group of mainly younger students who had not fully grasped the opportunities afforded by the course, focusing mainly on handing in their assignments but not much more.

A week in the field soon found them out, particularly two young ladies who got lost. The weather conditions in the North-Western Highlands were not suited to anyone getting lost, and after they were found safe there was a big discussion as to whether we felt the whole degree had now been brought into disrepute. This discussion was also symptomatic of how, after three years together, we were all now pulling in different directions, as many of us now were looking for new challenges. Once again we realised that while we were here we might as well try to have the best time possible anyway. So, with this in mind, Irish Graham and I teamed up and paddled an inflatable packable raft down a river; German Peter and I canoed across Loch Ewe; and English Mark and I walked in to Carnmore bothy in time for a midge infestation. It was a bit of an anti-climax after three years of non-stop action; but after the May Ball that was it: over.

I couldn't just stop; the hills were a way of life for me now, I no longer needed an excuse to go, the hills and mountains were home. It was over a year since I had had an address, so away to bothies in the Cairngorms I went, with Al, to climb whatever we could in the pouring rain. It had got to the point where I felt relaxed about finding and eating packet food in the bothies to supplement whatever I had found in friends' cupboards. Going back to the real world would be going to be hard, and I was determined to avoid it.

Chink got me some shop fitting work in London, labouring. Martin Hansen had sent me joining instructions for the trip to the Picos de Europa that I would be involved in with Shrewsbury School at the end of August. The rest of the summer was spent labouring and anticipating the return of Kate from Canada. She returned, with money from working on the summer camp, and we had a few days to rekindle our romance before I was away with the school, sailing down to Spain.

The Picos de Europa are limestone peaks, steep and challenging, cut by deep gorges. We backpacked the Cares Gorge and then up through a donkey track via the tiny hidden village of Bulnes into the heart of this small compact range, with ideas of scrambling up a few of the more amenable peaks. A great few days were spent in this way before the boys went home and Kate arrived. We were going to spend another week here, trekking and scrambling and climbing. The ultimate climb we did was the south face direct of Naranjo. This was a serious affair, not least because she had never climbed multi-pitch routes before, and there was no margin for error up here. We were glad to have started early as a Spanish south face gets very hot. There were bolts at 50m (160ft) intervals, but nothing in between, good for abseiling, but rock gear was sometimes difficult to place on the 'canaletta' features in the lower parts of the climb. Naranjo gets its name as the sun sets and the whole mountain glows a mellow orange. We watched it do this from the hut after our successful ascent.

The degree course offered a fourth, Honours, year and I was eligible as third year results reached the standard. Almost by default I gravitated back to Jordanhill, sure of another year's funding, as did a few others, including

Alan, Chris and Nina. Peter and Sylvia had gone to live in Mongolia, Mark had returned south.

Honours year at University allowed me to dictate my interests and build them into the timetable. After the travelling, I had seen and had lived adventure tourism, and that was the way I wanted to steer my dissertation. My lecturer was happy with my basic premise, and a research methodology was started. I wanted to visit some of the adventure tourism and trekking companies, interview their directors to try to correlate some answers, to look in depth at how they were run and how things might trend in the future. This seemed a logical step forward, tying my experiences into some research, and hopefully some work in this area.

The everyday nuts and bolts of life included delivering phonebooks around the local area in order to fund more climbing. A long drive north yielded me a solo ascent of Suilven, floating majestically in its own world. The first winter route of the season was done on 19th October 1998 in the Cairngorms on Coire Sneachda. I was in preparation for the Winter ML assessment and booked it for the following February, which meant everything done outdoors over the coming months, would be focussed on it. In early November we went into the Cairngorms and were pinned in the Hutchison Hut as the tail of the wrath of Hurricane Mitch scoured the peaks above. The door of the hut thrummed in its frame and was impossible to open. The best thing to do was to let it blow itself out. Eventually after four days and nights out we were able to navigate back over the plateau to Cairngorm (where the wind speed had been recorded at 156 mph) and eventually back to Aviemore. Several less eventful trips followed in the run-up to Christmas. Term had finished and phone book delivery had started in earnest to fund a festive season culminating in another crossing of Suilven's ridge on New Year's Eve, and the wondrous gift of a Brocken spectre on the summit to welcome in the last year of the century.

*****

The New Year in Peru found Liliana heavily pregnant with Ricardo's baby. The pregnancy had not been an easy one, but a beautiful baby girl was born on 26th January 1999 and was named Alexandra Xiomy Braithwaite Escudero. A nanny was arranged, and Liliana went back to work soon after.

*****

I felt that I was fully prepared for my Winter ML Assessment. The first day we went up around Aonach Mor to do some security on steep ground. My map blew away; I didn't have a spare one – a foolish mistake considering my experience. This unnerved me, and I made some schoolboy errors. Knowing I could not pass now, I relaxed into the rest of the week's assessment and did well enough; but the verdict at the end of a hard week was that I would have to return at some stage to re-sit a day of those units which I had failed.

With the weight of the Winter ML removed from my shoulders, I could concentrate fully on the run up to the end of the course. Part of this involved phoning and visiting Adventure Travel tour operators. Two of my 'victims' were John Biggar, who ran 'Andes' in Castle Douglas, Dumfries; and Bob Lancaster, who owned 'High Places' in Sheffield. On the phone to Bob, we discussed many things, including qualifications. I mentioned that I had recently been deferred on my Winter ML assessment. "Yes, I was when I did mine!" was his reply, and I'm sure this honesty helped me to secure a meeting with him.

My ex girlfriend from Shrewsbury had also been in touch. Was she aware that the course was coming to an end? She had refinanced the house and wanted to offer me £9,000 to buy me out. Had she known that I would be flat broke at the end of the course? She knew I knew the house was worth more than that. I knew she couldn't afford any more. She also knew I would snap her hand off. We could have done several things sensibly, but travel was in my blood now, and the tickets were booked for Peru. I would travel there in the summer and then see what happened. It felt great to have some money in the bank. I was a bit sensible, though: I bought a friend's tired old Volvo for £300.

Bob at High Places offered me a deal. As I would be in Peru, I could go along on one of his treks as an assistant leader, free but unpaid. That sounded like a foot in the door to me, and I agreed. Firstly though, I went to Huaraz, hired a guide/porter and transport to get to the trekking peak of Pisco (5752m, 18,870ft). Getting to the bottom of the mountain after a day's uphill trek then requires a down climb onto a glacier, weaving a way through house-sized blocks of granite fallen from the mountains over millennia. When through this, you have to ascend a dusty ridge to a relatively flattish spot where a few tents are huddled against the elements. An alpine start followed by four hours of climbing in the dark and a magnificent sunrise reveals the Central Andean peaks in all their glory. We were on the summit at 08:30 am local time on Saturday 19th June 1999, within a week of leaving the UK. Staggeringly beautiful peaks were all around us: Chacraraju, Piramide, Artesonraju, Alpamayo and the brooding twin peaks of Huascaran, highest in Peru, glinting pearls in the icy blue. With the headaches associated with not letting the body acclimatise properly, we soon had to leave this heavenly kingdom. Travelling south, and up to Cusco I met Dad, who was to accompany us on the Inca Trail to Machu Picchu.

Dad had recovered well from his kidney problems, and on the hills he was steady and slow but happy and very interested in everything around him. The Inca Trail was fantastic, crowned by visiting the ruined city. We travelled on into the desert to Arequipa, and Colca Canyon, famed for its condors. He travelled back to Lima and home and I went back to Huaraz to await the arrival of the High Places group, led by Richard Haszko. A Sheffield teacher, Richard arrived ahead of the group, and we went up the Ishinca Valley. As I was already acclimatised, I decided to solo Ishinca (5530m, 18,143ft). It was straightforward, I felt good going at my own pace and was on the snowcapped summit by 10:35 am.

I learnt a lot observing Richard and how he worked with a group. We did the Santa Cruz trek with eight clients. Coincidentally one of the clients was a Professor at the University of Strathclyde. I made notes each evening and wrote a full report. The trip was a success, although I had several recommendations for improvement.

Back in England, there were just four days to turn around before I left to lead a Shrewsbury School group to Norway with Martin Hansen. This didn't get off to the best of starts, as I had got drunk the night before we left and ended up back at Paul's flat with an attractive but older lady I had met in a pub.

By the time the Land Rover and minibus convoy had reached Norway I had sobered up. In true Shrewsbury School style the itinerary was full. Peaks included Galdhopiggen (Norway's highest at 2470m/8,100ft); then a drive into the Arctic Circle for the Solvagtind ridge, Juteshytta, and another peak, Blaho; then returning south to climb the excellent ridge of Glittertinden before departing home from Bergen. Some of the terrain was beyond my qualification level but Martin had a fun way to slow up some of the faster boys on the approach walks – they had to carry an aluminium ladder through undergrowth and towards any 'glaciers' we might encounter to bridge crevasses. We didn't take the ladders on Galdhopiggen; but Adam Booth was one of the 'keen lads' on my rope. Here he takes up the story:

'When we finally reached the glacier it was incredible: as I stepped onto the white, crisp snow that carried on until the horizon.

'We put on our crampons, took out our ice axes and roped up into groups of four. I was the front man, the crazy, light person who falls into the crevasse when the snow bridge collapses. Just as we were about to set off across the massive ice sheet, I read the sign that marked the division between rock and snow:

EXTREME DANGER. Glaciers are in motion and as a result crevasses several metres wide and 30-40 metres deep may be present. They may be covered with snow. DO NOT proceed unless accompanied by a competent guide. (Guides are available at Juvasshytta.)

'I looked around at our 'competent guide': our mountaineering instructor, Stewart Wellings. He was pulling faces and doing reindeer impressions. Everyone else in the group was greatly amused at watching me psyche myself up to go first. However I knew that, with Stewart at number two on my rope, I would be held, should I drop through the floor.

…Soon we reached snow again which fell away sharply to the left and joined the top of a cliff on the right: a kind of ice ridge. As we climbed we put pieces of protection in rocky outcrops, and then clipped the rope into them to save us if we fell. By now visibility and temperature had dropped substantially. When we reached rock again, what would have been an easy scramble turned into a hard climb, with the chilling wind coming over the top of the cliff to our right, constantly battering us. It was at that moment that the cloud cleared to our left to reveal an immense glacier riddled with gaping blue-black crevasses. Even as we watched they were getting bigger, and we saw snow collapsing into their deep darkness. I was thankful we hadn't attempted the peak via that route.

Finally, we reached our last stretch of snow which lead to the summit. It was steep, and the weather was starting to take its toll on some of us. However we plodded on and encouraged each other, and at last, through the white of the cloud, a hut appeared, and a short way beyond it, the summit pillar.

It felt incredible…

This was it…

The highest peak in Norway.

We had made it…

The Rovers had made it…

Everyone was ecstatic – to get a party of 28 to the summit was a major achievement, and we had done it in the Rovers way: as a team. I remember completing the highest peak in the Picos de Europa (Torre de Cerredo – 8686ft) with the Rovers one year before, little thinking that I would go on to climb the highest peak in Norway. Standing on Galdhoppingen, I stopped to consider where I might be in a year's time… Who knows?[11]

It had been good logbook experience, working with children in hostile environments and no incidents. But would insurance have been valid if an accident had happened, as it had in Alaska a few years earlier? Requirements and regulations for mountain leaders in these situations are constantly reviewed. This is the conundrum for the aspirant leader: how can experience and qualifications be gained through the proper channels?

---

11   Dr Adam Booth has gone on to summit Everest twice, Lhotse, Ama Dablam, El Capitan's Nose, Half Dome and many other immense achievements

My first port of call back in the UK was the High Places office in Sheffield. I met Bob and Paul Adams, the director, and others, including Remi, Operations Manager. I felt I left them with a good impression.

Egger had met a young research student, Andrea, whilst working in Hammersmith, London on his PhD in Medical Cell Biology. They were married in Durham a few years later and settled initially in Peterborough.

My Graduation was in the November. On stage, giving out the certificates that day was the Professor, my Peruvian trekking client from the summer. I wore a kilt, and Mum and Dad came along. At last I think Mum began to understand what my life was about.

John Biggar offered me a permanent full-time job working for his company, 'Andes' in Castle Douglas on the Scottish borders, and I made preparations to move there. It was a small business, just him and me. The big job on the horizon however was the trip I was to lead to Aconcagua in Argentina in January. Aconcagua, at 6959m (22,830 ft) is the highest mountain in the Southern and Western Hemispheres, the highest in the Americas, one of the windiest and coldest on earth. After Everest, it is the most prominent mountain on Earth. This was a challenge I could rise to.

The world continued to turn as the new millennium dawned, despite fears of digital disaster, and I returned safely from welcoming in the New Year in the Alps on a skiing trip with Mark. I was enjoying spending the money from my house sale. I needed a new sleeping bag and could now afford a top of the range down version at over £300, a necessity not a luxury now. There was a good community in Castle Douglas, and I felt welcome there.

At the end of January I left for Mendoza to meet my team. The acclimatisation went well, and we climbed a couple of 5000m peaks before the mule train led us up the quieter eastern approach of Aconcagua along the Relinchos valley. We established ourselves on the mountain, three clients and I, and then started the time-honoured mantra of "climb high, sleep low, rest" as shouldering loads gradually we moved up the mountain. Of the three clients, one was not adapting to the rarefied air and was not eating properly. On summit day a few hundred metres from the top he was feeling bad and had to turn round. I had to go with him, and had to make the decision that we should all go down. I had no way of knowing how bad he was and the other two had limited knowledge and experience. I couldn't take the chance of letting them go on into the unknown, with the possibility of their getting lost if a storm blew up. The pack I carried down was maybe a little less than 50 kg (110lb); I had taken a lot of the client's gear as he was struggling and became ill. It was a shame that we didn't summit, as the weather had been pretty good by Aconcagua standards.

My contract with Andes was terminated amicably, with notice. Paul Adams offered me the job of Operations Manager at High Places: the season was about to start and as I drove south I knew that I wouldn't be living back in Scotland. That made me sad: all the fun, the friends, the mountains just memories now as the old Volvo chugged down the M6 once more.

S7 is the Sheffield postcode for climbers. I was a mountaineer; I couldn't claim to be a beanie-wearing chalk fingered skinny lath of a climber; I liked my beer too much. I found a bedsit in Agden Road, an attic room in an imposing grey stone old house in a leafy lane. The shared toilet was downstairs, but for £195 a month this would do, especially as that would be dead money for several months whilst I was away on trips over the year. I was to head the South American part of the company in addition to my duties as Operations Manager. Everything seemed to have led up to this, and it felt great!

This summer I would be leading four trips in Peru back to back, leaving in May and returning at the end of August. My base over there would be The Andino Hotel, the best hotel in Huaraz. The itinerary was Pisco Trek, Huayhuash Trek, Pisco Trek and Huayhuash Trek; so, between trekking around some of the most beautiful mountains in the World, I would be travelling up and down to Lima, taking and bringing groups to this very special place. I could get used to this!

There were seven on the first Pisco trek. It went well, and High Places had acted on my earlier recommendations. The agency we worked with were the Morales family, who had been outfitting and guiding teams for several decades, knowing this part of the Andes, its flora and fauna, its *refugios* and high passes, its villages and stop-overs like no others. We were in safe hands. Everyone summited Pisco, and we all went down to Tambo's Night Club to celebrate before the long drive down to sea level for farewells and a quick turnaround: before picking the next group up. Always up or down this road we would stop at the same café, and always I would have the same Chinese Wanton Frito and soup. My base when in Lima was the famous faded splendour of The Bolivar Hotel, which occupies a whole block in old Lima, facing on to the square of Plaza de San Martin, notable as a gathering place for Peruvians in times of civil unrest.

There was a big demonstration taking place, and we had to run the gauntlet to get into the hotel, using the rear entrance, ringing in our ears chants of "Gringo! Gringo!" The next morning we were glad to leave the city for the peace of the mountains, to attempt one of the world's most beautiful treks – The Huayhuash circuit. A two week trip, after acclimatisation, we would be at over 4000m (13,120ft) for virtually the whole time, and there were many passes at over 5000m (16,400ft).

A few days into the trek we heard gunfire. Riding up the valley were horsemen firing the occasional volley into the air. As they approached, Freddy, their leader, announced himself, saying that he was the mayor of the local town, and that he and his entourage would be camping near our camp. They were brash, but they were fun, and they were the real deal. I was just glad they weren't here to rob us. In the night one of my clients was very ill with pulmonary oedema and started to breathe erratically. I stayed in the tent with him, but it was obvious that he would need to go down to lower altitudes. Freddy and his crowd were in a bell tent snoring loudly, whisky bottles and rifles piled up beside them. The tent flap was frozen solid, the Southern Cross constellation winked in the night sky.

Miguel the cook boy and I took our ill client down to the outpost where Freddy had agreed to evacuate him in the town's communal VW beetle back to Huaraz. Miguel would accompany him. I rode my horse back to join the remainder of the group, I had done my best for him. The rest of the trek continued uneventfully through this dramatic land. On the last day our now fully recovered client walked in to meet us at the roadhead village of Chiquian to let us know that he was safe, but had been robbed in Huaraz at gunpoint.

Showered and fed in the Andino Hotel, we ventured out to celebrate, and gravitated to Tambo's Nightclub. Later having summoned taxis, and returned the group safely to the Andino, not yet satiated, I returned to the club.

And there she was: Liliana Escudero Vasquez turning to smile, just for me, her big eyes brown and beautiful; her aura pervading perfume and pizzazz and personality, lighting up the dance floor. We looked across the room into each other's eyes, the swirling revellers moving blurring around us. In that moment did I dare imagine that everything that had gone before had been leading up to this moment of destiny, this new beginning?

<u>Part Two</u>

Chapter 13

Aurora Australis

Liliana had been travelling from her native town of Pomabamba to Huaraz, a long and treacherous journey, cooped up in a stifling overcrowded bus as it negotiated hairpin after hairpin and mountain pass after mountain pass. Youngest sister Mabel (May-belle), brother Jorge (aka Polaco) and Cousin Sylvia were with her. They broke their journey in Huaraz. There has to be a time to dance. A chance meeting; we were away to Lima the next morning too, all in our private bus. I was very surprised when the receptionist at The Bolivar Hotel in Lima called the room to say there was a young female visitor for me; there she was, Liliana, real and gorgeous and happy, with that dazzling heart-melting smile.

She remembered our shouted and whispered stilted conversation, fuelled with 'Cuba Libres'. My Spanish, learnt from *arrieros* (donkey drivers), was functional but basic. She had not one word of English, but she had tracked me down! She stayed for breakfast. I ordered room service for a Peruvian Beauty Queen, and she'd now seen me up close and personal, in the daylight, and hadn't been scared off! But before I knew it, I was back in the mountains with another group.

A typical trekking day would start by being awoken by an *arriero* with a bowl of warm water for washing and a cup of tea. Bag packed and left inside the tent, then sitting shivering in the mess tent, ready for egg baps and more tea at 06:00. By 06:30 we would all be stumbling along the trail, trying to warm ourselves up, still encased in down jacket, gloves and hats as the sun crept round the mountain. An hour or so later the first of the *arrieros* would catch us up: smiling gold teeth under moustache and a *'chollo'* felt hat leading a donkey or a mule, our tents and bags lashed on. A mid-morning break would be prepared for us, usually near a stream or perhaps on a ridge, and always with a view as we sat: blanket on the ground; a big metal teapot; bread, fruit, chocolate, sweets. Suitably revived, now daubed with sunscreen, headwear now sunhat, and layers removed as by now the sun would be high enough that we could resume our wanderings. Again the arrieros would leapfrog ahead of us, and camp would be set up for our arrival in the early afternoon, having covered between ten and fifteen miles.

It was usually at these times where I would be called upon to perform minor surgery on blisters or administer medicine for minor ailments, stomach problems or altitude sickness, or anxiety. Rehydrating in the mess tent we would discuss our day: a rare plant might have been seen; or a fox or a marmot spotted; or a condor had circled the thermals. A brief siesta gave chance to write the diary or read before the big meal. The team really pulled this off most nights: chicken, veg, potatoes, and usually a veggie or a gluten-free meal would be provided additionally for someone. And then there could be a card school, or a song, or even a poem, jokes and banter before an early night: always an early night and a try at keeping warm.

This rolling circus would continue wending its merry way up and down the passes of the Andes throughout the summer months, and all seemed to rise and fall in line with the daily rhythms, and life was simple and people were happy. Off they would go, and a new group would arrive, and I would see my beautiful Liliana in Lima before I would go away again with another group.

Liliana took me in a taxi into the area called Independencia: dirty concrete, the ubiquitous iron bars facing skyward in readiness for the next storey, more in hope than expectation, but spiking a grey polluted sky above brown leaden hillocks, overrun with shanty shacks. Vigilantes loitered on street corners; streets full of bustle, quietening down after dusk as lights flickered. I was led through a solid polished wooden door then through a small courtyard, and then into a well-presented but dark living room. Swarthy and handsome, suited, tieless, black hair slicked back: a man in his late fifties, strong, intelligent and clearly in charge - Jorge Valverde Escudero sat there, offering a handshake and a chair. With a clap of his hands, twelve bottles of beer in a dusty crate appeared at his feet. Jorge was strikingly different from the Andean people I was mixing with;

a tall mestizo gentleman. We were joined by Mabel's partner Giuseppe, from Sicily, very handsome and charming, with fairly good English, but giving nothing away. He and Jorge seemed like the interview team. A beer? Why of course! Jorge reached into the crate and lifted a bottle to his mouth and removed the top with his teeth. I took it from him and smiled back nervously. The three of us communicated well but then Giuseppe left us. Very soon after that Jorge and I were arm wrestling. I thought I had the measure of him, but I felt his strength as we locked grip. We drank more and more, kept repeating stock phrases. The tests continued, but by this time I had my dander up and every time slammed down either arm he offered me. At last Liliana came and rescued me and I was away again.

Liliana and I were growing together but the time was coming for me to return home. Liliana said she wanted to come and visit me. I was astonished: she had never ventured outside Peru before. I wasn't sure that she meant it but at the end of September I went to pick her up from Heathrow.

I managed a few days away from the office and we went to see the traction engines in the rain at the Michaelmas Fair in Bishops Castle. We climbed Snowdon and Cadair Idris. She loved our little mountains, she loved this green and pleasant land, she smiled all the time and she melted my heart.

Mum and Dad took her to London to see the sights, and they took in a musical, 'The King and I'.

Driving over to Sheffield, we stopped up on the Staffordshire moors and decided there and then unceremoniously to get married: that she would move over here, with her daughter Ali, now 20 months old. And that was that: simple as that. We even had time to look at what could be bought in Sheffield for around £30,000 before she flew back to Peru.

I knew now Liliana was the one for me. My days in the bedsit were numbered, my days of wild abandon would have to finish. It was time to change from a consenting adult into a responsible one. I thought deeply about how my life would be changing. I had had a notion to be settled down by about forty. It was time to change these habits of a lifetime.

A tussle with bureaucracy, paperwork, payments and in four months Liliana and Alexandra would be in the UK. A few weeks of single man bad behaviour seemed as just empty thrills: now a real new life was opening to me.

At work we were in the busy season, preparing 12,000 copies of next years' brochure and ensuring all the itineraries were up to date. My role was coordinating the images being sent in various formats from around the world (digital photography still being in its infancy). I led a trip to Wadi Rum in Jordan; we scrambled around the wadis and jebels in the desert. We crossed the Burdah Arch and slept under clear skies by the campfire, being serenaded by our local guide Sabbah on his one-stringed fiddle. Then at Christmas I was in Ecuador leading a group successfully to the summit of Cotopaxi 5,897m (19,142ft).

*****

25th January 2001. Manchester Airport. Tannoy announcement:

"Can Mr Stewart Wellings please make himself known at arrivals."

I ducked under the rail and spoke. And there they were, in summer clothes, luggage lost, Ali looking directly at me with a scowl that demanded answers – "Why am I here? Who are you? Why is it so cold?"

Our paperwork was scrutinised, Liliana and Ali were let into the country. Liliana's 'spouse visa' was dependent upon us getting married within the six month period permitted. The wedding had been booked for 19th May 2001. The little red Austin Maestro crossed the Pennines to Sheffield. From the back I heard a tiny voice: *"Donde es Mami Ina? Donde es Papi CoCo?"* In that wet cold January night, the night before Ali would celebrate her second birthday, I felt the full weight of responsibility for a young life, something I had never experienced before. This was different from herding adults up a mountain, this was the big one, and I hadn't done the course.

I had managed to get a mortgage on number 180 Edmund Road, Sheffield and collected the keys just three days before Liliana and Ali arrived: a mid-terrace ex-student house, with steep stairs, a postage stamp for a back garden and rising damp but at £34,000 the maximum I could afford. I had bought a yellow plastic baby bath from one of those shops, made a stair gate, tidied up, metaphorically threw my porn stash out, tried to respect myself and others and follow a 'straighter and narrower' path. "I *will* grow up!" I told myself. And suddenly there we were, and it was all happening.

New life meant things like trying to understand each other's languages, finding a job for Liliana, a nursery for Ali, shopping, keeping out of the pub, planning the wedding, and going to work. Mum and Dad came over, delighted and keen to help. Dad built a small picket fence out front round the 2m x 4m garden; Mum taught Ali nursery rhymes and counting.

Herlinda bravely crossed the ocean. Wild horses would not have stopped her. She was immediately wooed by old Cyril from down the road who wanted to take her to the chip shop. Leonora, our toothless old Jamaican neighbour, came round for endless cups of tea. Liliana had never seen snow before, and the wind and the rain were new to her. Whenever I went out in this weather she worried as she had not known winds like these and her English could now muster the phrase 'Skinny people in the sky!'

I was to lead a group to climb Chilean volcanoes at the end of February and all too soon had to leave my little ladies for three weeks. They were left with two cheques (for £20 each) and a £20 note. The cheques bounced, and the Bank of England chose this moment to withdraw the 'Faraday note'. Issues such as these are complicated enough for natives to deal with.

Liliana with Ali in her buggy, charged around the steep streets of Sheffield. People in the street smiled at these two exotic creatures and their golden aura as they discovered budget price Netto and charity shops. Voluntarily exiled, Liliana produced no stereotypical beauty queen hissy fit histrionics; she was just a calm tough purposeful stranger in a strange land. I was only really beginning to find out about the miraculous, resourceful woman who had chosen me.

I returned from a successful trip with a souvenir brand new lump of rock that had landed near me, the result of an eruptive sulphurous belch from the crater of the Volcano Villarica. And an engagement ring made of lapis lazuli.

The bread I cut with the breadknife in the kitchen had a greenish tinge to it. Liliana had cut the grass in the back garden with it!

The occasional jeering from passers-by was a result of Liliana painting the front of the house blue and white, the colour of Allianza Lima, her favourite team, and, coincidentally the same colours as Sheffield Wednesday. Unfortunately we lived one street behind Bramall Lane, home to the red and black of arch rivals Sheffield United. In my absence, Liliana had at least one offer of marriage (from a driver who stopped in the street).

Dad had found a deep religious view and was consecrated as a lay preacher in Lichfield, and the first time he had met Ali was when she rode her trike into his cassock below the steps of the cathedral. He was also church warden of St. Mary's Church, Broughton, Yorton Heath and his services were required to help us get hitched. There was a stag-do, hen-night, wedding, reception, night do and honeymoon to organise. All this had to be completed before I left for a summer of trek leading at the end of May. I would not be back until the end of August.

The stag do, I decided, could be nowhere other than the Long Mynd. Mick Boulton's hostel at The Bridges, Ratlinghope was booked, and the revellers began arriving on the Friday night. The plan was that we should all be transported in Mick's vintage charabanc to Bishops Castle and Ludlow and then back to Church Stretton for a curry before flouting the foot and mouth regulations to return over the Long Mynd to The Bridges. This we did. Musical accompaniment was supplied by Taff and his accordion and Stu and his penny whistle. The assembled all wore plastic nose-and-glasses disguises. Drink, as is the custom, was taken to excess. I, as groom, was furnished with a hard hat with antlers protruding, at the behest of Blutes, and, unsurprisingly, was debagged by the assembled merry band.

The Saturday after was the day of the wedding weekend. At lunchtime I parked up and went in to see Liz behind the bar at The Railway Inn for my 'last pint of freedom'. Crowding around the pub were my family, friends from childhood, friends from Scotland, friends from everywhere! We all went on to the church which was packed to capacity. Dad had always been a techno wizard, and had applied his brain to the problem of a bilingual church service. The first draft of the service sheets he printed in Spanish, read 'Father, Son and Holy Alcohol'!

Ali joined Kim and Blutes' daughters Sophie and Hannah as bridesmaids. Herlinda read a passage from the bible in Spanish but I think only she, Liliana and Ali were Spanish speakers. Liliana looked beautiful, radiant: her brown skin highlighted against her white dress, her smile confident, and her eyes happy. When the congregation were asked if they would support the newlyweds in their marriage vows they loudly professed that they would.

The reception was at Grinshill Village Hall under the hill, and then into town for a huge dance and sing and drink-up with Stu Altman's band This Way Up and a guest appearance from Jo Cairns, my old flatmate. A plastic ball and chain was clamped round my ankle as we do-si-do-ed and swung our partners and disappeared into the sweaty hazy night of alcohol and dance and laughter. At lunchtime the next day what was left of the party reconvened in the Quarry Park by the Bandstand for a picnic before Liliana, and I headed north for our honeymoon, with Ali and Herlinda.

In Glasgow we borrowed a high altitude small two person tent from Big Al and headed up to Glencoe to camp outside the King's House Hotel. Herlinda was shown how to operate the meths burning stove in order to keep Ali fed, and we went off to climb Curved Ridge; Liliana, Nina and I, very cosy on a honeymoon! Liliana proclaimed the experience, including the roped lower-off over the Laggan Garbh snow patch as *mantequilla*! or 'Butter!' – easy peasy! (It was then I thought to myself "Phew! This is going to be alright!") She was a formidable person and I should never have doubted that she would cope.

Back in Sheffield barely had I time to unpack again before I was away for three months. A night at the cinema to see 'Bridget Jones' Diary' but Gabrielle's song 'Out of Reach' reduced me to tears. Little Ali barred the door, imploring me not to go. It broke my heart but go I had to: this was how I earned our money.

The work was a re-run of the previous year: four treks back to back, with the same support crew. It went pretty smoothly this time; no hijacks or medical emergencies. The weather remained blue sky, dry and calm for the vast majority of the time. Jagged white peaks pierced the sky; the trails still wove their way through villages, over passes and above ravines. Both of the climbing trips to Pisco (5752m/18,870ft) were total successes: everyone summited. The trekkers were all strong and healthy, and stomach problems were minimal. Lessons had been learnt from previous trips.

I was back in Sheffield at the end of August. The work had been very rewarding, helping people achieve their dreams, putting a lot into the local economy, building bridges across cultures, making friends, keeping fit, taking photos, teaching and learning, reporting, reaping the reward from good planning and being prepared. I felt this was the culmination of everything I had strived for up to now, that I was on top of my game, things were really flowing. But now I faced a greater challenge at home, if I was to make the marriage work and not be just an absentee father and husband.

It felt so good to be home. I had missed Liliana and Ali, and they had missed me. They had found their feet in Sheffield: Liliana had worked as a carer, while Herlinda stayed and looked after Ali, taking her to and from nursery. Liliana had coped very well. When she first arrived, one of the first things she asked me was *'hay brujas aqui en Inglaterra?'* ('Are there witches in England?') And she was serious.

Although it is not obvious to visitors, many people in Peru live in constant fear of curses and evil spells, particularly spells that could make a child ill. Liliana was relieved that Ali was growing up away from that risk.

As she went about her daily business Liliana would smile happily. A lullaby for Ali never far from her lips was:

'Mamacita Linda, Yo te quiero mucho – mucho mucho mucho. Nadir como te'

'Beautiful Little Girl, I love you so much, so much, so much, nothing compares to you'.

She loved the singing of the Andean Superstar Dina Paucar and also Estrella de Pomabamba

'*Que Lindos Ojos*' – Such Beautiful Eyes.

*****

For my birthday, Liliana and Ali bought me a cycle helmet. I had never worn one before, but now I treasured it. I was straight back into work: the office side of things dictated that we had to get next year's brochure out as soon as possible. Once again my job was to collate photos and text and re-jig itineraries, ready for when the phone rang with queries and, hopefully, bookings.

Driving back from the printers, a news item came on the radio about a plane crashing into a tower in New York. Reports were unclear, the news was just breaking. I called in at home and turned on the TV. Liliana and I stood motionless, in horror as the footage showed a plane crashing into a tower and huge plumes of smoke billowing. US airspace was sealed off. President Bush spoke live to us all. He was going after these 'folk'; they would be tracked down. I had to return to the office immediately. We had groups of clients coming in from all over the place. Every flight was being grounded. Suddenly it seemed like the whole world was under attack.

Within a few days the dust began to settle. All our clients were home safely. But then came the big unexpected shock. Without realising it, I had witnessed the death of one of my childhood friends. Graham Berkeley from Bayston Hill, a lad we had all known as kids and had grown up with, had been in the plane that crashed into the second tower. In an instant the world had moved on its axis. It felt as if all the things I took for granted, even the village of my childhood, was under attack, and it was evidently us in the west against those in the east.

The implications for the business soon became very apparent. Next year's trips to places like Pakistan, Morocco, Nepal, Bhutan, Jordan, all good sellers in the past, we thought, would be very unlikely to run. We hoped people would want to book trips to mountainous areas like Peru and Ecuador and Bolivia, where we hoped it would be safer; but we would have to wait and see. My mind had been made up. The world had changed and I had changed with it. Liliana was now pregnant and I just didn't want to leave her and Ali again. I applied for a job at Cruckton Hall School, near Shrewsbury, as a houseparent, and would be starting in January 2002. I handed in my notice at High Places in the November and worked up until Christmas.

The house in Edmond Road made a profit of £8,000, selling for £42,000 - prices were on the up. Having this amount of money made me very wary as it always burnt a hole in my pocket so I booked us on a cruise. This 'cruise' was on a car ferry from Newcastle to Bergen, Norway. Our cabin was below decks next to the boiler, and it stank of diesel. The four day trip did not go down too well, particularly as neither Liliana nor Ali were allowed off the boat at Bergen, as they were not yet British citizens, and the fear was that they might seek asylum in Norway, or that the baby could be prematurely born Norwegian on the quayside.

Chapter 14

Venus and Mars and a Gift from God

Cruckton – Two Cultures Collaborate and Collide
Learning English In Our New Paradise

I found a three bedroom semi-detached ex-council house on 'The Green' at Cruckton, as Church Close is known locally, which, at £400 per month, we could just afford to rent. We moved in at the end of January. This was another huge change for Liliana. She seemed to trust me implicitly, but I hoped she would be able to adjust to this new rural life. Trees in Lima are a rarity in all but the more classy areas, places like San Isidro or Miraflores; here in the fields around were scores of ancient oaks surveying us with a natural wisdom, rustling in the breeze.

Liliana had another cultural shock when a local traveller family were rehoused across the green. When they visited, one poor child in a wheelchair had to be helped in, they were all ragged and clearly hungry, and she was appalled. She had not expected to encounter real poverty in 'Gringoland'.

My job at the school was to look after boys with behavioural problems, dyslexia, Attention Deficit Hyperactive Disorder (ADHD), autism and associated spectrum disorders. I had experience working with kids and was 'on their level' generally speaking, although in their eyes I would be an authority figure. There had been a promise that there would be plenty of outdoor activities for me to get involved with as the school understood the value of these. I had had the chance to detail my background and felt sure the management had heard me and understood what I could offer. During the school day, I would do domestic duties and cover supervision roles at breaks and lunchtimes, as there were often violent incidents to deal with. Training for restraints in these situations was compulsory.

Ali was three years old now and had started at the nursery at Hanwood School. Liliana was working at the Minsterley meat packing plant, ramming dead cows' tongues into tins for Marks and Spencer. I was having trouble adjusting too; my wings had been well and truly clipped. The staff at Cruckton Hall School, dedicated as they were, were also very down to earth as the job meant keeping a routine for the boys, keeping them safe from harming themselves or others. I had envisioned a different role, more time spent outside, using my skills and knowledge to teach and train these boys to be able to prepare for manhood. However the reality appeared to be more about constraining and restraining.

I handed in my resignation and left at the end of March. I couldn't relate to the culture. Opportunities to take a group off campus usually resulted in the boys misbehaving and little else being achieved. But the spring was here, and the opportunities to be a freelance self-employed outdoor instructor were coming my way. I picked up work with Red Ridge Outdoor Centre, helping them run climbing, abseiling and caving trips at Llanymynech, just half an hours' drive away. The problem was that, despite all my mountain experience, I didn't have the 'single pitch award' for instructors in these 'on site' situations, and so I could only be an assistant. I needed to somehow fit in further training and qualifications. I delivered newspapers and the admag to help keep our young family. A big 'paper round' like this could net me £85, a handsome wage for a day's work, although it was only one very big day a week, delivering to 1600 urban doorsteps.

On 6th June 2002 our baby boy was due to be delivered by Caesarean section. Liliana and I sat listening to the John Peel show on the radio. I emailed him, explaining what was happening. He read it out instantly and played us 'Meet on the Ledge' by Fairport Convention. He wished us all the best for the future. The next day at 10:30am in Shrewsbury Maternity Unit a healthy beautiful baby boy was born weighing 8lb 12 oz, or nearly 4kg. We named him Matthew (Matty) – 'Gift from God'.

Matty started his life being pushed around the countryside in his pram, delivering newspapers, meeting horses and sheep, gurgling and smiling

Our next-door neighbour Julie and her young daughters Hayley and Beth doted on Matty and Ali.

Liliana's grasp of English was slowly improving. She used what vocabulary she had to describe things or people she was unable to name. After our friend Nige had visited while I was out, I was informed that 'Big Carrot Man' had been. (Nige is 6' 1", with a shock of light ginger hair).

Stu Altman organised a trip to Peru in the September, to do the Inca Trail. They were all old friends, and I went as their guide. Whilst there, I took the opportunity to talk at length with Liliana's brother Julio. He was trapped in the frightening, dangerous life of a young man in Lima. Alcohol, drugs and gang wars had left their mark. I could see that he needed a direction and a purpose and helped him get a visa to come to the UK to visit us. In my naivety I thought he would return home after a few weeks when the visa expired. He stayed in our spare room, trying to come to terms with his demons. We introduced him to basketball with the lads on a Thursday night, which he loved. Football was his passion though, and he turned out for The Nag's Head Dodgers - suddenly a Shrewsbury town pub team had a mysterious South American midfield general with golden boots!

As Christmas approached Julio and I found work at Minsterley Creamery, on the trifle production line, upmarket products. The money was good for me, and for Julio it was amazing. As we togged up into white coats, hats, clogs and hairnets and walked onto the factory floor I suddenly felt at a disadvantage. The *'lingua franca'* appeared to be Portuguese. The place was staffed with migrant agency staff. Julio seemed to be adept at fixing parts of the production line when they broke down, which they often did, whereas I became trancelike in a waking daydream of Scottish winter climbing as I deftly flicked biscuits into pots as the trifle ingredients were dispensed along the line.

One morning I had to fish Julio out of the police station at 5:45 a.m. after one of his frequent all-night drinking bouts. I fed him chewing gum and coffee in a vain attempt at sobering him up. I shouldn't have bothered: Julio hurled the contents of his stomach into the empty trifle pots. The whole line had to be washed down and disinfected with a deep clean. Staff, many bussed in from Wolverhampton, were laid off.

Over the winter I had fallen a long way from my chosen career, and dropped back into the work I thought I had escaped for good.

After Christmas it was back to the deliveries. And this was when things started to get 'interesting' financially. We were paying private rent on the house, so I enquired whether we could buy it, and for how much. Yes; we could, at the knockdown price of £80,000. We had jumped off the property ladder in Sheffield and I hadn't realised that prices in Shrewsbury had doubled while I had been away. How could we do it?! A simple case of creative accounting was the answer, and the financial adviser asked:

"How much do you earn, Stewart?"

"Well, with the addition of tax credits and child benefit, currently I'm earning £85, but it's only one day a week," I replied.

"Yes, but you could earn that every day if the work was there."

"Yes…" I replied, puzzled by his question

Tap tap tap went the calculator buttons.

"OK, we can lend you £73,000. Can you get £7,000 as a deposit?"

"'Erm, I'll have to see if I can ask my dad for help."

My wonderful, long-suffering Dad found the money to keep a roof over his grandchildren. And that was that; signed and sealed. I had climbed the rickety money tree with wife and kids clinging on to my back, just managing to reach and grab the bottom rung of the housing rescue helicopter ladder as it skimmed the treetops of affordability, whisking us back to Thatcherland. As we were to learn a few years later, similar scenarios were being played out in many a dubious mortgage shop: fly-by-night money lenders, selling dreams no one realised they couldn't really afford and creaming in big arranger fees and bonuses for themselves. We were all happily bamboozled by the whole process. Now we would own our own little castle; renting had just been a blip, we were heading back to the joys of home ownership. Because that was what home ownership was about wasn't it? It was more than just a roof over your head, it was an investment, and we were playing this dangerous game now.

Things were looking good. Soon after, I got a job as the Outdoor Instructor at a school for children with special needs and behavioural issues. I would plan the daily off-site outdoor activities and present risk assessments at the staff meeting before the children arrived. When agreed, I would then load the people carrier with equipment and then, with the help of a teaching assistant, try and cajole the children into getting into the car to take part in the activity. Invariably there would be an issue – anything – behaviour, medication, problems transporting the children to the school on time, tantrums, jealousy, anything. It was like herding cats. Driving to the activity we would try and keep them entertained, always braced for the next explosive confrontation. Parking and then starting the activity would involve splitting up the children to avoid fights. An activity such as climbing had risks on top of risks, and quite often it would be abandoned before a rope had been uncoiled. We would have to phone for reinforcements and draft someone in to remove a child from the situation. Then there was the weather. There were very low expectations of what could be achieved. Despite all these variables, we did have some successes. A good day would simply be one with few or no physical fights. A rare day would be one where one or two would at least try a climb or an abseil or walk.

The children exhibited a lot of bravado and braggadocio around each other, a harsh exterior developed as a coping strategy hiding an inner self battered and bruised from a life in care. Underneath they were very vulnerable and sad, some so unloved and damaged they had huge problems relating to the idea that these adults were on their side and wanted to help them. They all had complex needs, triggers that we had to know– any 'signposts' pointing towards a potential flare up. Formal learning in a classroom was a goal, but many breaks were factored in to 'let off steam'. This was why there was such a large emphasis on the value of outdoor education. There was a structure and a framework for what we did, and ways of testing and measuring and evaluating the learning that could be done.

There were days when restraints went on for hours, followed by writing up reports of incidents, the detail of the type of restraint used, times, dates, incident numbers, witnesses, everything. Another part of my job was to organise residential trips. Camping was a favourite with the staff, who tried to sell the idea to the children. These had to take place at weekends due to the school week. All in all it was a very arduous way to earn £16,000 per year. We didn't get the long school holidays enjoyed by a mainstream teacher. School holidays meant supporting the care staff, running extra activities. Liliana was learning English; she enrolled on a hairdressing course and needed my help with her assignments.

Additionally I was undertaking a Post Graduate Certificate of Education (PGCE) but struggling to find the time to do it. Something had to give. It was me, I just hadn't had the time to complete any essays, and failed the course but my employer was less interested in my PGCE than my outdoor qualifications. I had passed my single pitch award for rock climbing. Almost five years ago I had been deferred for a one day re-sit for my Winter Mountain Leader Award. My employer wanted me to get the award to broaden what they could offer throughout the winter months, and agreed to pay the cost of £200. The re-sit had to be done within five years, so it was now or never. Amongst other things, I needed to revise 'security on steep ground'.

Tracey, now teaching in Scotland volunteered to be a mock student so I could practice, and so we went up onto Aonach Mor to set up some scenarios. I lowered her down a steep snow slope to where a platform had been cut with ice axes. As I down climbed to join her she fainted and slumped on the belay. My practice trip had turned into a real and serious emergency. Within a few fraught minutes she came round but was pale and ill. With steep snow below us I returned up the slope, having secured her on the platform, and kept her on a tight rope from above. She woozily climbed back up. At the chairlift cafe hot chocolate was administered, a long break and then the gondola down. Only later did Tracey find out that she was anaemic, but eventually made a good recovery and went on to be a very successful runner. The next day it was Louise from Plas y Brenin who again tested me on several topics as I led her over Bidean Nam Bian above Glencoe on good nevé,[12] in early spring sunshine. This time my skills, decisions and techniques were found to be satisfactory.

Back home I could still pick up other work and the mix would give me a break from the constant restraint culture of my School employer. I left and started work at a secure house. The children here had committed serious crimes and could be violent and highly sexualised.. They required a 2:1 staffing ratio. We tried to use up their energies in a creative way with almost constant physical activity. We were often away on residential trips, mainly camping, in any weather all year round. We chased up and down the Snowdonia hills, scrambling, walking and climbing and mountain biking around the Welsh centres. I completed an eight day shift cycling from Holyhead to Chepstow off-road virtually the whole way. My charge had wanted to raise some money for charity, and grittily completed his challenge in good spirits. I dared hope that this could be a turning point in his life. Other children from other units heard of this trip and wanted to try similar things themselves, and so we facilitated their ideas as best we could so as not to set them up to fail, but to succeed.

The management were happy with these arrangements and receptive to my next suggestion that a Mountain Instructor on the team would be beneficial. This award, the Mountain Instructor Award (M.I.A. now the Mountain Climbing Instructor – M.C.I.) sits above the Summer Mountain Leader and single-pitch awards. It qualifies the holder to take clients on longer more difficult multi-pitch climbs and also to teach climbing. I had the requisite logbook experience and went away to Plas y Brenin again for a nine day training course. There was so much to learn: this was a whole level above, and included things such as teaching a climber to lead, rescuing a climber stuck more than a rope's length above the ground, rescuing an immobilised climber, climbing a rope using a friction hitch, bypassing knots in the rope, and related problem solving. There were sessions on the dark art of short-roping, micro navigation and Tyrolean traverses. It was a great course, with lectures in the evenings and rain most

---

12   Nevé is the best type of snow

days. Without exception everyone was younger and a better climber than I was, but despite my arthritic aches and pains, I had the edge when it came to experience. I planned how I could distil this new knowledge and skill. I could move up in the outdoor world, run my own courses, and employ people. The only way to prepare for the five day assessment would be to climb harder and practice more.

My new main climbing partner now was my old friend, Nige, the Big Carrot Man who had been enticed away from his coarse fishing. It was great to rekindle this friendship after so many years away. Nige was strong and powerful, his day job was a ground worker digging sewers and trenches. He was a very steady solid character, intelligent and utterly reliable. And he was keen to go climbing summer and winter.

It was autumn 2004 and I had to pick up a new boy for the House from a secure unit where he had been serving time. He was to be taken away to a remote barn in the wilds of Yorkshire for a few days whilst some work was carried out at the unit in readiness for his arrival. I was advised to hide all the knives from the kitchen when we arrived at the barn! The boy appeared pretty timid and wanted to play on his computer games like any young teenager would. He didn't even put up any arguments against walking in the hills. After a few days of this a yellow van appeared over the horizon. The cavalry had come to relieve me in the shape of Matt. Matt was in his early twenties, a likeable, well-mannered tough guy, a dyed-in-the-wool 'monner' with a biting sense of humour. We got on well straight away. He told me of his plans to start his own outdoor company and, as we seemed to have so much in common, we discussed a business partnership.

Matt and I started our outdoor company, 'Gateway Outdoors'. We had completed our 'Adventurous Activity' paperwork, been inspected and given the go-ahead to trade. We were now buying equipment for our stores. Friends Paul Wynn and Richard 'Bish' Beddoes started a new shop in Shrewsbury called 'Spike Outdoor' to equip the discerning outdoor enthusiast. The two companies 'Gateway' and 'Spike' sought a symbiotic relationship, helping each other. Matt had a definite idea of how he wanted the company to perform; our target customers would be schools and colleges, delivering climbing and canoeing sessions and Duke of Edinburgh Award Expeditions. I brought my mountain experience to the partnership but Matt had more experience of this daily session work. I had a few contacts, Shrewsbury School and Concord College being the most lucrative ones. Although my ideas were more about expeditions, Matt's were the bread and butter of what we did. I was feeling bullish: now, a few years into self-employment, I had earned £17,849 that tax year, more than I had ever earned, and all from outdoor instructing.

Additionally I had managed to get another trip to Peru off the ground, and Matt wanted to come. The main peak we wanted to climb was Tocllaraju (6032m/19,790ft), one of the higher peaks in the Blanca area.

Matt and I endured a steep climb onto the North West Ridge, shivering and gasping, the cold thin air rasping our throats. Sunrise brought some warmth to our bodies but hunching over our ice axes, we stopped every twenty steps. The final pitch was a bergschrund headwall between us and the gleaming peak. Gasping and laughing, we summited a proper Andean peak with dizzying drops falling three thousand metres away to the *quebradas* below. We were up in the gods.

Our return flight on 7th July 2005 was delayed by the terrorist attacks in London. Thankful to be safe but saddened by the violence, we arrived a day later and got straight back to work. Really, we shouldn't have left our 'baby' Gateway Outdoors' so early in its infancy.

Gateway work had to blend in with other work we could get, mainly care work, which although decently paid was mentally and emotionally tiring. We ran a winter skills course in the Cairngorms for adults before school work came in for the Spring and the young company started to grow again.

*****

Liliana's British citizenship was granted at a ceremony at the Shirehall in Shrewsbury. Ali's situation was different. As I was not her biological father, social services had to be involved and their solicitor was appointed to the case. A letter to Ali's biological father's last known address in Lima was dispatched asking for his whereabouts and an advert was placed in 'The

Lima Times'. We went to the courts in Birmingham where Alexandra Xiomy Braithwaite Escudero was made a temporary Ward of Court as Liliana had to give her up for adoption. It was only then that she and I could both adopt her on an equal footing. She became Alexandra Xiomy Wellings on Friday 19th May 2006, our fifth wedding anniversary. Doing this meant that she could now become a British citizen and eligible for a passport.

I had been asked to start a Cub Pack in Hanwood. Ali was one of the first members, and three year old Matty would come along. On one of the first Pack nights, an assistant leader, an environmentalist, took some of the pack down to the Rea Brook to look at the wildlife. As I approached with my group I saw one of her Cubs floating away in the swollen fast running water. I jumped in and pulled him out to safety, although my feet could not touch the bottom. He never returned to Cubs.

*****

Out of the blue I was offered the 2006 summer season working in Peru for High Places. We had to rapidly adjust our plans. The trade-off was simple: Matt could have Gateway, 'his' business, and I could return to Peru – with my family — and get paid! In truth, Gateway was really Matt's: there wasn't really room, or work for two bosses. He refunded me the £5,000 I had put into the company, and we amicably went our separate ways. Except that it wasn't 'my' £5,000. I should have paid it back to the credit card; but we were living in the moment. I would fly out to run the trips in Peru, and Liliana would follow later with Ali and Matty. That £5,000 would help cement our family bond!

As soon as I had taken our seats for the flight from Birmingham to Schipol Amsterdam we had to 'deplane'. An incoming flight had crash landed on the runway. I found the one client who was travelling this route, and we caught the bus to Manchester and rerouted, arriving in Peru a day late. My luggage made it; the client's didn't. In Lima we had to get a public bus to Huaraz as our private transport had gone the day before. Pushing my way through the teeming travelling masses swarming around the ticket office, I literally bumped into Joe, an old pal from Scouts and Sixth Form.

"Joe! What are you doing here?"

"Scoob! What are the chances?"

We didn't do the maths. Joe had been drafted in to help run a trip for 'Andes', his first trip to Peru. Joe had been living and working in the Lake District for many years, at the forefront of long distance racing and navigating.

The Huayhuash circuit is one of the world's major treks. The Huayhuash (pronounced 'Why wash') is a compact mountain range to the south of Huaraz. It is a remote area, home to Jirishanca, Yerupaja (highest in the range and second highest in Peru at 6635m/21,770ft) and Siula Grande, where my predecessor at High Places, Joe Simpson, had 'Touched the Void' with Simon Yates. My first group on the Huayhuash this summer were a great group from the Austrian Alpine Club. We had stunning scenery all the way, and no hijackings or gunfire this time. I felt vindicated in the bold choices I had made. It was on the tenth day of the trip, the fifth of the trek proper, when over the hill came Elvis — yes, Elvis — carrying the client's luggage last seen at Birmingham International.

This trek diverted to the base camp used by Joe and Simon Yates on their first ascent of the west face of Siula Grande when it had gone so spectacularly wrong. The glacial rubble-strewn bleakness was broken only by our discovery of *Qallu qallu/ Llingli llingli*, a rare plant from the Valerian family. We climbed a 'small' peak of 5000m before completing the circuit.

Back in the Andino – the smartest hotel in Huaraz — showered and clean, I answered a call from reception and let my visitors in – Liliana, Ali and Matty! They had been out in Llamellin, Herlinda's home town, living in an adobe house with no windows, driving donkeys to fetch water and supplies. They were dusty and dirty, and hungry. They had walked miles and really enjoyed themselves.

The next trip was another successful ascent of Pisco. Then I was away with another group, to summit Huapi, Pisco and Tocllaraju, making it five out of six attempts on Pisco and two out of two on Tocllaraju. Having a great team around me was the key to success and I had enjoyed returning to trek leading, but the season was over for another year.

Now it was family time - we got the bus to Cusco, and headed to Machu Picchu. Liliana had never been, and neither had the kids. To them it was the biggest adventure playground in the world: they ran around all over it, laughing all the way. We were back in Lima for the Fiesta de Santa Rosa, Lima's patron saint day, a day of dancing drinking and eating guinea pigs. Together as a family we felt so happy.

The school term back in Hanwood had already started and the kids were late getting back. Somehow I felt under par, and didn't know why, until I passed a metre-long tapeworm and felt much better. I was on a bricklaying course at the time in a bid to 'expand my skill set', as I was picking up some work labouring for Nige, doing odd jobs, trying to make ends meet.

Ron and Else had visited but aunt Puss had been ill. She died on 14th October. We were devastated. Puss had meant so much to so many people. Her sister role to Ed, Ron and my dad Bob had taken on aspects of motherhood after their mother died in 1954, and she had continued to live with her dad Charlie until his death. That her little brother had three sons living round the corner gave her much pleasure. She doted on us, she didn't stand on ceremony and she always appeared fun and happy. Puss had welcomed Liliana and Ali into her heart unconditionally and she knew us and she loved us all.

Chapter 15

Like Icarus

Faltering and Failing

Puss' will stated that on her death 39 Lansdowne Road should be sold and the six surviving nieces and nephews would share the proceeds. Dad was the executor of the estate, and a few months later we all received £25,000 each. We had been expecting it, a wonderful gift from a wonderful person. Liliana and I really needed the money now as we had been living beyond our means. I had several credit cards and juggled them around. The minimum monthly payments had reached nearly £100 on a couple of them, most of that being interest. The mortgage payment was now £693 per month. Additionally I had overdrafts which had never been paid off from university days; I owed money for the log cabin we had built at the top of the garden and also owed for my van. Credit had been easy to obtain, and at that point I had had a credit history of paying loans back early. Now money was coming in, but money was going out faster. I decided to be proactive and ease the financial burden. Without consulting Liliana, I decided to roll all the debts up into a big sum and pay them off with a loan. The interest was just less than 10%. My argument was that when Puss' money came in I would pay the deficit off and have a clean slate. It didn't work out like that though.

The van and the log cabin loans were paid off. We spent money doing up the house and buying materials for me to build a patio. I bought myself a motorbike, a brand new Royal Enfield 350 Bullet, made in India, for £2,500. I bought a brand new drum kit. Why not? I could learn! I opened another credit card, using it to import a bulk load of Peruvian hats and jumpers to sell on a pedlar's licence in Shrewsbury on the run-up to Christmas when other work was quiet. Money was flying around everywhere, and suddenly there was not enough to pay off the expensive loan that I had intended as a short-term measure. I had fumbled it: we had wanted to pay off most of our debt, keep it at manageable levels, but instead it had increased. We had had a fun time, doing the things we had always wanted to, but now everything was proving to be unsustainable through my mismanagement.

Work diversified again in 2007. I did shifts at a care home south of Knighton. An Adventure Rope Course near Shrewsbury sprang up and I was in, running sessions here for school and corporate groups. It was orderly, organised and easy, and well paid. I got work with another outdoor adventure team over the border in Welshpool through Powys County Council educating children excluded from school. Most weekdays we would drive round collecting them, from outposts off the beaten track, from Welshpool and sometimes as far away as Brecon. Once we had everyone together, we would attempt an outdoor activity before the long process of delivering them all back home again.

The mix of work also included Duke of Edinburgh Expedition training for Shrewsbury School. On 17th November Shrewsbury School had their annual freelancers' dinner, and it was here my right leg was broken during some horseplay among staff. I was plastered from upper thigh to toe and I was not Liliana's favourite person on her birthday the next day.

Would I be fit enough to take us all skiing? £1,500 from Puss had gone on that, buying skis, ski boots and ski clothing too. We were leaving on 5th January; I had just over a month. I could at least wheel a trolley up Pride Hill and sell Peruvian hats and jumpers even with a broken leg. The healing process worked quickly enough, and we did go, the bindings kept the foot solid and I skied the famous Kandahar slope. Matty and Ali learnt to ski and whizzed all over the place, laughing all the way. Liliana loved being in the mountains, soaking up the atmosphere.

Back at work, mountain biking was on the roster. This activity seemed to be the best for getting results, keeping the kids moving, using their energies productively. Even a 'mechanical' or a puncture was a learning opportunity. Among the staff there were some great characters: Rob, hard

drinking artist producer of pub murals; JJ, an old friend from school days
— which kid would argue with a giggling 26 stone giant? Jim, young
Yorkshire backwoodsman; Andy - dedicated senior instructor: we were
thrown together in this work, and pretty quickly gelled as a team. The
pupils were completing the requisite paperwork towards awards. Informal
outdoor education seemed to be working. There were days though when
you found yourself working on your own with two pupils who realised
they could run amok. Trying to restrain a child on the top of a cliff in
freezing rain in January is not easy. Help takes a long time to arrive. How
much emotional capital could I sink into working with these kids before
I burnt out?

This was at the back of my mind when I was approached to work as
an assistant for a job in the Atacama Desert. After that he had a couple
of clients who wanted to climb Aconcagua. I would be away for two
months. Fitness had been ticking over with the day job, but it would
need to improve. I started carrying paving slabs up Pontesford Hill in the
winter darkness and running laps up and down the steps when working at
Outward Bound in Aberdovey.

A group of ten of us flew into Calama, northern Chile, and made our
way out to San Pedro de Atacama. It rained. It never rains in the Atacama,
driest desert on earth — ever; but it rained for over an hour! We would
acclimatise here, visit the Valley of the Moon and Taito Geysers, and then
head out into the empty desert to camp. Rheas, guanacos and flamingos
swayed in the shifting filtering colours of the *lagunas* before sparkling
starlit nights surrounded by mountains. We climbed two peaks of around
5,000m (16,400ft) before attempting the volcano of Lascar.

Lascar is one of the Andes' most volatile volcanoes. Ash from its
eruptions has reached as far as Buenos Aires, 2000 miles away. We
pitched camp 15 km (10 miles) to the south and drove across the dusty
plain and over the Tropic of Capricorn. We zigzagged steadily east of
the summit cone, breathing the rotten egg sulphur smell of SO_2. The
crater is 500m (1640ft) deep, and smouldering fumaroles are everywhere.
We felt like time travellers: meeting a dinosaur here would not have

come as a surprise. We climbed west to the summit proper, and then back, descending away from this environment, the stench of primordial elements overpowering us.

We climbed another small peak, and then loaded up the 4x4 and drove through mineral rich desert to attempt one of the twin peaks of San Pedro and San Pablo, both c. 5,800m (c.19,000ft). Here we had to haul 20 litres of water on our backs as there was not a drop to be had. The only water we passed was a vibrant turquoise colour: the highly mineralised, poisonous outfall from an abandoned mine.

Within a week all clients had flown back home. I had some time to kill before the long haul down to Mendoza via Santiago so I cycled out into the desert, trying to combat homesickness. I arrived in Mendoza as ready for Aconcagua as I could be, a few days before the clients - a father and son team. Client Senior acted like a headmaster, and his son was something to do with serious banking. Both were 'ex-pats'. This was going to be a long trip. Over the next few days I took them up into the Cordon del Plata to acclimatise, acting as chief cook, guide, bottle washer, medic, navigator and entertainment officer. They were supposed to be on a bonding mission, but slept in separate tents: Junior on his own, Senior in with me. It was like going on a camping trip with your headmaster, for three weeks!

My focus was to overcome these personality issues. I can get on with anyone. The three of us were on our own, dropped by our agent next to the roadhouse on the Pan American Highway that marked the start of the trek in to Aconcagua. Gauchos on horseback approached us at Puenta Vacas, and we loaded up three mules for our three-day trek to base camp. Our route followed a wide dry river valley through small outposts: Las Lenas, Ameghino and Casa de Piedra (House of Stones). We arrived at the second night's camp in a thunderstorm sharing it with two Scotsmen, recently returned from Antarctica. After fording a wide river to ford the next morning, feet cold and wet from the onset, we pushed on up across the red earth of the Relinchos Valley. Base camp was a small tented village; we arrived at 3pm and camped in a polytunnel at

4200m (13,800ft). Next day a load carry to Camp 1, where we dumped a Hyperspace and a Quasar tent there before returning to base, where the showers are US$20. I stayed dirty.

Camp 1 sits on a tongue of land, the lip of a huge steep hanging valley above with fresh water, only accessible from a small stream when it thaws in the afternoon. We had brought our third tent up with us in readiness to push further up the mountain.

'No water, so spent 5 hours melting snow. Then bag leaked over my sleeping bag. Waste of time. Couldn't breathe properly. Losing sense of humour somewhat!'

As we had reached High Camp, the infamous Aconcagua winds were slamming down the Polish Glacier on to us. We had wasted a lot of precious fuel thawing the water which was lost when the bag leaked. The tent poles flexed madly and the tent fabric pressed down on us making it difficult to move inside the tent for long periods of time.

*'**Friday 20th February 2009**. Day 17 (Day 44). Jnr and I did not sleep all night. Got packed up and headed back to Camp 1. Needed crampons for 2x snowpatches with big fall potential. Camped at Camp 1. Did not sleep all night due to winds.*

*'**Saturday 21st February 2009**. Day 18 (Day 45). Rest Day. Stayed around camp all day, brewing and eating. Camped @ Camp 1. Did not sleep all night. Still windy.*

*'**Sunday 22nd February 2009**. Day 19 (Day 46). Wind abating. Today I had not slept for 3 days so headed to B.C. S+J went up to Camp 2 with Hernan + Nita. Went to see Dr. but he said I'm OK. Felt better @ B.C. v. homesick.*

Hernan and Nita were part of the wandering teams of porters that work and live on the mountain over the season. Since they were young and monstrously fit, Senior offered them some money to get them higher up the mountain.

*'**Monday 23rd February 2009**. Day 20 (Day 47). S+J summit bid (they got to 6500m). The plan was to walk to Camp 2 with water for S+J and then camp at Camp 1. I got to Camp 1, dropped kit, started to go to Camp 2, but felt bad so dropped back to Camp 1. Then decided to drop camp, carry it all back to B.C. Heavy but worthwhile, shit n' all. Got back put Quasar up for J.*

'Tuesday 24th February 2009. Day 21 (Day 48). Acon. I cooked pasta and coffee+ carried them up to Camp1 to meet S+J. They were there by lunchtime. Long drop back down.

'Wednesday 25th February 2009. Day 22 (Day 49). They left early as. Jnr keen to get back home. Acon (4 day trip?) I spent the day sorting out our kit for the mules… Nita cooked me a hamburger (=$10US). Last night at B.C.

'Thursday 26th February 2009. Day 23 (Day 50). Trek out to Punta de Vacas. Solo. Little deviation but sorted it out. Crossed river OK, long trek to Punta in thunder, lightning and rain. Cleared up in evening, and so I got gorgeous BBQ from David (Gaucho) as I'd pretty well run out of food. Great sleep.

'Friday 27th February 2009. Day 24 (Day 51). Trek out to Punta de Vacas solo 3hrs 40 min (8am-1140am). Pick up @ Vacas <u>1pm.</u> Mules via other direction kept us waiting for 2hrs til we found out. Got back to MDZ by 6pm. Then sort out tents, kit etc.'

The clients had been near to the summit but ultimately it eluded them. This had been a very hard trip physically, emotionally and mentally. I needed a break. I headed for the lights of Mendoza to get some relief, feeling exhausted and defeated.

Back in the UK spring was starting to push its way through the dead leaves of winter, and the thing I noticed most was the lack of wind. Living in it for weeks, I felt raw, and the sentient feel and smell of the green grass and the warmth of the sun on the back of my neck slowly restored my energies over the coming days. Any pocket of stillness particularly gave me overwhelming joy.

Liliana had cracked on regardless while I had been away, organising Foxy and Bob to construct the conservatory she'd bought from Ebay. I was physically and emotionally drained, but she was growing in strength and confidence. Somehow our relationship had survived and was now growing again. The kids were glad to have me back and I loved being with them. Spring was here, and there was plenty of work to do.

I started converting the attic. Working with wood, creating actual things that I could see and touch, was therapeutic, but I knew I had neither the skills nor the speed to be able to do it as a tradesman. That was good, because it couldn't be ruined by having to 'call it work'. That always spoils things. In effect, I was spending time and money to make our house worth less, but this was how we wanted it to look. What were a few structural considerations? I wasn't going too mad; at least I had some appreciation for what was involved. My admiration for Chink and his carpentry business grew. Not only did they have brilliant '*craic*' at work, but they produced things that people wanted, to a deadline, and were paid well to do it. I did some 'gofering' for Chink – delivering across the country, 'gofer' this and 'gofer' that - bits of easy shop assembly work, that sort of thing. There seemed plenty of work around and I had been paid well for the Andes trip, but that didn't stop me from my ongoing constant obsession with 'real' work- jobs with terms and conditions, paid holidays, sick pay, pension, advancement opportunities and being part of a team. Irregular income had affected my creditworthiness: I remained and remain a bad bet – unable to obtain overdrafts credit card loans or hire purchase.

For years now there had been a job application from me in someone's in-tray somewhere, a reference to ask for, and an interview to prepare for but always the bridesmaid, never the bride. The results from these were all filed in the bin, and nothing ever said.

One night after Cubs one of the dads stayed behind and we talked about mountains. Sean had climbed many Alpine 4000m peaks and was a member of the Alpine Club. Blimey, I thought, this guy is impressive; he drove a posh car, in fact he had a small fleet of them. He was suave and Southern and über-confident. He asked me if I fancied a trip to the Alps in the summer. How could I say no? But when I got home I worried that at last I would be found out. Could he drag me somewhere well outside of my comfort zone and mock me. But I didn't really care; it could be interesting… and hopefully fun…

Ali had petitioned us for a dog for a very long time. Ten year olds have this way of grinding you down, and Liliana was her usual ambivalent self: "Up to you, my darling," was her stock response. On 29th May, down by the Severn, upstream from Pentre on the border, we met a Welsh Collie crossed with Jack Russell and maybe Arctic Fox, the runt of the litter, she simpered sweetly up at us. £50 bought her, a bale of hay and a tin of dog food. This made up for the fact that I had been away for Ali's tenth birthday: back in the good books again! This pup we named Danni.

Summer continued in unabated energised semi-controlled mayhem: a great mix of local day work, weekend Duke of Edinburgh camps, evenings at Cubs and up on the crag at Pontesford or Grinshill. I had a great three-days-a-week job that I could work around in late summer running a mobile climbing tower up at Bulthy Hill Farm. I ran sessions of speed climbing and coached novices, surrounded by rolling hills and a rare view towards Long Mountain. I cycled there and back every day in readiness for the trip with Sean to the Alps.

Thursday 27th August found me in Geneva airport renting a car, and the next day, having picked up Sean, we caught the rack and pinion railway to Nid D'Aigle and shouldered our fairly heavy packs up to the Tête Rousse Hut at 3167m (10,400ft), where we sweated in the stifling dormitories. Next day racing across the 'shooting gallery' of the Grand Couloir, dodging rocks, and we were at the Gouter Hut perched precariously on the top of its ridge by 9 a.m. Now at 3817m (12,520 ft), we set up camp, expecting to be moved on by the *gendarmerie* at any time. Our plan was to climb Mont Blanc by the ridge above us, the standard Gouter Route, and then descend the other side of the mountain to the Midi and make our way back from there.

Having not slept a wink, we left at 2:20 a.m. without any breakfast fuel inside us. I led fast and furiously to the Vallot Hut, where Sean took over to guide us over the Bosses Ridge, the only semi-technical part of the route. We summited at 8 am, a busy Sunday morning. The wind was by now really strong, so we opted for Plan B and simply reversed our route. Things eased as we returned to the Gouter hut, before the loose rocky descent to the Tête Rousse. We were back in Sean's chalet the next afternoon, Monday: a fun way to spend a long weekend, reaching 4808m (15,775ft), and highest point in Western Europe. It was very far removed from life in the Andes. My tally was Alps 1, Andes 28.

Manic work sucked me straight back in, but a family weekend up to the coast the next weekend was blissful: crabbing off the pier and scrambling around rocks and abseiling the kids into a cave. But on Wednesday 30th September 2009 it all suddenly changed. We heard that Herlinda was really ill in Peru. Liliana acted fast, maxing out two credit cards to buy tickets for her, Matty and Ali. The kids were whisked out of school, and Danni and I returned to an empty house.

Chapter 16

Returning to Mamacita

Stretching Us to Breaking Point

A daughter's love is stronger than time and tide and continent. Herlinda had been living with cancer for a very long time. Very little good news seemed to come to us from Peru. Liliana's very presence there would have bolstered her mum and the family. Her organising and practical nature and her amazing smile would roust everyone from the doldrums. Back on my side of the ocean, I was alone without my family and the sun had gone out.

Half-term meant one thing: foreign students. For several years now we had been guardians. Foreign students, usually Chinese, would come to us for short breaks during term time. Three could fit in the attic room now it was finished. A week lodging at half term netted over £800. The next thing was to sell the drum-kit and the motorbike. It went for half what I paid for it last year; but it was: "Peru, here I come for Christmas!"

The day before her 41st birthday Liliana met me at Jorge Chavez Airport, Lima dressed in a lime green trouser suit, stunning as usual, and looking like the modern businesswoman she had always been. She always worked hard and long hours but I didn't see her gain personally from what she did. It was for solidarity with her mum and her sister Mabel, brother Jorge (Polaco) and father Jorge and their family business.

Ali and Matty were very pleased to see me. With Liliana and Mabel, they were living on the eighth floor of an apartment block in the fashionable area of Miraflores. I liked it here, there was a cool café and even a climbing wall over the road, and I had bought climbing shoes for the kids and myself from home. They were well settled in, having been in Peru for eight weeks already.

The kids went to school every day, but it was all a bit hit and miss: the teachers came most days but there were strikes and walk-outs. Matty and Ali had friends and their Spanish improved but there was disruption and new plans daily. Liliana's family, our family is close-knit, other family members would sometimes be there; but our bedroom door within our apartment had to be kept locked when we were away. The climbing wall would wobble alarmingly as we bouldered outside under the smoggy Lima night sky. Liliana was working long hours at 'Bella Fruta', Mabel's fruit shake café business. The kids would walk there after school, crossing a huge 8 lane highway in a throng of people, all jostling and taking their chances. I was appalled by this place, but proud of how my kids, just 10 and 7 years old, took to it like a daily adventure.

We fell into a sort of pattern of living. I became the house-husband, being around for the kids, so if we arrived at school to find no teachers, then at least I was there for them, drawing, stories, the climbing wall, games of chess in a café; I even had a 'local' where I went a couple of nights a week for a beer. Because the kids' education was so sporadic now, I decided to take them on a trip down south to Arequipa.

Arequipa is a desert city high in the Andes. The overnight bus arrived at 8 am, and we found a hostel. Arequipa's architecture is stunning, with a huge *Plaza de Armas*. The next day we went on a sightseeing trip to the Colca Canyon, where we hoped to see condors. The bouncing bus upset Matty and he didn't cope well with the altitude and the dust. We saw condors from a distance. We sat out in the café, with the volcano *El Misti* shining above us. This had been a very important bonding trip for me, Ali and Matty.

The fruit markets of Lima are a riot of colour, texture, bustle and business. We would load the taxi up with boxes of fruit strapped on the roof and pushed through the crowds back to 'Bella Fruta' where the *jugueros* prepared it.

Tuesday 8th December 2009. *Kids up and ready, but no school today! OK – let's go to work. Busy, busy, busy! I left @ 1pm w' Matty + splitting headache. Got home, relaxed, felt better, played chess, climbing wall not open, Burgers* *(yuck!) chess @ La Maquina. Matty asleep 9pm. Listening to iPod wondering where L+A were. They got back @ 12m.n. with tales of football hooligans, knives, idiots, big battle, trying to get in the shop, 100 people barricaded in, v. scary, horrible, police on horses broke it up! Scary!'*

Back 'home' in the apartment the kids wanted to know whether 'Cheese on toast' was a good name for a hamster! Bizarre and surreal.

*'**Thursday December 17th 2009.** M+A to school. I'm beginning to realise how much we trust each other in daily life. Certainly in my UK job I can trust people with my life within mins of meeting them – and vice versa. Here there really seems to be a hardened culture of mistrust that pervades everyday life- it throws up issues all the time, makes it so difficult to avoid conflict.*

Separately, why does L jump into these ventures without thinking/planning them thru' properly first? Ostensibly, she is here for her mum, but it is the business. And she is using me as a sort of manager/dogsbody. I do not cope well in this environment, but she just gives me Hobson's choice. She needs to recruit some staff and not rely on the goodwill of her husband, which she totally takes for granted.

Change Matty's tix….?'

Isolated and paranoid, I feared that our family would be torn apart, with perhaps Liliana and Ali remaining in Peru and Matty and I returning to the UK.

*'**Friday December 18th 2009.** Diarrhoea and sleep all morning! BF?(Bella Fruta) (School break up for Xmas (until 6/1/10)). Ali school prom. Excellent occasion. Ali looked so grown up. It went on late, but good do.*

*'**Sunday 20th December 2009.** Family. Saw the water fountains+ lights again; got v. wet!*

*'**Monday 21st December 2009.** Round Presidential Palace. Saw the changing of the guard close up – v.good! Didn't go to Huaraz due to stomach – had diarrhoea for over a week now + L's insistence that the road will be dangerous. Came back to Apt.'*

*'**Tuesday 22nd December 2009**. Went into BF after failed attempt to take kids to school (L thought there was something happening today). Managed to escape BF and went to La Muralla Park – an area of concrete down by the*

polluted river with a café and bike hire under the road bridge. (NB – do not go there in case of earthquake!) Kids hired bikes for ½ hr, then we went for good session @ the climbing wall. L back v. late as usual.

'**Thursday 24th December 2009**. I was supposed to look after the shop for 1-2 hours. It turned out to be 10 hours! What was supposed to be an Xmas shopping trip with A+M was hijacked. Another day of 'why am I here?'

'…Still contemplating divorce – or at best separation. I cannot believe she enjoys all this shit, but she apparently does! Happy Christmas! PS – We got to Mami Ina's house about 10:30-11pm. I managed to stand around in the street drinking with the neighbours for a while. L,A,M, Mabel and Ina – sleeping.'

'**Friday 25th December 2009.** Christmas Day. All slept in late. Not much in the way of presents (from me) I'm afraid. Mabel bought Matty a skateboard and Fabricio and Ali hand-held computer games. The corner shop open today, so I got some beers for me + Polaco. I bought fireworks for the kids (traditional). Mami Ina cooked us cow's stomach soup and suckling pig with spuds, veg. We ate sitting up by the washing line on the top floor.

Later Polaco and I went in search of Agualito (Great Grandad) but @ 95 yrs old he was in bed by 8 pm. We drank some beers and a couple of bottles of sweet wine outside a corner shop with Sebastian - one of Polaco's/Julio's mates,! L has a bad throat and is taking amoxycilin + amplex?

'**Saturday 26th December 2009.** Today I had promised Matty we would buy the remote control cars, and we did – but not before traipsing round the fruit market with L for several hours and then taking it to BF. We bought the cars from some sort of underground post apocalyptic manic trading bunker absolutely rammed with people. Scary to see the S-Sismo signs down here. You wouldn't stand a chance in an earthquake. I insisted we went back to Miraflores where I had t-d up a meeting with old friend Eudes Morales about running an Alpamayo trip next year. We then went to visit Harry Hildebrand of Markham College to talk about Outdoor Education. Lots of chat, lots of ideas which could result in odd bits of work next yr… Got home late and had a quick go with the cars before we all fell asleep.

'**Sunday 27th December 2009.** The proposed night of passion for L+S failed to materialise… The morning spent packing, then a taxi via the flower sellers

*en route to Mami Ina's. IB 6650 LIM-Mad Dep 2055 Arr 1425 +1. Mami
had made papa la Huancaina and chicken + rice – nice! We packed some presents
and opened the ones from Mum + Andrea which had been hidden. This was
great – happy campers, but sadly time for me to go. I hugged Matty + Ali + L @
the airport, and with a heavy heart headed thru the departure gate.'*

I would never see Herlinda -'Mami Ina'- again. Leaving Matty and Ali
gave me pain, but I knew I couldn't stay as I needed to earn money to keep
our house in Cruckton viable. Back home I had to keep moving. I picked
up the £200 cash I had stashed with a friend and went out to for a mad
New Year. Double bonus! PPI refunded money was paid directly into my
account: £660. I packed the Peugeot 306 and headed north just as the best
winter conditions in decades hit the UK – The Big Freeze of 2010.

Big Al was married now and living with Jane and the kids up by
Corpach, north of Fort William. Al had passed all his mountain badges
and was working as a M.I.C. – Mountain Instructor Certificated, training
and assessing aspirant mountain leaders, guiding and climbing summer
and winter. He had flourished since our University days. But he didn't
drive, which meant I could drive him to his assignments. Al doesn't really
differentiate between work days and his own climbing; it's all climbing to
him, all fun. Once again we climbed Curved Ridge on Buachaille Etive
Mor in good snow conditions, something Al must have done at least 100
times by then. It was a great day out, and the client enjoyed it. On days
without work we skidded the car up to Fort Augustus to climb a small
ephemeral waterfall, frozen solid. I took myself up to play around on the
frozen Steall Falls at the head of Glen Nevis; I went skiing, called to see
Nina and had a go at curling on a frozen loch. But all too soon I was spent
up and had to start working again.

Getting to Welshpool, get the minibus defrosted, and I was back on
the merry-go-round of taking the excluded students out for outdoor
education. The big freeze lasted until well into April as so much snow had
been blown off the fields and hills into the lanes that they were impassable
for months. Huge diversions had to be taken to try and keep contact with

everyone. Activities in the snow and my winter survival skills were being used, balancing safety, fun, learning, paperwork and timekeeping.

We spoke most days - the family in Peru were doing it their way as I continued to 'hold the fort' in Cruckton. In March I went on a lads' ski trip to Aviemore with Rob 'The Ferret', dependable practical and unflappable, Clive 'Dirty Uncle', the roughest of diamonds, and Al 'Glasses Up', used car-dealer maverick and raconteur. This marauding band of misfits benefited by driving from Oswestry to Aviemore with synchronised bladders, and therefore we were well early for the pub. The trouble started on the street when, like a fool, I lobbed a snowball into a group of Irish girls. From their reaction it might as well have been a Molotov cocktail! I was recognised in The Vault nightclub later and, by nefarious methods still unknown although highly plausibly related to alcohol, I found myself unconscious on the floor, blood pouring from a wound in the base of my skull where I had hit it on the corner of a metal step during an uncontrolled descent. The skiing was pretty uncontrolled too, and my head as well as my body had now started to feel wrong on a daily basis.

Liliana Ali and Matty were all due back at the end of April. Ali needed to be registered again with Hanwood School ready to start Secondary in September up in Pontesbury. Liliana, perhaps through this recent experience, now better understood the kids' situation regarding education and that they had to be the priority. A volcanic eruption was the random delayer to flights. This time it was the Eyjafjallajokull volcano in Iceland that caused it. They landed at Gatwick, not Manchester; but most importantly they were safely back, my adorable lovely kids and exasperating but well-meaning wife were home.

Chapter 17

Hiding the Bad Times

Finding the Good Times

The General Election of May 2010: Labour lost power to a coalition of Conservatives and Liberal Democrats. Liliana and I volunteered to be stewards at the Shrewsbury Folk Festival, to save the massive expense of the tickets. In front of a crowd of 5,000 festival-goers I drunkenly heckled socialist Billy Bragg as to why he had advised people to vote Liberal. His reasoned articulate response about tactical voting was no match for my impassioned incoherence, and I was summarily ushered out by my fellow stewards but Bragg's interpretation of 'Union Miner' still remains hollow to me. What had riled me? I was in a bad way. I felt emasculated, disempowered, drifting with the tide. Not all the reasons were political, but I had to vent my spleen somewhere. I hadn't been able to secure a decent job, despite a constant stream of applications; debt was crippling me; I felt powerless regarding my family; my health was deteriorating; Mum was ill; and Liliana and I were struggling, unable to see my way clearly, bizarrely and for no sane reason, I blamed it all on Billy Bragg.

A groin pain that had developed earlier in the year was now permanent, hampering my driving ability. I didn't yet know, but my hip joint was wearing out. Any physical work was becoming very difficult. Mum had succumbed to arthritis and was now wheelchair bound at best, and mostly bedridden. Dad had mobility problems too, and I went out to help them at Yorton when I could. Dad paid me an hourly rate, but I felt beholden. I was nearly 50 and any career I had hoped to kick-start at this late stage seemed further away than ever. The next generation, people in their forties, thirties and even twenties, were now established in roles with the companies I had worked for, and I felt like I was sinking to the bottom of the tank, no more than a 'gofer', a substitute, just filling in, with no way of moving up. As soon as the work stopped the money stopped, and I had to rethink and act every time. I had tried every job from British Antarctic Survey to vending machine operative and everything in between, but I was just making up the numbers, not doing what I wanted to do work-wise or going where I wanted any more: thrashing about with no strategy, no plan. Career success had eluded me. I made mistakes and began to lose confidence in my abilities.

Herlinda died on Saturday September 4th 2010. Liliana flew to Peru the next day and arrived just in time for the funeral on Monday 6th. That was Ali's first day at Secondary School. Bravely she and Matty went in to school, no crying. Their amazing mother had brought them up to be tough. Our relationship was under pressure, and our parenting partnership was stretched paper thin, across two hemispheres, but it was just about holding out.

Liliana was away for two weeks, and upon her return had to appear before a tribunal to explain why she had left work at such short notice. There was no compassion from her employer: she lost her job. Things were now at a very low ebb. Immediately there was an impact on our finances.

Then Lem Kirby contacted me out of the blue. Here he was now, over twenty years down the line, a mate from Alaska. Friendships forged in situations like that run deep. Now a rich and successful vascular surgeon, he and his wife and sister were flying into London, staying with friends who lived in a castle, and they had VIP tickets for us and them to see our hero, Van Morrison, at The Albert Hall. Liliana would not come, so I took Matty with me and he loved the castle they were staying in and his new friends. These lovely people were doing very well, thank you, but I was vague when discussing our circumstances, not brave enough to admit that Liliana and I were struggling and also had been on a financial roller coaster for a long time, barely holding on. Sitting in the box I cried through Van's performance, not sobbing, but unable to stop the tears, wiping them away unseen. Live music was a luxury we had not been able to afford for a long time, and I felt the poignancy of his songs, the lyrics of the song writing genius that had been in the soundtrack to my life. I sat there, an imposter in a plush velvet box, with my free t-shirt, free canapés and champagne unable to even afford a round, feeling vulnerable and small.

When we got back Liliana was nowhere to be seen. This was unlike her: she would never usually venture out at night, especially on a Sunday night. I put the kids to bed, read them the customary story and fended off questions as to where she was. Next morning there was still no sign of her, but we ate breakfast, and Matty and Ali went to school as usual. I cycled into town to make the usual requests for more time to pay. I had no work that day, but sometimes the penalties for missing payments could add up to more than a day's pay, so it was always stressful trying to keep up the dialogue of debt. At least if you pay something, even as little as £1, it can buy a bit of extra time.

Liliana was so fed up with me that she had just decided to take herself away for the night. Liliana and I were trying to understand each other. We both wanted the best for our kids – that's what had kept us together. Deciding what 'the best' was often a source of arguments, but we would try and resolve them amicably. She found work working for the NHS, initially as a cleaner. I found myself having to travel further for work and doing jobs like shop-fitting and labouring, but hardly any instructing. My hip and groin pain was getting more and more painful.

This really came home to me during a trip to the Cairngorms. Mountaineering, which had been virtually a way of life a few years ago, was now just a few days away snatched perhaps twice a year. I was ploughing through deep snow towards Coire Lochain when my phone rang. It was the current boss. There was no more work, government funding withdrawn with immediate effect. Don't come in next week.

I continued up on to the top of the ridge. The increasing wind meant that I had to lean on my poles. I had reached the Fiacaill a' Coire Cas and was about to begin the fairly innocuous descent towards the ski station when I froze. A crampon came off: a common enough occurrence, but looking down, I struggled to bend and reach to fix it. I looked at my gear: everything was old, second-hand, repaired or else lashed up - me included.

The young climbing bucks were streaming off the hill now, leaving me in their wake. Slowly I limped down, ready for a slip or a fall, tense, not relaxed. And then I had to go back home to someone who was annoyed I had been away, and break it to her that I had no work.

Feeling sorry for yourself is a warm feeling, a little cocoon, but it doesn't pay the bills. However there were other labouring jobs coming at me, and I was working in various parts of the country in a variety of jobs, and some money was coming in. Liliana got a job working in the Pharmacy at Redwoods, part of Royal Shrewsbury Hospital: at last something she was trained for and she very much wanted to do.

My blitz of job applications was just drawing a blank. Then there was a call from Nina in Scotland. I went up, was interviewed and suddenly I was employed, on a contract! Venture Trust is a youth charity supported by the Scottish Parliament. It aims to change young people's lives through a programme of outreach and planned outdoor residential activities in which they are challenged to work together to complete a task. Never mind that the weather was foul most of the time; never mind we were out all the time, and that the pace of the group was glacial. I was part of a team. I could see a point to it all again, using my skills and experience. Yes, the lines of communication back to Cruckton were stretched, and my hip pain continued; but I felt valued as a team player, and my confidence was returning.

Unfortunately within a few weeks they could see that I was struggling, and I was called into the office. The issue was that I wasn't helping the team: with my stiffness, hobbling and limping I was a liability more than a leader. What if something went wrong in the Cairngorms, with a group? The risk just couldn't be taken. Mr Karlakki, my consultant, had told me before I went to Venture Trust that a hip replacement was the answer; nothing else would do, and the sooner the better, but I had been in denial. Venture Trust promised me that when it was all done and dusted and I was able again they could offer me work, but this was looking like next year now. There was nothing else for it. It was 3rd May 2012: time to go back home after seven weeks, try and find a vehicle that would last a while, look for any available work and try to keep smiling.

Matty and Ali were doing well at school. Ali had discovered running, and won Inter School Gold in the 1000 metres race. She read books all the time and she questioned everything. Matty's 10th birthday party involved him and a group of his friends climbing, abseiling and caving at Llanymynech. I managed the day. That's the thing about arthritis: some days you are well enough to function, but many days you are not.

The date for my hip replacement was set for 17th October 2012. On the run-up to this I felt increasingly nervous. I convinced myself that I had to do things with the family before October while we were all together. This resulted in a few walks into Snowdonia, Ali doing the Cwfwry Arête with me and Nige, The Nantlle Ridge, and Matty and me walking to Farmer Phil's Festival. Strange as it sounds, I had also managed to lead a few Three Peak Challenges for friends Oggy and Maria, as either driver or mountain leader but with many painkillers. After this the operation seemed so final somehow.

Inevitably the time came, and I was admitted to Oswestry Orthopaedic Hospital. I didn't know what to expect after the operation: what I would or wouldn't be capable of. All I remember is waking up on the ward full of old men, singing at the top of my voice in the middle of the night – sing or scream, I remembered, sing or scream. Of course I was shushed and sedated, medicated and moved. The hospital staff were understanding, dedicated and professional. I was kept in for four days. At home I had to inject anticoagulants into my stomach daily, and there was a long list of do's and don'ts. To my worried mind the walk outside down the drive had gained the significance of trying to descend the North Face of the Eiger. My chair had been raised on blocks as my bending was limited. There was even a commode set over the toilet.

Gradually over the weeks things started to move forward. The pain in my hip had gone completely, and the swelling and pain from the operation subsided. Every day I set myself a target to walk a little further. The North Face of the Eiger morphed back into a steep driveway, and the crutches were replaced by a single stick. Matty was brilliant, helping me put my socks and pants on, but it was not something he bragged to his mates about!

It was November now, and financially we were marooned, but help came from out of the blue. An old friend heard about my hip trouble and offered me a soft loan. We agreed for it to be paid in instalments through the winter. When I asked how I could pay it back I was told to just 'wait and see' there was no hurry. Time is money and now they had bought me time: time to recover fully and look to the future. There was hope.

I applied for a job as Lettings Agent, Estate Agent and Funeral Director and as a houseparent at Concord College. I didn't get any of them, but at Concord I met with the Principal who remembered I had worked for them before. I made a passing comment about how 'My daughter would love it here!'

'I'd have to see her reports' he replied matter-of-factly. I was there the next day with them and handed them in to his secretary. By time I got home there was an email in my inbox inviting Ali for a tour of the campus and an interview. She impressed them, and on January 29th 2013 she returned for some tests. Although she didn't shine, the principal was so impressed with her work ethic, her confidence and ambition that he offered her a place, starting on Monday 25th February.

My mobility was improving daily, spring was round the corner, and things seemed good again. I had even managed to get some contract work before the half term. Things were going so well that we planned a family trip to Scotland. We packed up with winter survival gear and drove up to Glenmore Lodge in the Cairngorms, where we loaded up and crunched our way through the snow along the track to Ryvoan Bothy. Danni pulled our gear, which we had secured onto a little cart that Rob the Ferret had helped us make. At the bothy we roasted by a fire with a few other bothiers as the mercury plummeted below minus ten outside. Matty skied, Ali read and Liliana and I walked in crampons. My confidence was definitely returning. We had fun before Ali's big new beginning.

Concord College is one of the premier International English Language Colleges in the UK. Situated eight miles south of Shrewsbury in Acton Burnell Hall, the campus boasts incredible facilities. Students come from all over the world, but mainly from the Far East. They are from rich, famous, influential, powerful families. They are studious, and live on campus. The college is a charitable trust. This means many things, but the most important for us was to do with tax and fees. Because the students don't come with a broad knowledge of English, bright local native speaking students are admitted as day students through a bursary scheme. Perhaps even without knowing it, they earn their places here, acting as monitors for the teachers, helping by speaking the language fluently and prompting debate and discussion within the classroom. We were immensely proud that Ali, whose native tongue was Spanish, had scaled these heights and was studying alongside these international students.

Venture Trust Scotland was true to its word. On April 1st 2013 at 9am there I was back working with them. My efforts to get back to fitness over the winter had paid off. VT started me on a steady lowland expedition. The young clients, arriving with their emotional baggage and low self-esteem seemed like people I could empathise with.

Having been through months of physical and emotional trauma and coming to terms with the ups and downs of life, just part of my life's graph, I felt I was well-placed to listen to these young people and their stories. Individually they had come forward to join in, sign up and abide by the basic rules we had; it was an admission that things in their lives needed to change, a chance for a new beginning, to break old habits. As we walked in to camp up near Derry Lodge one night a man was camping near the bothy, casually observing us all. Later we fell into conversation. The man was an academic, and praised what we were doing.

"You're fishing upstream!" he said "The NHS is positioned just above the waterfall! They try and help people when things speed up and before they fall over." He continued: "You are trying to help people see the journey they can take from an early age, helping them look out for the waterfall and find a less turbulent path."

His comments rang true. We knew these children would be going back into the communities that had helped form them straight after the expedition. They would face all the same privations and temptations, the same destructive daily grind. To break out of the cycle would be an on-going challenge for young people, many with invisible scars. The expedition phase is only part of a longer contact period with the VT outreach team, who try to help them use the experience of the expedition to build survival tactics, improve communication, and establish healthy friendships back in their communities.

Noble ideals like these could sound hollow when bandied around and put into actions by people with their own life problems; but really are we not all just leaning on each other, helping each other? Someone who is being helped may not realise that the person who is helping them needs help too.

Back home I had started a youth club in Hanwood in 2010, and it was now flourishing with leaders Will and Lyn taking the helm. I had managed to do this within the relative chaos of my own existence, helped by the parents and carers who also wanted to bring their children together for fun and the future of the community. The lily grows out of the mire.

Venture Trust work is issued in small parcels, as it is intense mentally and emotionally. I had offers of other work which were going to be more fun and would give me a break.

James Hickman and Dan Cassidy, the laconic American bluegrass fiddler from Maryland (brother of the late Eva Cassidy): a guitar/fiddle duo, had lined up a short tour of Scotland to promote their CD. Dan doesn't drive, and James didn't want to, especially since one of the gigs was in Bradford, with the next one being at Loch Torridon Community Centre. I became their roadie and driver in my rattly van, and they gigged round the Highlands. It was a great tour; the lads were very well received. I had known James and Dan for many years. James learnt his craft at a young age in and around the folk club in Shrewsbury with his dad Cedric, where he met Dan, whose slow southern drawl belied his incredible musical talent

James liked to keep fit, and wanted me to introduce him to hillwalking. The long daylight hours allowed us to spend a few hours out on the hills without interfering with the gigs. A highlight of the week was an ascent of Bla Bheinn on the Isle of Skye. This mountain sits apart, offering views towards the Cuillin Ridge. Other peaks followed. We posted the photos on social media. Without me realising it, the pictures were promoting me and advertising my mountain skills.

Jim at Adventurous Ewe and the Mountain Challenge Events Company had picked up on what I was doing from my facebook posts and offered me leading work on some Three Peak Events. The National Three Peaks is to be completed within 24 hours, climbing the three highest mountains of Scotland, England and Wales. Being asked to do this galvanised my confidence, and soon I was back in the mountains again, feeling strong and secure.

My motivation for being in the mountains had always come from within, from my passion to be out amongst it all. Leading people, whoever they were - youths, adults, people with disabilities - in the outdoors is when I had felt most at home and most at ease. When I was growing up 'doing The Three Peaks' had meant a bunch of mates in the pub banding together – using someone's car, maybe a Ford Capri; someone else had the map; we all chipped in for fuel and food; and off we would go after work on a Friday. A different breed of people now seemed to be emerging into this outdoor industry.

Now the Three Peaks had captured the public's imagination. People could buy the experience with the click of a mouse. Many times, before the start, we would check a client's kit and send them back to buy proper boots or other essentials before allowing them out on to the hills. They wanted to be guided and some did not know where they were being led. I am convinced a large section of the population remain unaware how to access the countryside, and fewer know how to look after themselves or navigate. Whilst this is very good for us, as we get paid to guide them, an element of education helps these events. The Three Peaks are looked upon scornfully by some mountain people, and I can see why: it can feel like herding people along at times; but you do keep fit, you meet new people and teach, instruct and advise them and each time it is a challenge.

Many clients are doing the event for charity which adds another variable, the 'must complete it at all costs' mindset. This is a brave but dangerous approach. They need a mountain leader who can make decisions about safety without being skewed by outside moral concerns.

Sleep and nutrition are the key elements, so minibus tactics have to be good, being able to switch off and snooze as best you can. Of the mountains, Scafell Pike is the hardest: the path through Hollowstones and on to the summit is non-existent, and it is invariably dark, wet, foggy, windy and cold. After successful completion of this spiteful little mountain, the technical aspects seem to drop away, with only a stumble up and down Snowdon to be completed.

The original Three Peaks Challenge was completed in 1926. The 24 hour timing was from the top of Ben Nevis to the top of Snowdon. We would often bring this information to our clients' attention if it looked like they were flagging on the latter stages. As clients descended in dribs and drabs into Llanberis, we had to then organise forward transport, usually via Chester, then drive back to the depot near Oswestry biting knuckles to stay awake, swigging energy drinks. The bus had to be cleaned before we could drive home, hopefully with enough time and energy left to at least acknowledge the existence of our loved ones before falling asleep on the settee.

On weekdays there was Red Ridge work; caving, climbing and abseiling instruction with groups of primary school children at the disused quarries and mines of Llanymynech. These days were very well organised and the kids would step back on the bus at the end of the day tired and happy.

An offer of a two week contract to assist with a Land's End to John O'Groats bike ride came up with 'High Places/Pedal Nation'. This was a full-on-no-rest-days-day-after-day trip, working with Nick Mitchell, who had written the new 'LEJOG' guidebook. Nick was a great character, knowledgeable down-to-earth and fun to work with, and we worked long and hard to ensure the event went well. An average of 80 miles had to be covered daily. This is a steady doable amount, but the slower you are the longer you are out each day and that attrition can start to take its toll. We had to be the last ones in; we couldn't leave anyone out on their own. Nick and I took it in turns to ride with the clients and drive the van.

The days in the van involved buying and preparing food, running errands, fixing easy mechanicals, dealing with navigational challenges, general chores and humping luggage into rooms. By the time the group reached the wider horizons into the Scottish Highlands a better sense of camaraderie existed as we and our ten cyclists rolled along. A day's work was typically fourteen hours, with up to eight or ten in the saddle. High Places/Pedal Nation were paying me £50 per day plus free food and lodging.

While working on this, I managed to use the internet and lots of texts to cobble together a small music festival at our local pub, The Lea Cross Tavern, for the weekend after we returned. Who needs Glastonbury?! Ten bands played, and the Saturday night headline on the back of a tractor was 'Blues Boy Dan'- Dan Owen our local young hope hero. About two hundred people braved the rain that night (the first rain after thirty-five dry straight days) but we didn't care, we were having fun, running on full throttle, living life fast and furiously.

Summers were so much fun and our local festival, Farmer Phil's Festival was always much anticipated by friends and family alike. Egger would come over with Andrea and their boys Adam and Jamie and Chink would bring Dan and Rosie. Liliana's brother Julio would appear from Manchester with his family – Yani, Oksana, Gabriel and Junior. We would all camp, cook and drink together, full size barrels of beer shaded on trestle tables; circled round a campfire.

All the cousins would play together, usually in fancy dress, roaming this family friendly festival site safely, leaving the adults to enjoy the fun, the occasional sunshine, the spectacle of it all framed between the Longmynd and the Stiperstones. The music was an eclectic mix of local bands and artists plus semi famous headliners. We strolled around the site bumping into old friends as we drank ourselves even more sillier, laughing and joking all the way. In the evening after the bands had finished we would stumble around and eventually sit, sing and laugh round our our fires. It was just brilliant and so relaxing we didn't want those summers to end. Events like these confirmed our deep friendships and love for each other.

Liliana and I were finding our way better now. Matty was ready for secondary school, and Ali had spent the summer back in Peru with her auntie Mabel and the family. I felt so good and strong, working the Three Peaking most weekends now, so I entered the Long Mynd Hike and went round easily in 17 hours, just 51 weeks after the new hip replacement. My body had passed its test.

But the nights were drawing in and outdoor work would soon end. Millets outdoor shop offered me a retail job in their Shrewsbury store, which, although only a basic hourly rate, did have the advantage of being paid weekly. Work patterns here were strange, though: every day a different start and finish time, four hours most days. Six hours were the maximum legal amount you could work without a break, and sure enough no break was allowed. Four hours would pay me £24.76 before tax. I began to understand how zero hours contracts worked. How and why had it come to this situation? When I had worked for BT we had earned more and that was 34 years earlier!

How employment had taken a dive since then! I could only find work for minimum wage and with bad terms and conditions. Although I still applied for 'proper' jobs, the reality of the situation was that I could not get these jobs, an interview being my best result. Perhaps it was fate reminding me to be careful what I wished for. Could I have really returned to a 'real' job and seriously stuck at it?

Venture Trust believed in me, however, even though their contracts were short term. I needed the money too: I left Millets and arrived in Scotland on February 6th 2014 with £3.26 to my name. VT's £115 per day was decent, but you earned it camping out in the wilds in a filthy February, dealing with troubled youths, technically and in reality on call 24/7. Results from this work were intangible and unquantifiable but there were rewarding days.

Ed Wellings was taken into hospital. I called in to Liverpool on my way home from working up north to wish him well. It was the last time I ever saw this lovely man; an unsung war veteran, uncle, devoted family man and friend, he died in his sleep on March 23rd 2014 aged 93.

Spring brought gardening work at £7 per hour, if paid by cheque, otherwise cash at £6.50; and there was the conundrum that it was below minimum wage but more hours than zero hour contract shop work. I hadn't the funds to wait for a cheque to clear so I was back in the cash-in-hand economy. Eventually the better work came in: another tour of Scotland with James and Dan, then another LEJOG bike ride with Nick Mitchell with a good bunch of cyclists and good weather for two weeks.

I got a job, in a factory, five days a week making roof trusses and bespoke wood panels for timber frame buildings. A big order had come in and I was amongst an influx of new starters. A few days later it had all fallen through; the foreman saw how awkwardly arthritic I was, slow jarring movements getting up and down on the bench to screw components together; and out I was again. At least I got a "sorry, mate!"

Still I could walk well, and working with the Soldier's Charity guiding army veterans along the route of The First World War Western Front in France was something I was honoured to be part of. This was in September to commemorate 100 years since the Great War started. The cemeteries, and there were so many of them, all stood pristine, mute in testament to the hundreds of thousands of men who made the ultimate sacrifice to secure our future freedoms. The love and compassion of our War Graves Commission and other nations help keep the reverence to these holy places. We walked between them, the small towns and villages so quiet now.

The season of mellow fruitfulness was upon us back in Blighty, precursor to the inevitability of winter. As a counter point, Pantomime, I reasoned, would be a good way to get through the dark winter months, which of late seemed to be having an increasingly negative impact on my body, mind and soul. Twice a week rehearsals for the Pontesbury Players' Pantomime would be good for my mental health, I figured. This was a tacit admission that life had been taking its toll recently but this was fun. Three months of learning lines, singing songs and acting then a buzz from 'the roar of the greasepaint and the smell of the crowd!' as the banter repartee adlibbing and knockabout comedy lifted us all up to a grand finale. And Spring!

By December I was able to look back on the year and take stock of what I had done. The list I committed to my diary on 4th December 2014 makes for interesting reading:

'Retail, VT (Venture Trust), Labourer, Gardener, Roadie, Driver, Bike Leader, Mountain Leader (summer), Alpinist (amateur), Summer School Tutor, Slabber, Tour Guide, Photographer, Singer, Actor, Youth Worker, SPA/ High Ropes, Bushcraft Instructor, Tiler, Skip Lorry Driver, Chinese Delivery Driver, Vending Machine Stockist, Guardian'.

Chapter 18

The AM in SLAM

Alexandra and Matthew

Our chaotic financial existence became something that we had adapted to; we took the rough with the smooth but gradually we were establishing ourselves. True, all the adventure and excitement had left me with my wonderful wife and family but nonetheless very precariously perched – for instance, I could not afford to be ill.

Ali and Matty had their own energies needs and lives to lead. Ali had blossomed at Concord College. Early starts and late nights of studying were now paying off. Every Saturday morning there had been tests to familiarise the students with exam conditions. Ali learnt strategies and tactics to help her get the most from these situations and sure enough she became a straight A student, gaining 7 A's and 4 A stars in her GCSE's in the summer of 2015. Since the age of 13 Ali had moved into a netherworld – living in a semi detached ex-council house in Cruckton but having a friendship group of extremely wealthy international school friends. Her Peruvian heritage and her confident manner carried her through this juxtaposition. A friend invited and paid for her to go to Hong Kong. Whilst they were there they went to China and then to Thailand for the Full Moon Party at Ko Pha-ngan. A fleet of limos complete with bodyguards picked her and her friend up at Bangkok Airport. Ali was moving in interesting circles, aged 15.

Despite having friends in high places Ali showed a compassionate side. With a great help from her mum, the Ali Wellings Foundation was launched, a charity to offer help and support to those in Peru who have less than others. The way they worked to do this mainly involved using social media to get their message across. Ali had been to Peru to teach English after finishing her GCSE's. The next year the town of San Jacinto where she had been working was hit by floods and mud slides, wiping houses out of its way. These torrents displaced many people. Ali's Peruvian head teacher assessed the damage and sent out a call for funds to help repair homes. Ali's foundation, through social media was able not only to raise £2,000 but to get it over to the people who needed it within 48 hours. This showed how the power of these platforms can best be used. There were many other local fund raising events too and a steady stream of help has been sent to Peru over the intervening years.

Matty's strengths lay in more practical subjects. To Ali's mastery of English Spanish History and Economics, Matty, not squeamish, could fish, skin a rabbit, walk and climb; he could make and mend things: Design Technology, Art, Maths and Physics were his strong points. However they both shared an independent flare and were strong and confident, friendly and hard working. We were very proud parents.

Matty was packed off on a summer tour. Liliana had found a flight to Canada for him for £150, but obviously there was a catch – there were 6 planes to catch – Iceland – Greenland – Newfoundland – Montreal – Toronto – Vancouver. Unsurprisingly this odyssey fell apart but the airline was true to its' word and found him a direct flight for the same price. As a 14 year old this was Matty's right-of-passage. He was away on his own for over 2 months staying with relatives and friends - both Anglo-Canadian and Peruvian-American but all people that he had never met. Matty's journey took him to Vancouver Island then to Boston USA, New York and Puerto Rico – staying firstly with our family in Canada and then Liliana's family friends in USA. He even worked as a waiter in Boston and as a 14 year old these experiences gave him immense life lessons.

What a family we were becoming: Matty and Ali globetrotting confident young teenagers – Ali a global citizen, serious but happy to move in the circles of the movers and shakers: family loving and devastatingly witty when the mood took her. Matty: a happy–go–lucky down to earth practical cool kid with a smile that could melt icebergs. Liliana was a pharmacy worker, Peruvian social media influencer; model, arbiter of taste and Queen of 19 Cruckton Pichu. And me: jobbing outdoor instructor, low grade climber, taxi driver, wannabee folk singing pub dweller and dog walker.

They say opposites attract!

Ch 19

Life, Death and Storms

There wasn't much work around Shrewsbury in January, but the taxi work money dripped in. To pass the time between fares I would text fellow night owls like Nick my old mate (and brother to Ashley who had died in a skiing accident years before) and was now struggling with his health. His malignant melanoma, treated five years previously, had returned, this time in the lymph nodes. We texted the usual banal funny nonsense and jokes we had grown up together sharing.

We were now both married, our kids of similar ages. Nick knew he hadn't got long to live, and a walk and picnic up upon The Stiperstones was organised for friends and family on May 7th 2016. At this gathering were people whom I had not seen for nearly thirty years, notably Nige, who I had not seen since his wedding to Claire in 1989, and Geoff, an old climbing partner of mine from the 1970s. Nick's mortality weighed heavy. He texted:

To Stiperstones the friends they came,
To walk with the devil, without the rain,
O'er stoney path and heath and grass
We tarry a while to talk and laugh.
Then to The Horseshoes to sup an ale:
I shan't forget this happy tale!

Nick died at home a few weeks later. He was 54.

Nick's death was part of the catalyst for the trip we planned for 2017. No one on their death bed has said: "I wish I'd worked more." But work I did that winter, and the goal was to buy tickets for us all to go to Peru before Ali left home to go to university in the autumn. Every time my bank account approached £700 to £800, as it did now finances were healthier, Liliana would look for a flight to Lima and book it. Ali would go out first, and Matty and I would follow, then Liliana would come out separately two weeks later. It was heads down, nose to the grindstone, night shifts, earning money. I went back to phone book deliveries to make a bit more money between taxi shifts, and Matty and Ali helped. A Peru and Bolivia trip was definitely viable now.

Mrs May called a snap General Election, as a cunning plan to strengthen her Brexit bargaining position. I made sure I voted this time. Ali had her first chance to vote, and she, Liliana and I walked down to the village hall together to mark our ballot papers.

Ali's last A level exam was on Thursday 22 June. She flew out to Peru on 24th June to stay with her Aunt Mabel. Matty and I joined them in Lima on Wednesday 26th July. From experience I knew we had to get out of Lima as soon as we could before our travelling funds were sucked from us. The next day Ali, Matty and I were on a very hot bus with only two stops in over 26 hours of travel. Matty, particularly, was struggling, feeling nauseous and vomiting. Three nights in Cusco would give us chance to relax a little; but I hadn't planned on being stalked on the Internet by Liliana! The kids refused to disconnect from the wi-fi, and Liliana constantly sent messages about every aspect of the trip. This was not travelling. I felt more like the kids were merely puppets being manipulated by Liliana's Latina Mother über presence. Thankfully the wi-fi was only good around central Cusco. As soon as we travelled away her virtual presence disappeared into the ether. On Rainbow Mountain (Wilkanuta in Quechua), we climbed up to 5,200m (17,060ft) to join the throng of tourists at this iconic site.

The bus from Cusco to La Paz, the world's highest capital city, was very comfortable, with reclining seats. Matty was more himself, smiling and cured now, and Ali was inscrutably buoyant and tough. Travelling overnight saves accommodation money. A few hours lay-over in a hip bookstore café, and another overnight bus deposited us, twelve hours later at sunrise, in the iron cold town of Uyuni, the gateway to the unique Salar Salt Desert.

I wanted the kids to experience this magical dusty outermost desert as I had done twenty years earlier. An other-worldliness still pervaded this dry moonscape. Blistering bright salt flats stretched as far as the eye could see, skewing perspective and virtually burning the retina. Colours and shades muted as we reached the volcanoes, and the twisted hues of the salt lakes mirrored and rippled in the wind. I wanted them to see the pink flamingos. Again the cold night air rasped our lungs as our breath steam billowed out.

I wanted to show them the geysers in the Laguna Colorado National Park. Entry fees of 450 Bolivianos were payable; I had 460. For maximum impact geysers had to be visited before dawn when they are at their most active. We scrambled around the Salvador Dali rocks and other giant natural masterpieces shaped by the wind; then we hugged Roro and Joanna, our fabulous female French travelling companions, before boarding the overnight bus to La Paz with our return tickets to Lima and sea level and oxygen rich air.

Back in Lima on Sunday 6th August, my Plan B worked. Emailing my next job, they advanced me £200. Chance-taking thin-ice skater that I was, I was solvent again. Liliana arrived and the next day we surrendered to her leadership and boarded another bus for thirty-two hours of travel to Pomabamba, ancestral home of the Escudero Valverde family. Anderson Acero Giraldo was to be our guide. Anderson, a friend of Mabel's, is an architect with aspirations of becoming Mayor of Pomabamba. He wanted us to help him film a promotional video to lure tourists there. Pomabamba is an out-of-the way destination, I felt sure I was the only gringo this side of the Andes.

We climbed up to the ruins of the lost city of Jaino with Anderson and his small entourage. Mabel struggled with the altitude, and I accompanied her and Liliana down to a small settlement, whilst Matty and Ali joined the stronger more adventurous team. A new bus rendezvous had to be organised, as the driver who had taken us here, had scarpered back in search of Pomabamban Liquor and Loves the minute he had been paid. Trust and integrity can be variable concepts to some. The small settlement we reached boasted one public telephone to link it to the outside world. Utilising this lifeline, we hoped we had managed to organise another lift and settled down in a cold back room to wait and wait. And wait. Eventually the wreck of a bus that had been sent forth into the night to retrieve us bumped us along tracks so wild that animators for 'Beep Beep the Road Runner' would have judged them fanciful. We retrieved the adventurous group en route. We found them in a one room shepherd's hut, Matty cuddling a lamb to keep warm. I helped repair the bus tyre; the driver carried small patches of rubber and superglue for these inevitabilities. Passengers took it in turns to inflate the tyre with a bike pump. Three more similar incidents later we finally rolled back into Pomabamba.

Next day Anderson wanted to show us his mountain hut at Safuna below the east side of Alpamayo. Another HiAce bus took us there. We were travelling in such a remote area that we had to stop to repair, or even build the road as we went. A final river crossing brought us to a thatched mud hut at 4,600m/15,000ft as alpenglow suffused the rarefied atmosphere. We climbed higher in the dusk. Ali Matty and Fabricio looked the part as genuine *Chollos* posing in their ponchos and hats, a rifle crooked in the arm for effect: great pictures grabbed just as the light optimised.

Darkness ushered us back down to an open fire back in the primitive kitchen at Safuna. A cooking pot hung over the fire and a couple of *cuy* (guinea pigs) squeaked under our feet as we huddled there together for warmth. Anderson butchered a lamb carcass, chunks flung into the salty water. Hungry as we were, it was vile. I joined Liliana and Mabel, huddling: so uncomfortably tired and cold.

Back in Pomabamba the next evening a party was in full swing in the '*Hotel Jacob*' where we danced *Huayno,* and the locals watched with interest: the first time that they had seen a gringo dancing their own traditional dance. At breakfast the next morning we were presented to the elderly mayor, the *alcalde*. We felt privileged to be in Liliana's ancestral town. I understood now her passion for the place, its history and culture and the strength needed to live with poverty. We had seen first-hand how they live; it is a hard life.

We boarded the bus for that journey again to Huaraz. Here we received the news that Ali had attained 3 A's at A level. We were all aware of the shocking gulf that lay between her opportunities and the future life of our hosts.

Onwards - to San Jacinto, where aged 16 Ali had previously taught English. Since she had been there, the village had been hit by a huge mudslide after the winter rains. We had crowd-funded a disaster appeal earlier in the year, Facebook friends generously raising money to help with repairing and re-roofing adobe houses. Pedro showed us what had been achieved; but we were introduced to mainly women children and elders, the grinding poverty had forced the men to travel for work and send money home. Having met these suffering families we were determined to keep in touch and to keep raising money.

Matty and I flew home a week ahead of Liliana and Ali. We got back to the house on Thursday evening. The next morning, my 55th birthday, I was in a minibus heading north to lead a National Three Peaks. As I summited Ben Nevis with my group, sweating and trying to remember why I was doing this, there was Big Al, my old climbing partner from university days, fresh off Tower Ridge with clients. We hugged, and he laughed at my madness. Scafell Pike followed, and a blast up and down Snowdon and later that day I was singing at Shrewsbury Folk Festival. I had already had a £200 advance deducted leaving me with £150 as all the money I had in the world; just that, family and friends and a huge vault of memories, rich beyond my wildest dreams.

There was no let-up, I was on a roll, earning money by walking: Oxfordshire, The Berwyns, Yorkshire, Snowdonia, Scotland. Ali had narrowly missed out on a place at Oxford University after a three day interview. She had been accepted at Manchester, Durham Bristol and London, she chose to study Law at Bristol. The course, the city and the community all seemed to offer what she wanted, and she got a good flat in the new halls of residence.

Matty came up with me for our last Yorkshire Three Peaks of the season, and we were engulfed in an absolute hooley! Even finding our way out of the campsite was a mission: you could not see a thing, the fog in the dark just bouncing the headtorch light back into your eyes. Some light eventually seeped into the sky, but the torrent kept pouring from above. We had to group as many as possible together. Spouts of water were issuing forth out of the limestone sinkholes, and we had to be very directive, keeping clients safe. A lower level route was the only option, with flash floods everywhere. Matty thought it was great fun, but it sapped us, and we earned our chips that evening. Unbelievably, the rest of the country seemed to have missed out on this deluge.

As I drove down to Egger's house on the edge of the Peak District, Paul Wilson, our dear friend, called me. He was living near his father in Bradford, having returned from time in Tunisia. He wanted to join us over at Eggers that night. Although he felt like a brother to us, Egger, Chink and I felt the evening might become a bit 'full on' and I was tired. Saying no to Paul was to be a decision I would regret.

Before the year was out there were two more trips to be made. Dad and I went to Denmark to see Ron, his last remaining brother, age now fast catching up with him. His love of people and of conversation had not deserted him; he loved to talk, and his memory was very sharp for detail of growing up in his 'Poor Man's Paradise', and of his time working on the railways. We left him surrounded by his loving family, happy that he was spending his dotage amongst admiring family and friends.

Ron, Ed and Puss had all played their part in the commitment the older generation had made in the fight against Fascism. Liliana had grown up in Peru with little knowledge of the Holocaust. When she had read and heard about what Ron, Ed, Puss and their generation had fought against, she went with Ali to Auschwitz to try and understand something of it. This experience deeply moved her.

The winter tactic for me was to keep busy with Panto and taxi work, fighting the dark depressing nights, keep the blues at bay and have something planned to look forward to when the weather got better, remembering that those who went before us had given so much so that we could live in peace and prosperity.

The Folk Walk is always a ray of sunshine in the bleak mid winter; it involves friends, old and new, walking lots of beer, laughing and singing.

Cabin fever came to visit anyway, it always comes to visit at this time of year, and I couldn't shake it off. Liliana ensconces herself in the home, but at this time of year I go stir-crazy. I needed a break, and planned to go away to Scotland to clear my head in the March. There would more chance of decent snow then, and I reasoned that camping in it would require focus, help repair body and mind and gain fitness for the coming season of work. A big storm struck on the day I was supposed to leave – 'The Beast from the East'. It didn't seem reasonable to drive into the teeth of it. Turning round at Whitchurch I came back south, feeling vulnerable and weak, and so diverted nearer home to the Caradoc, to walk with the spirits of brothers Nick and Ashley for comfort.

Driving through Leebotwood, with Danni in the car, the traffic slowed into a convoy as the snow blew in. A 44 tonne truck rear-ended me and instead of a contemplative walk I ended up spending the night in hospital with nerve damage to my spine, neck and shoulder.

I found it difficult to pick myself up from this incident; but reasoned I was only 'walking wounded' but both Danni and I were nervous about getting into cars now. The Spring was a long time coming but gradually it shook away that long cold snowy winter, and I went back to work for Red Ridge. My shoulder was really sore, and coiling ropes at the end of a session was nigh on impossible. Gradually it eased over the coming weeks but I had to compromise my technique and find unorthodox ways to do things. Liliana went back to Peru at Easter, as Jorge had not been well. I missed her, and melancholy added to my physical pain.

By May I was feeling strong enough to join 'The Folk Collective', our merry band of Paul Wynn (Guitar and Vocals), Rob 'The Ferret' Guy (Kajon drum) and Rich Pharo (Guitar, Fiddle and Vocals) on our much anticipated Scottish trip. We camped north of Fort William and in midge-free sunny days climbed Ben Nevis via Ledge Route and saw skiers in the gullies enjoying unseasonably good snow conditions. We walked the hills of Glencoe too. Drinking, singing and playing in the pubs of Fort William in the evenings, we thought we had found Nirvana. It was a great way to recuperate until we heard the news from home: Paul Wilson was dead.

Paul had been living in Bradford, having just returned from Sfax in Tunisia. His funeral on 31st May 2018 was in Shrewsbury, and he was buried in the cemetery on Roman Road.

The day after Paul's funeral Egger and I shouldered packs and embarked on the ferry to the Isle of Rum, making our way around the narrow coastal sheep track above the sea haze to the Dibidil bothy tucked tightly under Askival and the Rum Cuillin where Manx Shearwaters nest. Here we toasted Paul and reminisced about him; a force of nature, a mover and shaker, a man by turns amazing or cantankerous, a maverick, bohemian, warm, kind and wonderful.

Chapter 20

The Quiet After The Storm

"Drop your ice axe, let's go!" I yelled at Nige.

Lightning bolts were all around us, apocalyptic flaming columns thrown from Zeus himself, electric tongues flicking around the mountain bowl. Thunderclaps so close - you could smell it all.

Calmly he placed his axe near mine, already jettisoned in a snow patch by some rocks. Mental note to self: grey rocks by snow – should be easy to find tomorrow (not!). Down we went, scanning through the mist for the hut. Zeus was angry! "Just keep your head down and pray!" I told my atheist self. We couldn't have gone any quicker; stumbling and post-holing, down we went, wallowing through the thawing snowpack, the sense of urgency clawing at my mind, forcing me on and down to the hut. But where was it? Back and forward we looked, straining; when suddenly off far to the right the mothership loomed through the mist, partially hidden by a low ridge. Tacking across, we lumbered, boiling turmoil zinging all around us. Then "clank clank" up the metal steps and under the canopy and into the 'airlock' where we slumped and breathed a sigh of relief.

We were in the Conscrits Refuge above the Tres la Tête glacier and under the Dom du Miage Ridge near Mont Blanc. There had been no let-up of the storm. After a taxing crevasse laden approach, Nige and I had completed the Dom du Miage Traverse, a glorious sharp straightforward snowy ridge, apparently; not that we saw much of it through the mist. A descent across very unstable wet snow, threatening to avalanche at any moment, led us to more instability, to gain the ridge of La Berangère where, after a couple of roped pitches, we had escaped to the more benign slopes above the refuge as the storm vented at us.

Nige found the axes the next morning and we started our descent to the glacier. The storm had blown itself out overnight to be replaced by the hollow sounds of rock fall and avalanche. Everywhere everything was melting. Rocks on the glacier were exposed, sinkholes opened up and water gurgled and cascaded all around us and deep below us. A steepening required us to keep roped together. Squinting through fogged up glasses I spied glimpses of the route through the swirling mist. Below the *Mauvais Pas* the waters were rising and the glacier was feeding small icebergs into the bloated river. Getting past this would put us on the right side of the mountain with only the Bad Step left to negotiate. But first there was a small crevasse on the open icy terrain now stripped of snow, then a drop down into that hanging valley river.

As soon as I jumped I knew it was wrong. It was barely a jump, not much more than a long stride to clear the crevasse; but this innocuous slip did maximum damage. I roared with uncontrollable rage as the searing pain ripped through my shoulder. The weight of the pack came tight on to my left side as it slumped to the uphill side of the jagged rock strewn ice. My bellowing was lost in the wind and I, suddenly a wild-eyed wounded creature, a speck of humanity in a world of pain, within another world of torment, seized the heat of injury, roiled it, sucked it and swallowed it down and carried it forward inside me. I would only allow myself the luxury of dealing with it in the still of quiet dry warmth; but not now, not here. Now was to keep moving, get away from here. Get safe, stay safe, find drugs, eat drugs, stop shivering, drink, keep moving, cinch the pack strap tight to my shoulder, grip the poles hold it all together, keep moving, get away from here.

We had been lucky. Later news arrived that three Spanish mountaineers, roped together, had fallen to their deaths on that route.

The next day back in Chamonix the sun warmed the back of my neck, and every single item we had taken with us dripped drying on the fence. I chewed cocodamol and ibuprofen well above maximum dose but needed something stronger.

Back home in England, x-rays and scans confirmed that I had a complete tear of the 'rotator cuff' of my shoulder, a more serious injury than a fracture. The pain made me nauseous and I couldn't sleep properly for five months. I was operated on, a tendon removed, pins inserted, bones scraped and then I was in for a long period of recuperation and physiotherapy. I couldn't turn down work so I struggled on through the summer season, but for once I was glad work dried up in August.

Shooglenifty, Paul Wilson's adored band, were headlining Shrewsbury Folk Festival and were collaborating with Dhun Dhora, famous drummers from Rajasthan. We were hosting Malcolm and Quee from the band, and a full party was swinging at our house on my birthday weekend. Malcolm asked me if we had room for these Rajasthani drummers in our attic space. Of course I said yes. The lads had hoped to camp at the festival, but the rainstorm was intense and they had never seen weather like it. Six of them came in to shelter. The next morning those of us still standing watched as they sat cross legged in our dining room and sang to us. What a superb exotic birthday present! That evening we were on the guest list to see them perform in all their turbaned splendour in front of 5,000 festival goers. The collaboration of Scottish Acid Croft and Indian singing and drumming brought the house down. The spirits of Paul Wilson and Angus Grant were amongst us that night.

The summer of 2018 was drawing to a close. We had almost lived out on the patio, but now the nights started drawing in. Dad called me to say that Ron had had a stroke, and that we had better get over to Denmark quickly. We visited him in the hospice with his family round him. Ron had nodded to say that he understood Dad and I were here, but he never regained consciousness. Ron died at 3pm on Friday 2nd November 2018. Jean and Else and his granddaughter Nina were there as he slipped peacefully away, aged 93.

Ron had been a great chronicler of life in Bayston Hill in the 1920s and 30s, and his writings in 'Poor Man's Paradise' form the beginnings of this book. He was a funny happy family man, well loved by friends and family. He knew what was right and what was wrong, and the poverty and struggle he saw his parents endure had a profound effect upon him. This informed his politics, which he saw as the only sure way to make change. He saw the NHS come into being and the beginnings of the Welfare State after the war that he, Puss and Eddie had had to fight. He did not want to see a repeat of the struggles of the First World War that his dad had gone through, only to be betrayed and see their generation then thrown into the Depression, dole and indignity. Ron had been a gentleman all his life, but fought for the things he believed in. Gradually things got better for his generation, but they had had to fight for it all the way. Ron was an Internationalist, a peace-lover, a gardener, a correspondent, a raconteur and historian. He worked for many years in Denmark with people with learning disabilities. He was a man of the people.

I admired his integrity; but my impetuous nature has not allowed me to live as simple and honest life as he did. I have looked for my happiness and satisfaction in action and adventure, whereas Ron seemed to find them in the simplest things of life, quietly and thoughtfully, seemingly without looking.

Epilogue

When the world lost its innocence in the First World War, the repercussions were vast: many of those in Europe were returned to a 'peace' of poverty and pestilence, depression, deference, upheaval. Growing up and struggling out of this, they sent their children out into a century of rapid change; new technologies and ideas, moving from horses to motor power, and social change from deference towards empowerment. In the twentieth century world population increased from below two billion to seven billion and, in general, people's lives improved in terms of health, opportunity and longevity.

The changes someone like my grandfather Charlie witnessed and experienced were mind boggling – from an agrarian society little changed for centuries to mechanised farming, declining rural populations, a free National Health Service, jetliners shrinking the world, space exploration and the birth of the internet within one lifetime. How did his generation take to these advances? Now they were allowed to dream; now they had hopes and ideals. They laughed, they sang, they followed the plough, they were sometimes cowed; but they knew that they were stronger together. But what about their children and grandchildren?

What about us? With our different lives and aspirations, what would they think of us and the way we approach things? Have we taken our peace, our easier physical lives for granted, at the unseen expense of stress, debt and consumerism, unsustainable for our tired planet?

I had the chance to be hedonistic and carefree in my youth because of the sacrifices my grandparents and parents made. Eventually I found myself in the right place at the right time, a cushioned fall. Redundancy even left me able to choose to travel, such a modern luxury. Would they have approved of my choices?

I turned to a carefree life because at BT I had felt locked into the wage-slave society that had been created. Then I was made redundant and told to go away. Supposing I had had more status, more rank, more investment in the system, would I have had the courage to take the money and set off on my adventures? And if I hadn't, where would I be now?

My adventures led to experience and qualification; but still I wanted to return to what surely everyone wants: happiness, contentment, love, satisfaction, success.

I made my own way through the world, to have travelled is to have had your eyes opened, to return awakened with new insight to confront challenges, often of one's own making.

Our parents had limited options. Things had to be done a certain way, in so many ways that we now forget; you had to fit in then, less so today. We really have all the freedoms, but we can create our own obstacles: lack of imagination for what is possible with little money. I chose to be involved in many independent things and had the energy and enthusiasm to go my own way.

That way led me to Liliana and Ali and then gave us Matty. Living in Shropshire, trying to keep a roof over our heads and food on the table involved gritting teeth and working hard, or leaving, and I wasn't going to leave.

Our children: great grandchildren of Charlie, Jean, Julio and Agualita face a new century. These 'Millennials' - what challenges will they face, what opportunities will they have, what will be their ambitions? What will they learn from their family's history?

Travel, migration and inclusivity made my family. We should be making bigger tables, not putting up barriers and walls between us.

I have a plan (there have been many others on the way through). I'm not sure if it is a good plan; time will tell. Physically I am deteriorating, just as my ancestors deteriorated. But I didn't waste any time; I seized the days when I had my youth to climb the high summits but is my time as an outdoor, physical worker coming to an end.

'A man walks down the street
He says why am I soft in the middle now
The rest of my life is so hard
I need a photo opportunity

I want a shot at redemption
Don't want to end up a cartoon
In a cartoon graveyard'
(Paul Simon)

The voice in my head still whispers 'Come on, Stewart!' and I hear it and I get ready for another attempt; but I also yearn for comfort and security now.

Comfort and security in old age come at a price: the price of conformity compliance and obedience – staying with a job and reaping its rewards. Friends and acquaintances are slowing up and retiring from long careers now; well-deserved their nests feathered. Could I have done what they did? Could I have stayed there?

And those that didn't make it that far – Ashley and Nick, and Paul amongst them, their spirits will live on in our memories, in the breeze or when we hear a song or see their children growing up into fine human beings. I cherish the honour of just still being alive. We didn't all get that option.

Ron's legacy to me and others was his book 'Poor Man's Paradise'. In it, our ancestors come alive. The conversations I had with him in his later years informed and humbled me. Understanding our history is a privilege when we have the humility to learn.

My infamous stolen mantra had been:
'You can retake an exam but you can't retake a party!'
But maybe now (in the words of John Stuart Mill):
'I have learned to seek my happiness by limiting my desires, rather than attempting to satisfy them.'
The truth may lie somewhere, unfathomably between these two quotes.

Reviewing this life history, it is clear to me that I was saved by the love of a good woman. Liliana is my rock. Despite my transgressions, temper tantrums and tiredness, she is with me. We continue to grow together, she steers our boat; knows how we are navigating as a family, and where we are going. Her impetuous decision to dance with a mad gringo that night in Tambo's nightclub allowed her to save Ali from an overriding superstitious society where the *'broohis'* ('the witches') still hold sway, and to bear Matty away from the violence and drugs of Lima. While introducing them to their Peruvian heritage, she has made sure they make the most of the education that England has offered them.

Her strength and resilience and her forgiveness have kept us together. My Peruvian beauty queen, she could have had anyone yet she chose me and has stayed loyal to me through thick and thin.

Just when her greatest supporter, her mother, died, I fell to pieces and turned on her, but she rose above it and forgave me despite her grief.

She has believed in me, she has supported my writing, my painting, believed and understood my non-lucrative but rewarding work, the old bus I bought on a whim, the sheds, the pantomimes, drinking, singing, climbing: my family and friends, my aches and pains and my impulsive ideas.

When she acted on her dreams, I believed in her and supported her too. My dreams could have taken me somewhere else but I would have been alone. Where do we go from here now that the children have grown?

Wherever we go, we can go secure in the knowledge that all that we have experienced together has strengthened us. As a family, we have survived, we have bloomed, we have not been crushed.

We will walk far and wide again, but especially to Lyth Hill once more to take in that view and remember all that has gone before and to think of all that will carry on, and we can think for a moment and be thankful for our friendship, love and life. That view south, away to those Stretton hills, and the world we know, far beyond the horizon, in the cool of a summers evening far in the future we can sit and rest: and we won't weep for all the songs we did not sing, or the jokes we did not tell or for all the money we did not keep or for all the things we did not do. And the spirits of our ancestors will be looking over our shoulders, willing the story to go on.

Afterword

Friday 21ˢᵗ February 2020. Drove Home. I drove Chris's car as his foot is sore. The conditions were as worse than anything I've seen in last 40 years of coming up here. Got home 7pm. Peace.Love.Happiness.

This trip to Scotland had been aborted a day early due to the weather:

Monday 24ᵗʰ February2020. TAXI. Back to Go-Carz. River Severn flood levels highest ever recorded.

Friday 13ᵗʰ March. My bank a/c £0.56. Red Ridge

Saturday 14ᵗʰ March 2020. Covid 19. The corona virus is very serious now. Will schools cancel work? Overseas work looks unlikely... Very worrying. Mum and Dad are very at risk – i.e. – should not go to B's funeral on Monday.

Sunday 15ᵗʰ March 2020. Me + Nige – Nameless Cwm above Idwal Glyderau Snowdonia. Found a tiny snow-patch. Misty all day. Down Cneifion/Football pitch. It stayed drier in p.m.

Monday 16ᵗʰ March 2020. B's funeral (85) 130. Bayston Hill.

Wednesday 18ᵗʰ March 2020. RR. Couldn't sleep 3am – 530 am. – wrote to Ali. Westbury Youth Club £13.50 per hour. CANX.CANCELLED

Thursday 19ᵗʰ March 2020. RR. This was the last days' work at Red Ridge. We had delivered full-day climbing session as the cave/mine trip involved being in too close proximity and would spread the Corona Virus – c.v. easier. So there is no more work for me. I have been paid for what I have done only. I have an interview on Tuesday for some youth work. Fingers crossed. My main application currently is for BAS (British Antarctic Survey) – 4th time

I've applied since 1989! I've set my ambition lower this time – as a General Assistant.

Friday 20th March 2020. Matty's college has closed indefinitely due to C.V. Matty had a night out with his mates before the pubs, restaurants and clubs all closed – probably for months.

-Very uncertain times. Poor Matty. Ali still in Bristol but has had notices about possible civil unrest so is nervous.

Saturday 21st March 2020. I went to pick Ali up from Bristol. Lovely sunny day. Streets quiet – noticeably people wear face-masks now more. We got back to Shrewsbury c. 4pm. Most places closing down although relatively calm in Supermarkets. Night in. Meal all together.

Monday March 23rd 2020. Invoiced SYA (no. 2). BAS – sent application. SYA – Zoom app. Go-Carz. NHS. Delivery drivers. Hignetts – R+R Stores.

Boris Johnson addressed the nation: 3 WEEKS LOCKDOWN STARTS.

Prime Minister Boris Johnson addressed the nation on March 23rd 2020. A national three week lockdown was implemented to counter the Covid 19 Corona virus pandemic. But that's another story.

Stewart Liliana Ali and Matty: SLAM

There's a race of men that don't fit in,
A race that can't stay still;
So they break the hearts of kith and kin,
And they roam the world at will.
They range the field and they rove the flood,
And they climb the mountain's crest;
Theirs is the curse of the gypsy blood,
And they don't know how to rest.

If they just went straight they might go far;
They are strong and brave and true;
But they're always tired of the things that are,
And they want the strange and new.
They say: "Could I find my proper groove,
What a deep mark I would make!"
So they chop and change, and each fresh move
Is only a fresh mistake.

And each forgets, as he strips and runs
With a brilliant, fitful pace,
It's the steady, quiet, plodding ones
Who win in the lifelong race.
And each forgets that his youth has fled,
Forgets that his prime is past,
Till he stands one day, with a hope that's dead,
In the glare of the truth at last.

He has failed, he has failed; he has missed his chance;
He has just done things by half.
Life's been a jolly good joke on him,
And now is the time to laugh.
Ha, ha! He is one of the Legion Lost;
He was never meant to win;
He's a rolling stone, and it's bred in the bone;
He's a man who won't fit in.

Robert Service